# Christ in Crisis

# Christ in Crisis

## Why We Need to Reclaim Jesus

**Jim Wallis**
**Foreword by Bishop Michael Curry**

HARPER LUXE
*An Imprint of* HarperCollins*Publishers*

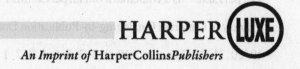

 For information, address HarperCollins Publishers, 195 Broadway, New York, NY 10007.

HarperCollins books may be purchased for educational, business, or sales promotional use. For information, please e-mail the Special Markets Department at SPsales@harpercollins.com.

FIRST HARPERLUXE EDITION

ISBN: 978-0-06-294481-8



Library of Congress Cataloging-in-Publication Data is available upon request.

19 20 21 22 23 LSC 10 9 8 7 6 5 4 3 2 1

This book is dedicated to the Reclaiming Jesus "elders," whose collective spiritual discernment and courage led to a fresh confession of faith for these times, helping to ignite a movement that has already inspired millions to reclaim Jesus from cultural, religious, and political captivity (the elders are all listed at the end of the "Reclaiming Jesus" declaration on page 401). This book is also dedicated to all those young pastors and leaders I meet, around the country and the world, who are already reclaiming Jesus in their local communities and churches. They are the ones who now inspire me and give me hope.

# Contents

Foreword by Bishop Michael Curry ix

**Prologue:** Reclaiming Jesus 1

1. What About Jesus? 5
2. The Neighbor Question 31
3. The Image Question 63
4. The Truth Question 123
5. The Power Question 161
6. The Fear Question 193
7. The Caesar Question 227
8. The Peacemaker Question 267

9. The Discipleship Question 299

10. Becoming Salt, Light, and Hope 347

**Epilogue:** The Light of the World 387

The "Reclaiming Jesus" Declaration 401
Acknowledgments 415
Notes 419

# Foreword

## SOUL FOOD

Two thousand years ago Jesus of Nazareth began a movement. It was a movement of people for whom Jesus was the very center of their lives, and his way of unselfish, sacrificial love, their way of life. Scholars sometimes call this the Jesus Movement. And it is the earliest origin of Christianity.

A few years ago, Jim Wallis and I ran into each other after a service in Washington's National Cathedral. We each knew of the other, but we didn't really know each other. Soon after that, we got together for a quick bite to eat and for some conversation.

But that quick bite quickly turned into a soul-food feast. While we were not eating at a soul-food restaurant, the conversation we had was food for the soul. And we discovered that we are soul brothers, if you will, brothers in Christ. We talked about Jesus of Nazareth, his teachings, his example, his Spirit, and the cultural complicity of much of contemporary Christianity.

We realized that we shared real concern for the soul of Christianity in America. It's not an exaggeration to say that Christianity in America is in danger of being hijacked—not by emergent secularism, but by being popularly identified with right-wing political agendas; by the propagation of a so-called prosperity gospel; and, far too often, by being associated with thinly veiled religious animosity, often directed at Muslims, by sometimes subtle, religiously disguised racial bigotry and supremacy, nationalism and nativism instead of genuine patriotism, the exaltation of narrow-mindedness, antipathy toward scientific knowledge and learning, sexism, homophobia, and on and on. While this may not be the reality of Christianity on the ground, so to speak, and while genuine Christianity is not in the pocket of either the left or the right wing, or any other human ideology for that matter, the perception is very real. And perceptions often become reality, unless a counternarrative emerges. Hence, the "crisis" of which Jim speaks so articulately and profoundly.

That meeting and meal between Jim and me also led us to ongoing conversations and the formation of a larger group of church "elders" to discuss and discern the challenge of these times, which resulted in a fresh confession of faith called "Reclaiming Jesus," which Jim will say more about as you read on.

A few centuries ago Fyodor Dostoyevsky warned the church and Christians of this kind of crisis as an ever-present danger to genuine faith that would follow Jesus and his way of love. In his story within a story, "The Grand Inquisitor," in his masterpiece *The Brothers Karamazov*, he makes it plain. In that tale, Jesus returns to earth during the days of the Inquisition, when religious leaders were controlling, imprisoning, and killing their fellow Christians and Jews, all in the name of Christ. It was evangelism by persecution. The unwelcome return of Jesus results in his arrest, and the Grand Inquisitor himself comes down to Jesus's cell to confront him.

The Inquisitor explains that the church of that time had been able to keep the people in line and therefore create an organized and complacent society. Everything is working perfectly, the Inquisitor argues, without allowing the people free will with all its messiness. If Jesus is released, all he will do is mess things up! Throughout the encounter Jesus says nothing, but simply responds with the kiss of peace.

The contrast is a powerful one! There stands Jesus of Nazareth, whose life and teachings are a threat not only to the surrounding society but, sadly, to a church that professes his name but tries everything possible to keep him and his message hidden away from view.

Dostoyevsky was writing a piece of fiction . . . but oh, how familiar that tale is in our own time and our own context. It has been so easy for the church in various generations, including our own, to disregard, disarm, and domesticate Jesus to the point that he may not even resemble the Jesus of the New Testament.

Not long before I wrote this, Jim sent an email saying that he had finished the book. I sent him a congratulatory email and said, "I really do think your book is going to be a major contribution to the radical reformation of the face and the reality of a way of being Christian that looks like Jesus." Whenever Jesus of Nazareth—his actual teachings, his lived example, and his loving, liberating, and life-giving way—takes center stage, a revolution of love, a reformation of life, and a renewal of our relationship with God, each other, and all of creation is at hand.

This moment, fraught with problems and complexity, is likewise pregnant with a new possibility for the church and those called Christians.

This crisis may be a genuine opportunity to reclaim our roots, our origins, our true identity as Christians, by reclaiming Jesus of Nazareth and his way of love.

Now is the time to reclaim that bold and counter-cultural Jesus who said things such as "blessed are the peacemakers," "love your enemies and pray for those who persecute you," "you cannot serve God and wealth," and "love your neighbor as yourself."

Now is the time to reclaim that Jesus who turned expectations upside down with parables about a good Samaritan, a prodigal son, a persistent widow, and the Last Judgment.

Now is the time to reclaim that Jesus who was unafraid to sit with those who others considered unacceptable, unwilling to be co-opted by the powers that be, undeterred in reaching out to the friendless and the needy, the cast down, the put down, and the disinherited.

Now is the time to reclaim that Jesus who Dietrich Bonhoeffer called "the man for others." The Jesus who showed what love looks like, giving up his own life not for anything he could get, but for the good, the well-being, the welfare, the salvation and redemption of others.

Yes, there is a crisis of Christianity. But Jim, like the angelic messengers in the Christmas story, brings us good news of great joy. For the Jesus, born of Mary, can, as the Christmas carol "O Little Town of Bethlehem" says, "be born in us today."

Yes, there is a crisis, but this crisis is an opportunity. An opportunity to reclaim Jesus and to be reclaimed by him. An opportunity for a way of being Christian that actually looks something like Jesus of Nazareth and his way of love to emerge as the face of Christianity in America.

Yes, there is a crisis. This can be an opportunity for the church to reclaim its roots, its true origins. Now is the time for the church to become more than merely the church as culture perceives us.

This may be an opportunity for us to become the twenty-first-century realization of the Jesus Movement of old. And in so doing, to find our soul.

May your reading of this book be for you what that conversation I had with Jim a while back was for me: a real soul-food dinner!

—Bishop Michael Curry,
*Presiding Bishop of the*
*Episcopal Church*

# Christ in Crisis

# Prologue
# Reclaiming Jesus

When I used to visit one of my mentors, Dorothy Day, the founder of the Catholic Worker movement and perhaps now headed toward sainthood, at the movement's Mary House on the Lower East Side of Manhattan, a big graffiti quote on the side of a building always caught my attention. It read,

> **Reporter:** "Mr. Gandhi, what do you think of Western Civilization?"
> **Gandhi:** "I think it would be a good idea."

Perhaps what many young people today—of many faiths or no religion at all—think would be a good question right now might sound something like this:

**Reporter:** "What do you think of Christians following Jesus?"
**Millennial:** "I think it would be a good idea."

Who is Jesus? What did he say? Did he mean it? These are questions inside and outside the boundaries of Christian faith, including among those who check the box that says "none of the above" when asked about their religious affiliation. Many people who can no longer associate themselves with "religion" wish somebody would talk more about what the first-century, brown-skinned Jewish rabbi born in what is now Palestinian territory had to say. They still want to listen to him. It's always amazing to me how Jesus has apparently survived all of us Christians. These are also the most important questions that people can ask inside the churches, especially with so many outside the churches and across the globe wondering how American Christians can call themselves followers of Jesus while saying and doing the things they do; or not saying and doing what they think Jesus might. And when most people now acknowledge that Christianity is indeed in crisis, many are longing to ask and hungry for the answer to the question "How might we get back to Jesus?"

I believe the questions Jesus asked or prompted are vital to our lives and our society—especially right now—both to Christians and to those who are of different faiths or no faith at all. Given our cultural conformities to starkly different values than he proclaimed, I think Jesus indeed needs to be reclaimed and is worth reclaiming. That's why I wrote this book, that's what it is about, and that is what I hope you, and I, will take away from it.

On Ash Wednesday 2018, a group of church leaders, all old enough to be called "elders," met in response to mounting political and moral concerns to ask the question "Which Jesus will we choose to follow?" The church was as divided as the culture around political issues. And because the church's politics seemed so disconnected from its convictions, we needed a fresh confession of faith, not another political strategy.

As the early Christians had done, we decided to create a confession of what we thought it means to follow Jesus's kingdom today and take it to the streets, threading through communities and congregations with a proclamation that it was time to "reclaim Jesus." (You can read more about this movement, which started in Lent in February 2018 and culminated on Pentecost, later in May, and how five million people responded, in the epilogue, "The Light of the World.")

This book has emerged from this challenge to close the gaping distance that presently exists between Christians and a Jesus that too many Christians desperately try to avoid. What are the fundamental truths of Jesus's ministry that can help us find our way back to him, even and especially amid this fearful time?

Perhaps the best way to diagnose and discuss this distance from Jesus is to go back to Jesus himself. What are the questions he asked or provoked that show us most vividly the difference between choosing the triumphalism of wealth and power or the way of Jesus with his servanthood and solidarity with the poor and vulnerable?

I hope that with this book we can explore what it means to follow Jesus in a world in crisis, just as his followers before us have done in their own crucibles of choosing, and how we can reestablish a deep and passionate connection with the meaning and message of Jesus Christ.

# Chapter 1
# What About Jesus?

"Why do you call me 'Lord, Lord,'
and do not do what I tell you?"

—LUKE 6:46

For the first six months of 2017, I was waking up many days at 4:30 or 5:00 a.m. and finding it hard to get back to sleep. Astonishing and alarming political events were happening on a near daily basis. They seemed to me to threaten the most poor and vulnerable, the progress of racial justice, the status and safety of women, the rationality of government, and even the idea of truth. And I heard fear animating many other people in the United States: fear of the changing demographics of the country, insecurity about their economic future, fear and resentment of elites who had no concern for them, and concern about their religious liberty. I was being flooded with calls and emails from friends and pastors, and people unknown to me who didn't know what to do. They came from around the country and, interestingly, included international Christian leaders around the world asking what I made of what was going on at the highest levels of power in America—and the lack of a serious Christian response thus far.

People often approached me as a veteran sage of Christian activism (which just comes after doing this work for a long time and getting old!), but I was feeling the fear, too, understood what I was hearing, and didn't always know what to say or tell other people. Both church leaders and political leaders were expressing fear and confusion and feeling stressed about what to do. I could easily relate. Community organizers were reporting to me the fear of immigrants who were already under new deportation attacks, with families in danger of being destroyed. Churches who had refugees on their way to them had those refugees blocked by the new administration. Black pastors were fearing the targeting of their young people by the police. Muslim leaders were afraid of the consequences of travel bans that seemed aimed at their communities. Some white pastors were afraid to speak up on these and other issues of justice for fear of being attacked as "political" and dividing their polarized congregations. Some black pastors called that a "white veto."

I vividly remember a phone call with evangelical leaders where some white evangelicals said they voted the way they did (81 percent) not because of the racial bigotry used by their candidate but because of other moral issues so central to them. To which black evangelicals replied, "So racism wasn't a deal breaker for you." I hadn't seen such a racial divide in the body of Christ for decades. Fear and despair were ruling the days and nights for many.

Unable to rest in the early hours of the day in those first several months of the new presidency, I began to go downstairs just to think, be alone, and pray. I wondered what scriptures I should be reflecting on. Reading the gospels, which I love to do, was making me more discouraged as I saw how the good news of Jesus Christ and his transformative teachings about the kingdom of God seemed so far away in our public life and even in our churches. My favorite biblical prophets, of course, made me even more concerned in the face of churches and faith leaders being so silent about speaking truth to power.

Eventually I was drawn to the Acts of the Apostles, the story of the earliest Christians, after the death and Resurrection of Christ. I came to the texts with my questions about how *they* responded to their first crisis and challenge—of presenting their new faith in the one called Jesus to a world full of both political injustice and religious hypocrisy, like ours.

I've continually found that when I go back to the scriptures, even those I have read many times before—but with new questions and concerns—there is always something new. That happened again this time.

Early in Acts, of course, is the coming of the Holy Spirit upon the disciples who were hiding and afraid, yet the astounding events of Pentecost overcame their fears and empowered them to take the message of Jesus to the streets. After many converts, the early believers of "the Way," as they were first called, settled into a new life together characterized by radical economic sharing, deep fellowship, great joy, and transforming worship in an increasingly diverse community of rich and poor, men and women, old and young, and even free and slave.

Peter, who had infamously and painfully denied Jesus, now had the courage to rise and speak to all the people in Jerusalem's public squares by quoting the prophet Joel (Acts 2:17–18):

*In the last days it will be, God declares,*
*that I will pour out my Spirit upon all flesh,*
*and your sons and your daughters shall prophesy,*
*and your young men shall see visions,*
*and your old men shall dream dreams.*
*Even upon my slaves, both men and women,*
*in those days I will pour out my Spirit;*
*and they shall prophesy.*

Clearly something new was happening. Peter described Jesus as the one whom God had raised up, who made known "the Way," who had been freed from death, and in whose name their sins would be forgiven—to all who welcomed his message.

As I went on reading, I kept noticing that everything the disciples did and said was always done and spoken *in the name of Jesus.* That was so clear and central in every narrative. In Acts 3, when Peter and John met the disabled beggar who always sat just outside the city gate, they healed him in the name of Jesus. Peter said, "I have no silver or gold, but what I have I give to you; in the name of Jesus Christ of Nazareth, stand up and walk." The people, the text says, were "filled with wonder and amazement" (verses 6–10). When Peter saw that response, he addressed the people, "You killed the Author of life, whom God raised from the dead. To this we are witnesses. And by faith in his name, his name itself has made this man strong, whom you see and know; and the faith that is through Jesus has given him perfect health in the presence of all of you" (verses 15–16).

Peter and John kept teaching and preaching to the people in Jesus's name—three thousand converts the first time, five thousand the second time—and the people kept coming. The authorities were "annoyed," the scripture says, so they arrested these first disciples and held them overnight. "The next day their rulers, elders, and scribes assembled in Jerusalem. . . . When they had made the prisoners stand in their midst, they inquired, 'By what power or by what name did you do this?' " Then Peter, "filled with the Holy Spirit," addressed the "Rulers of the people and elders," telling them that this man they saw before them was healed "by the name of Jesus Christ of Nazareth, whom you crucified, whom God raised from the dead. This Jesus is 'the stone that was rejected by you, the builders; it has become the cornerstone' " (Acts 4:5–11).

The story goes on to say that the rulers who "saw the boldness" of these "uneducated and ordinary men" were "amazed by them and recognized them as companions of Jesus." The authorities pushed Jesus's disciples out of the council meeting to discuss the problem. "What shall we do with them?" they asked each other, and finally decided how to handle the problem. They thought they couldn't deny what had happened, "But to keep it from spreading further among the people, let us warn them to speak no more to anyone in *this name*" (emphasis added). Then they called Peter and John back in and "ordered them not to speak or teach at all in the name of Jesus" (verses 13–18). They didn't seem as nervous about these "uneducated and ordinary men"; instead, they were worried about the name of Jesus.

"But Peter and John answered them, 'Whether is it right in God's sight to listen to you rather than to God, you must judge; for we cannot keep from speaking about what we have seen and heard' " (verses 19–20). I think that is always the question for those who call themselves "followers of Jesus": How can we not speak out after what we have seen and heard? Or have we forgotten what we have seen and heard? Or in our churches, did we ever even hear the things that Jesus said and did while he was on this earth?

After "threatening" them some more, the rulers had to let them go because of the people. It was only in Jesus's name in which the first disciples healed, taught, and preached, not in the names of the new celebrity religious leaders, or their nonprofit faith-based organizations, or to help raise funds for their various causes. The name people heard was that of Jesus; and the religious and political authorities began to realize that this name could become a threat to them. But invoking Jesus's name did not work as a magic formula. These Christians trusted that Jesus was there with them, which gave them confidence to act boldly.

The Acts readings struck me deeply and prompted me to ask, "Where do we see people speaking and working in the name of Jesus today?" And given how religious people can sometimes just speak words or even just a name, where is the clear presence of Jesus with them that these first disciples felt when they named the name of Jesus? Where are those people speaking now to our growing moral and political crises in Jesus's name? Or is Jesus's name being forgotten, silenced, or co-opted for temporal political power, or even hijacked by the powers that be? How might Jesus be named today in opposition or resistance to the dangerous values, behaviors, and policies being seen, along with the attacks on so many vulnerable people by those at the highest levels of political power? Where do we look for Jesus's name, either in the public square or even in the churches? The loudest voices of some religious leaders had been, ironically, in direct support of some of the most disconcerting things that have been said and done by the new regime in power. And why has there been such perceived silence from many other religious voices? How did what it means to stand with Jesus get so distorted?

My fresh reading of the early chapters of the book of Acts showed me once again that the early Christians acted with boldness, confidence, and courage in the face of hostility from the ruling powers. They could do this because they did everything in the name of Jesus, which means they were in sync and felt deeply connected with Jesus's passions, teachings, and presence. And here is the hard truth that my reading of Acts showed me, which also serves as the diagnosis for why we are in the present crisis: *We have become disconnected from Jesus.* We are not standing and acting in his name, with his values, action, and inspiration. We have lost Jesus—lost our connection to him. This explains why our actions and words lack the power evident in the early church.

Can we reconnect with Jesus? Is that possible? How might we do that?

If we name the problem as becoming disconnected from Jesus, that helps us to focus and clarify the crises before us and guide us as we think through what we must do. If the followers of Jesus are not acting like the "salt" and the "light" that he intended us to be, it is no wonder that a society can easily unravel and polarize around fear and divisions. When we fail to be the "yeast" or the "leaven" a culture needs, we should not be surprised when individualism, selfishness, power, and wealth predominate over any commitment to serve each other and the common good.

It is not news that we are in a political crisis, but the answers to it are more than political, especially for people of faith and others with moral sensibility. This political crisis has revealed not only the weaknesses and frailties of our political system—it also reveals much more. The election of Donald Trump in the presidential election of 2016 and the presidency that has followed—and the Christian response to all of it—have revealed how disconnected many American Christians have become from Jesus. Therefore, the greatest opportunity, even a redemptive one, to the present political crisis is that it could be a wake-up call for many Christians to how much we have disconnected from Jesus and how we could find the ways to be connected again to the one whose name should be above every name—our Lord and Savior, Jesus Christ.

This question of how we know whether we are connected to Jesus led me back to the Bible, especially the gospels. This book is the result of that study. I found eight distinctive teachings of Jesus, usually in the form of questions asked of him or questions he asked of his followers. By measuring ourselves against these questions or themes—one for each chapter—we can test whether we are connected to Jesus and operating in his name. These questions are not meant to imply that there is only one Christian position on any political topic before us. The questions are meant to make sure we are aligned with Jesus before we determine how best to incarnate his values in the world today. Christians have disagreed politically throughout our history, but this does not mean we cannot use Jesus as the measure for judging what motivates and drives our politics. At the heart of this book's message I am saying, *don't go right, don't go left; go deeper.*

Are we standing with Jesus? Are we listening to what he said? Are we following that? Are we watching what he did? Can we answer honestly and affirmatively? That will be the continuing drumbeat throughout this book: Are we wanting, needing, longing to reconnect with Jesus in a time of crisis like this one?

I was not the only one asking these questions. For many months, I'd been having a legion of conversations with leaders from many sectors; ordinary people, pastors, and politicians; and, most importantly, with young people, people of color, and women. A president at one of the nation's leading universities, and a devout person of faith who is usually very upbeat, talked to me while he was feeling quite overwhelmed and discouraged. "Things are happening every day that affect my university and our community, and I just don't know what to do," he said. A very thoughtful and always morally sensitive US senator, also a Christian, called me to say, "There are too many things to fight at the same time; how do I choose what to fight?" A bishop of a national church called with deep concerns: "I find myself just reacting all the time—to what is happening with refugees and immigrants and to so many other things. How do I act and not just react? How do we *assert* our faith in a time like this?"

## WHAT DOES RECLAIMING JESUS MEAN?

I remember a breakfast conversation with a member of Congress in Washington, DC, in 2017 about the relationship between faith and politics. He asked, with deep puzzlement in his eyes, how so many Christians could possibly justify accepting and even supporting so many fundamentally immoral policies, statements, and behaviors coming from the White House, or at least why they were being so silent about many things they never had been quiet about before. It really wasn't a partisan query. He just couldn't understand, so he asked me respectfully and quite sincerely, "What about Jesus?"

This lawmaker, as a committed Christian himself, is also concerned about how too few of his colleagues, on both sides of the political aisle, are willing to seriously grapple with this same question, or even care to ask it at all. For many years I have said, "The right gets it wrong and the left doesn't get it." That would seem true now more than ever—especially with the departure of so many white evangelicals from many of Jesus's core teachings, which is genuinely baffling to many people beyond my lawmaker friend, and to people like me who are from the evangelical tradition. Even other Christians all over the world are asking the same question: How have American Christians forgotten about Jesus? In particular, many American Christians of color and a new generation of young people of all colors and creeds who are trying make their own decisions about faith are shaking their heads in confusion and even disgust.

Fear has become very bipartisan. Many respond more to what they are afraid of than to what they are for. I believe most people voted in the 2016 presidential election out of their fears more than out of their values.

Most were voting against someone, something, some others. And the results just increased the sense and spread of fear and division.

We are indeed in a crisis, and the disorienting and dangerous state of our nation's present reality is rapidly being normalized, which is even more frightening. Many people experience an ongoing crisis of safety and lack of opportunity in communities of color; many women and marginalized people feel afraid in the United States and around the world. And many of us—across the political spectrum—are alarmed at the lack of public civility and decency; the growing dangers to the protocols, procedures, and practices of governance; and even threats to the rule of law, which collectively put both the common good and even democracy in jeopardy. Going beyond and deeper than politics, many across the ideological spectrum sense the sharp decline of values, health, and human flourishing in our cultural and civic lives, which morally undermines the quality of our public life and society. By morally accepting things that we should not, we help to undermine the spiritual fabric of our personal, family, and social lives.

As many have pointed out, the symbol for the word "crisis" in Chinese is a combination of the symbols for two Chinese words: "danger" and "opportunity." The dangers of the present crisis are obvious and growing by the day—especially for those people on the margins, such as immigrants and their families; young people of color, especially in relation to our policing, criminal justice, economic, educational, and electoral systems; all the poor and vulnerable among us; people who face cruelty, oppression, and violence because of who they are, how they worship, who they love; and women in every category. Democracy itself, the rule of law, and the very idea of objective truth are all in danger now, as our nation and world face an emerging and spreading autocratic style of leadership.

What is the opportunity? Most fundamentally, reconnecting to the person and teachings of Jesus. Christians, in other historical moments, have often remembered, rediscovered, returned, and gone back to their obedient discipleship to Jesus Christ—both personal and public—in times of crisis. It's called coming home. Even Americans of other faiths hunger for this return. Muslims and Jews regularly tell me how grateful they are when Christians start talking about Jesus again, as that makes them feel safer! People who don't identify with any faith system wonder why Christians are not talking about the actual person and teachings of Jesus more and wish they would.

Reclaiming Jesus is not merely about making more

Christians as much as it is about making Christians more genuinely and redemptively human, as God made us and as Christ calls us to be. For people of faith, along with their neighbors of other faiths or no faith at all, this is an opportunity to remember and return to our best personal convictions and choices. And it is also a time to recommit to the best founding values and aspirations of our democracy—sometimes called our civil religion.

This crisis of faith and politics thus presents us an opportunity to go deeper—deeper into what we call faith; deeper into our relationships with each other, especially across racial lines; and deeper into our proximity to the most marginalized, whom we often don't think about or whose faces we don't see. Crisis can take us deeper into the moral, spiritual, or faith commitments that can and do shape both our personal and public existence.

I believe two things are now at stake: *the soul of the nation* and *the integrity of faith.* Who we are and want to be and what we truly believe about God and our purposes in the world must be made clear in a time such as this. Much is at stake in this crisis. How we answer key questions will determine whether we go deeper and use this opportunity to create a better world or not: Who are we as a nation? Who do we want to be and become?

What is our identity as Americans? What is our identity as people of faith or moral conscience, and how does that relate both to our personal lives and our public posture and participation in the world? Will what we say we believe compel us to reject other things—behaviors, practices, and policies—that are contrary to our faith and moral values? These questions can serve as the moral test of what now lies before us.

In his first inaugural address, President Abraham Lincoln appealed to "the better angels of our nature." That is what our political and religious leaders should always do—appeal to our best angels. But at the other end of the moral spectrum, political and even religious leaders often appeal to our worst demons: fear, anger, resentment, greed, prejudice, division, and hatred. And the danger we are discovering is that our demons in America have been lying just below the surface and have been aggressively brought forth in recent years. The crank of the jack-in-the-box has been turned, and Jack's not going back into the box. *So mere political activism (as important as that is) won't defeat our demons alone.* The moral, religious, and political battles between our angels and our demons have become the "spiritual warfare" of this fearful time.

In such a moral confrontation, our true identities must be made clear. If we are truly the followers of Jesus, then our identity as Jesus followers is first before any other identity—racial, ethnic, cultural, national, class, or gender. It means belonging to his "body," a beloved multiracial and international community—with everything else put down the line. It means that "America First," or any other arrogated version of the phrase, is literally a heresy. For example, when the operative word in the phrase "white Christian" is "white" instead of "Christian," the gospel message of Jesus Christ that reconciles us to God and to each other is in great jeopardy.

But here again is the opportunity. The recovery of our primary identity in Christ and the potential power of the most diverse global community on the planet could help spark a spiritual renewal and moral revival of the churches and our societies. This is an extraordinary opportunity born of a dangerous crisis. Jesus is our embodiment of God's love, justice, grace, and mercy—which is exactly the formula for what could bring healing and unity for our hurting and frightened world.

That is not to say that the road ahead will be easy. Indeed, we now see daily barrages of tweets and news reports that appeal to people's fears and reinforce people's very sense of identity as "us" against "them." Many kinds of people are being "othered," and each one of us experiences being "othered" by some number of other people. Yet, Jesus was quite clear about how we are to treat "the other." "Fake news" reinforces false identities—making us think of ourselves as members of conflicting tribal groups. There should be no surprise in the predictable shift of reality-television values, now dominant in the popular culture, into the government sector. The political news of the day is now quite deliberately conflated with entertainment news, often becoming the same.

Unfortunately, America's white nationalism is always present with those "demons" in our history and national life that lie just beneath the surface. Xenophobia and racism are being stoked more openly today than at any time in decades, including animosity toward immigrants and refugees, as well as toward many young black victims of lethal police violence; and even toward black athletes who take a knee—not to protest the national anthem or the flag or veterans, as is falsely accused—but rather to take a public stand against racialized police brutality. Those historic demons have been enlisted to build and maintain an empowered white nationalist political base that feels stronger now than in many years, and is dangerously well armed. And as evidenced by the brutal murders of Muslims at worship in Christchurch, New Zealand; the cold-blooded killing of black church worshippers in Charleston, South Carolina; and the massacre of Jews at worship in their Pittsburgh temple, the white nationalist movement is growing globally.

So, we ask, what about Jesus? More of us are coming to realize that reclaiming Jesus is a better pathway than devolving into increasing political polarization and its ugly entertainment. That means that Jesus *needs* to be reclaimed, as he has been silenced, stolen, and even hijacked for political purposes. It also says that Jesus is indeed *worth* reclaiming, especially at a time such as this.

It was with these questions and in this spirit that our group of elder church leaders met at the beginning of Lent in 2018, eventually producing the document "Reclaiming Jesus: A Declaration of Faith in a Time of Crisis" (see page 401). From the beginning of our prayer and discussion, we were adamant that this not be just another "statement" for people to sign or not, but then ignore. Instead, it would reflect our deep commitment to commend a fresh call to reclaim Jesus in our time and act on it ourselves as we called others to do the same. A moment then became a movement, with five million people responding thus far.

We need this reconnection movement more than ever in the days ahead as we face both a moral test for our faith and, increasingly, a moral test for our democracy. It seems that each week, and sometimes each day, brings further erosions of our norms about truth and morality, our constitutional structure and the role that checks and balances have traditionally played in our nation, and a growing danger to racial and religious minorities.

Attacks on the truth and the rule of law are being accompanied by both rhetoric and policy that consistently and callously demean and attack the most vulnerable members of our society, whom Jesus specifically instructs us to protect, in ways that are truly dehumanizing and thus extremely dangerous.

To reclaim Jesus is a quest that is always both timeless and timely—and time is of the essence here. For me it springs directly from my own spiritual struggle to understand this moment in our history, to reflect on where we have lost touch with our Lord, and it is deeply shaped by my conversations and prayer with many others as we are trying to ask and answer the right questions for us today.

## A BATTLE FOR THE SOUL OF A NATION

The United States of America, and many other places around the globe, are currently in a deep cultural, political, and growing crisis—all undergirded, in my view, by a moral and spiritual crisis that the Apostle Paul might describe as spiritual warfare. Although the state and outcome of this many-layered crisis is continuing to change, the fundamental questions—the ones Jesus asks of us— will remain the same. These will not change regardless of the outcomes of elections, as important as those are.

This moral crisis in politics has also catalyzed a crisis of faith, and that is why both the soul of the nation and the integrity of faith are indeed both now at stake. This crisis is fundamentally about our chance and our choice of whether those who call themselves Christians are ready to go back to Jesus, and whether such a call might be taken up by others. I believe that many of us share a deep hunger for reclaiming Jesus instead of falling into more political polarization—for theology to trump politics.

The questions Jesus asked or prompted are as relevant as ever today. And they are questions we need to answer if we want to be followers of Jesus. They go to the heart of matters today, as they always do. In the midst of this crisis, returning to Jesus's teachings clarifies where we should stand.

**To sum up those questions:** In an environment where the question of whether we will love or hate our neighbor is dangerously at stake, Jesus told us what it means to love our neighbor, which includes, according to Jesus's definition, those who are different from us. When the number of official lies told becomes legion to the point that people doubt the existence of truth anymore, Jesus says, "You will know the truth and the truth will make you free." When people don't just fear the things that are reasonable to be concerned about but are now living in the "spirit of fear," Jesus repeats this phrase more than almost any other: "Be not afraid." When leadership becomes utterly defined by power and by winning and losing, Jesus says leadership is about service and washing each other's feet. When accusation, slander, and attack become the norms of public discourse, Jesus says that those who are the peacemakers, the conflict resolvers, will be called "the children of God." When the "Caesar test" is being defined by strongmen who say everything is about them, Jesus instructs his followers to render to Caesar only the limited things that belong to him; and to God, everything else. When wealth and power become the definitions of society and politics, Jesus makes the extraordinary judgment that the ultimate measure of our lives, including God's evaluation of the kings of the nations, is what we have done for "the least of these." To live in answer to these ways of Jesus is to become the "salt" and "light" that societies desperately need, especially when they are in crisis.

What would reclaiming Jesus mean going forward? We will take gospel texts and seek to apply them to some of the pressing issues now facing us. Each chapter will ask a question that Jesus asked or raised as he walked and lived among us. And he expected a response—both then and now. Who is my neighbor? Who is the greatest? What is truth?, just to name a few. These questions are for us today, too, and we all need to answer them again—right now.

Readers will have several choices.

Some may respond to Jesus by insisting that his teachings are just for our private lives, not for our public behavior, or he is irrelevant to our times—but that is hard to do for those who call themselves Christians, if God so loved the world.

Others will argue over how to interpret all the teachings of Jesus that are lifted up in this book; but that is the very conversation we need to have.

Finally, if the things Jesus said and did do urgently need to be reclaimed and applied today, then we can all join the road together to explore and discover what our discipleship to Jesus means for us in this moment of great danger and uncertainty. And we will not be alone; we can take that journey with our brothers and sisters in a pilgrimage—a sojourn—of prayer, study, discernment, and action.

It is time to take seriously the questions Jesus asked or prompted others to ask, weigh the choices we need to make, and consider what this all means for our response. We may not all have the same answers to these questions, but they must be asked; and perhaps it is our conversation about them together that could help heal a broken nation. I invite you to join the conversation, remembering that reflection must always lead to action.

# Chapter 2
# The Neighbor Question

But wanting to justify himself, he asked Jesus,
"And who is my neighbor?"
—LUKE 10:29

The question "And who is my neighbor?" that was asked of Jesus and then answered by him is both timeless and painfully timely. Who will we love and who will we hate? And what does it really mean to love our neighbor as ourselves? We can either listen to what Jesus says or ignore him at our spiritual, moral, and political peril.

One of the most key gospel texts for our times is so

familiar that even people who aren't Christian have heard of it: the Good Samaritan.

A young inquisitor of Jesus asks what he must do "to inherit eternal life." To which Jesus gives a quite simple answer: Love God and your neighbor. There you have it, says Jesus. But the young lawyer asks Jesus a follow-up question, "And who is my neighbor?" (Lk. 10:25–37). It's clear from the context that this lawyer (who I suspect might have been a Washington lawyer from the tone of his voice, which is very familiar to me) was seeking to diminish or limit the scope of who his neighbor was. The tone isn't one of expanding the reach of loving his neighbor but of restricting it.

Jesus answers with the exemplary story of the Good Samaritan in a way that upends everyone's expectations and that gets to the heart of this question. The lesson of Jesus's parable is much deeper than the traditional ideas about the Good Samaritan—that Jesus is simply commending the act of reaching out to another in need, like the Samaritan does—or even deeper than going out of your way. Some say that the parable means investing time and money to take care of a person who has been hurt and even interrupting and inconveniencing your own schedule, unlike the priest and Levite in Jesus's story who famously passed the man by the side of the road because they were too busy or preoccupied or afraid of getting dirty, or late to an important religious meeting. These are all good lessons to learn from the story of the Good Samaritan.

But what Jesus is trying to teach us here goes much deeper than simple compassion and time-consuming service to the needy. The Samaritans were not "good" as far as the Judeans of Jesus's day were concerned. They were a despised mixed race, considered half-breeds and "foreigners" to the Jewish tribe. Nobody liked them, and most tried to avoid them. They were an example that usually provoked disgust, not admiration. But Jesus chooses the hated "other" as *his example* of who our neighbor is. Jesus then describes the Samaritan taking actions that show us what it means to be a neighbor to others as the Samaritan reaches out to someone who was also an "other" to him with practical assistance, self-sacrifice, and even at risk to himself on the dangerous highway of the Jericho Road. Read what the Reverend Dr. Martin Luther King Jr. said in the final sermon of his life, the day before he was assassinated, about the dangers of the Jericho Road:

> It's a winding, meandering road. It's really conducive for ambushing. . . . In the day of Jesus it came to be known as the "Bloody Pass." And you know, it's possible that the priest and the Levite looked

over that man on the ground and wondered if the robbers were still around. Or it's possible that they felt that the man on the ground was merely faking. And he was acting like he had been robbed and hurt, in order to seize them over there, lure them there for quick and easy seizure. And so the first question that the Levite asked was, "If I stop to help this man, what will happen to me?" But then the Good Samaritan came by. And he reversed the question: "If I do not stop to help this man, what will happen to him?"[1]

Jesus's parable of the Good Samaritan, as told to the young lawyer, was meant not just to call people to service and self-sacrifice, but also to disrupt and challenge their concept of *who their neighbors were and were not.* It was a direct attack on the tribalism of the Jews and all of us, and a proclamation that those who would choose to join Jesus's tribe would be known for reaching out to and standing with all the other tribes. According to Jesus, the test of who your neighbor is will be shown by how you treat someone who is *different* from you. I believe that when Jesus's lesson of difference becomes the measure of who our neighbors are and how we treat them, this story can change cultures and even politics.

One of my favorite gospel commentators, N. T. Wright, says it well:

> When Jesus told the story of the Good Samaritan, he did so deliberately to shock his audience. Who is my neighbour? asked the lawyer. Jesus turned the question back on him: in this story, who turned out to be neighbour to the man in the ditch? Like so many of Jesus's brilliant stories, it operates at several levels. At the simplest level, of course, it is a spectacular invitation to a life of self-giving love, love in action, love that's prepared to roll up its sleeves and help no matter what it takes: yes, precisely the kind of work we associate with the work of this Order. But at the next level down, it's a story designed to split open the worldview of its hearers and let in a shaft of new and unexpected light. Instead of the closed world of Jesus's hearers, in which only their own kith and kin were properly to be counted as neighbours, Jesus demands that they recognise that even the hated and feared Samaritan is to be seen as a neighbour.[2]

Jesus is truly brilliant here, as N. T. Wright suggests. First, the best example of a neighbor is a hated outsider, a Samaritan, who demonstrates in the clearest way what a good neighbor is: someone who crosses boundaries to help someone else in need, risks his own safety and security, takes time out from his routine and certainly the schedule for his day, changes the plan for his whole trip, invests not only his time but also his resources, enlists others in his strategy; and then comes back to check to make sure that the injured man is being taken care of and healed of his wounds—all across rigid ethnic lines and national borders. Now, *that* is a neighbor, says Jesus. You can imagine the young lawyer's face when the concept of his neighbor just got expanded more than he ever could have imagined.

## OUTSIDE YOUR PATH

Perhaps theologian Gustavo Gutiérrez says it best: "Who is my neighbor? The neighbor was the Samaritan who *approached* the wounded man and *made him his neighbor.* The neighbor . . . is not he whom I find in my path, but rather he in whose path I place myself, he whom I approach and actively seek."[3]

Who is in our daily path and who is not? And is that part of the problem—how we are so limited in loving our neighbor by our narrow pathways of the "neighbors" around us, our people, our tribe, "us"? Jesus is saying we have to go outside the boundaries of our normal path to find the people who he says are the ultimate test of the question "And who is my neighbor?" The "neighbor" we need most to reach out to will only be found if we actively seek them out, by deliberately placing ourselves in different pathways than those that are normal to us and our people, and where our lives predictably and sociologically tread. The clear call of Jesus to love the neighbors outside our path is seriously challenged and regularly compromised by our *racial geography* (which is done, not by accident, but by public policy and deliberate strategy), which prevents people from finding their "neighbors."

Given the residential, economic, and even religious segregation that literally defines where most of our lives tread, we can't really do what Jesus says until we disrupt our normal pathways by moving outside of them. And given that such racial and socioeconomic geography isn't accidental but accomplished by deliberate social policies and structures, we need to ask ourselves whether we are willing and ready to transgress those boundaries—the ones that make it impossible to follow the answer to the question to Jesus "And who is my neighbor?"

Let me give you a personal example. My father, Jim Wallis Sr., was a naval officer in World War II, sent out to the Pacific after graduating from college, getting married, and being commissioned as an officer in the navy on one very busy day! The country was in a hurry to try to win the war—and they did. Most returning veterans, like my dad, came home to an enormous opportunity following the war. Our young family, like many others, received two huge things: the GI Bill for education, and an FHA loan for a house. When you get a free education and the chance to afford your first home, you immediately become middle class—and that's what our government did for us. We moved onto a nice little street called River Park in a lovely little neighborhood in the Detroit area called Redford Township, with every home a three-bedroom ranch house headed by a World War II veteran. My siblings and I were able to walk easily and safely to the wonderful Mason elementary school.

Everyone in our neighborhood, school, and nearby church looked just like us. You see, black World War II veterans, like the black sailors aboard my dad's destroyer fighting to take back islands in the Pacific, never got the GI Bill or an FHA loan. Jim Crow laws prevented that in the South, and segregated education and banking policies did in the North. No Detroit banks would lend money to black families for a new home, and the schools their kids went to, of course, were not nearly as good as our Mason school. But we never thought about it or talked about it. No one did in the white community, schools, or churches. We were all in and on the same path.

I remember when, as a teenager, I started to feel and ask some questions about all that, why we seemed to live very differently and separately in white and black Detroit—as that was what I was sensing from the newspapers I was starting to read and the news I was now listening to. The hard questions weren't welcome and were never honestly answered in my all-white world. If I really wanted to find the answers to those questions, I realized I would need to step outside of the boundaries of my path and ask the same questions elsewhere. I always tell young people to trust and follow their questions until they get to places where they will find the answers to them.

My questions took me into the city of Detroit, where I got low-paying summer jobs alongside other young men my age—but they were black, and I was white, and I began to realize that was what made all the difference—that while we were all born in Detroit, we had been raised in different countries. I was making money for college and they were supporting their families. I also sought out the black churches, which I had heard existed, but I had never been to, nor had black Christians from one of those churches come to ours. Of course, there were many moments that became great eye openers for me, what in the faith community are sometimes called "epiphanies."

One was the story I often tell about my friend Butch, a fellow janitor in a downtown office building who brought me home for dinner one night to meet his family. I will never forget as long as I live what his mother (who seemed just like my mother, who mostly just cared about her kids) said to me about the Detroit police when I asked her what she thought: "I tell my children, if you're ever lost and can't find your way home, and you see a policeman, hide behind a building or duck under a stairwell; wait until he passes and then find your way home." As she spoke, my mother's words to all of us five kids just echoed in my head, "If you are ever lost and can't find your way back home, *look for a policeman*; he is your friend and will hold you by the hand and bring you home safely." That story from fifty years ago is, of course, still painfully contemporary, and the reason I believe stories from black parents today is that I found a place, outside my path, where I heard those stories a long time ago.

People often ask me how I got started in the work I still do today. It was then—when I began to wander outside the path I was in because of the questions I had. Changing my pathway and the places I would go became what has continually changed my life—over and over again. *My worldview has always been most changed by two things: being in places I was never supposed to be, and meeting people I was never supposed to know,* much less become "neighbors" with.

I wasn't always sure what I was doing back then, but have since realized that this is what Jesus meant when he said to love our neighbor—to get outside of our tribal pathways and listen to the lives of the ones whose pathways have been so "different" from ours and whom Jesus defines as our neighbor. They are the test of loving our neighbor—not merely the people we meet on our narrow pathways every day. That biblical and spiritual reality has never been more true in my lifetime than it is right now. We need to reclaim Jesus's message here, by seeking and finding our true neighbors, if we are going to have any integrity for our faith or any health in our democracy.

## WHAT RELIGION AND LAW BOTH HANG ON

When asked by the religious leaders of his day what the greatest commandment was, Jesus answered, "'You shall love the Lord your God with all your heart, and with all your soul, and with all your mind.' This is the first and greatest commandment. And a second is like it: 'You shall love your neighbor as yourself.' On these two commandments hang all the law and the prophets" (Matt. 22:37–40). Loving God and loving your neighbor sum up both religion and law; everything starts and goes back to these two great loves.

Again, and very importantly, these vital questions must not become reduced to political and partisan issues between left and right, liberals and conservatives. They must become matters of faith that can bring us together across political boundaries too. Conservative evangelical New Testament commentator Darrell L. Bock, from Dallas Theological Seminary, writes that Jesus meant "that our neighbors can come from surprising places."

> Jesus simply says, "Go and do likewise." Jesus' point is, Simply be a neighbor. Do not rule out certain people as neighbors. And his parable makes the point emphatically by providing a model from a group the lawyer had probably excluded as possible neighbors.

To love God means to show mercy to those in need. An authentic life is found in serving God and caring for others. This is a central tenet of discipleship. Here human beings fulfill their cre-

> ated role—to love God and be a neighbor to others by meeting their needs. Neighbors are not determined by race, creed or gender; neighbors consist of anyone in need made in the image of God.[4]

Well said. This is a conclusion that could unite us across both theological and political lines, which have become so polarized now.

New Testament theologian and former Wesley Seminary professor Sharon Ringe, in her commentary on Luke, emphasizes the active requirements of loving one's neighbor: "No one can simply *have* a neighbor; one must also *be* a neighbor. . . . The story simply stands as yet another challenge to the transformation of daily life and business as usual which lies at the heart of the practice of discipleship."[5] And that means to cross boundaries.

As simple and familiar as this all is, the practice of the two great commandments that cannot be separated is both astounding and transformational, both in our lives and in the world. A quote that stands on the Friends Committee on National Legislation (FCNL) Quaker headquarters building on Capitol Hill in Washington, DC, prophetically reads, "Love Your Neighbor—No Exceptions." What does that mean right now? How do we explore how honestly answering the question the lawyer and the religious authorities asked Jesus is the key to moving forward now in such a perilously divided society and world?

## THE SHIFT OF NEIGHBORS

In America today, there is an elephant in the room during almost all of our public debates and conflicts. The underlying question beneath many of our political battles now is that by 2045, America will no longer be a majority white nation, but instead will be made up of a majority of minorities. How does a white majority used to, even unconsciously, "white" always being the norm, learn how to be one of the nation's minorities? How can we navigate that enormous cultural and political demographic change?

Europe is now dealing with many of the same issues. In the most compelling studies of current migration patterns in both the United States and Europe, the details of policy issues regarding immigration and refugees are unique and different. But the moral and spiritual heart of the public attitudes surveyed regarding each are exactly the same: "otherness," our feelings and treatment of those we believe are "other" to us. For example, Tim Dixon and his colleagues at More in Common—a new international initiative designed to help communities around the world overcome polarization and social division—have conducted extensive research in a number of European nations and found identical concerns expressed by 40 to 60 percent of the population in France, Germany, and Italy about the loss of "traditional cultural identity" due to immigration, a concern that migrants and refugees do not "integrate into [French, German, or Italian] society" or that "[French, German, or Italian] identity and Islam are incompatible."[6] Jesus's teachings about who our neighbors are, and how we should treat them if we truly love God, are so powerfully relevant right now, not just in the United States, but also all over the world.

Meanwhile, we are moving into a whole new ecclesial reality as the location of the heart of the church—the epicenter—has moved from the United States and Europe to the global south (and to Africa in particular), which changes everything about our churches' future. As Wes Granberg-Michaelson, author of the powerful and insightful book *Future Faith*, explains,

> The story of world Christianity's recent pilgrimage is dramatic and historically unprecedented. The "center of gravity" of Christianity's presence in the world rested comfortably in Europe for centuries. In 1500, 95 percent of all Christians were in that

region, and four centuries later, in 1910, 80 percent of all Christians were in Europe or North America.

But then, world Christianity began the most dramatic geographical shift in its history, moving rapidly toward the global South, and then also toward the East. By 1980, for the first time in 1,000 years, more Christians were found in the global South than the North. Growth in Africa was and remains incredible, with one out of four Christians now an African, and moving toward 40 percent of world Christianity by 2025. Asia's Christian population, now at 350 million, will grow to 460 million by that same time. Even today, it's estimated that more Christians worship on any given Sunday in churches in China than in the U.S.[7]

Learning to love our neighbors as brothers and sisters different from us is the key to guiding us into the new and diverse world we are becoming.

## SEPARATING THE CHILDREN

One of the most dramatic, and hopeful, examples of a different and better public response to these issues was the huge public outcry in the United States and around the world against the US government's policy of separating migrant children from their parents who were coming to America seeking asylum from the violence of their own countries. This inhumane practice was directly and admittedly part of the new administration's "zero-tolerance" immigration policy designed to deter immigrant families from coming to America, and to systemically decrease immigration to the United States—not just undocumented immigrants but legal immigration too—especially from nations of color. All this derived from their overall white nationalist agenda, which appeals to their select political base—like similar political strategies of other allegedly populist strongmen around the world. I wish that were a hyperbolic statement, but it is tragically supported by all the facts.

But the stories of the separated children, in the spring and summer of 2018, were too much for most Americans to handle. Despite the government's efforts to hide what was happening, the American people saw and heard of parents and children put into separate lines and parents watching their kids being taken away with no explanation as to why or where. Children were taken from their mothers while breastfeeding. Babies were put on planes to travel to detention centers thousands of miles away from their parents. We were horrified to see children held in caged detention facilities where holding or touching crying children was prohibited, even among siblings. Some toddlers had to go into court for legal proceedings against them without their parents or lawyers to defend them (some volunteer lawyers did try to step in pro bono), with some of the children literally climbing up on tables during the hearings, as toddlers do. Nearly three thousand children were taken away from their mothers and fathers as a direct result of the "zero-tolerance" policy in 2018. Subsequent investigations and reporting strongly suggest that many more children, possibly thousands more, may have been forcibly separated from their parents or guardians for many months before the official zero-tolerance policy went into effect.[8] This was literally child abuse as a matter of public policy, and most parents understood that.

We saw an incredible outpouring of support for immigrants and asylum seekers to the United States. The most powerful moments for me were the candlelight vigils that many of us helped organize and the more than seven hundred rallies that took place nationwide, as hundreds of thousands of protesters came together to urge the administration to reunite children with their parents and to go much further to protect vulnerable families. These protests and vigils demonstrated the unity in moral outrage and compassionate responses since the administration enacted its zero-tolerance policies; and it offered a reminder of the need for continued advocacy in the days to come going forward—with a special focus on the separated children and the urgent need to reunite them with their mothers and fathers. These rallies and vigils were attended by tens of thousands of parents holding their own children in their arms—and essentially saying that those brown immigrant children "are our children too!" That virtually illustrated the scriptural teachings about who is our neighbor, with powerful images of parents grasping their own children while insisting on protecting other people's children as well and providing practical demands that all the migrant children be immediately returned and restored to their families. Shameless and cruel policies created a new discussion of "who is my neighbor?" both within and outside the faith community and even across political boundaries.

In a statement issued by the Reclaiming Jesus church elders, we called this "an unbiblical sacrilege that is cruelly contrary to the love of Jesus Christ" and "a terror to families and an infliction of evil on children."[9] As *Christianity Today* wrote, "believers of all stripes were united on this one point of public policy. When Jim Wallis and Franklin Graham, and nearly everyone in between, condemn the administration's policy, it's practically a miracle. And for this, we should be grateful."[10]

Some people from government agencies working on the inside of some of those systems and facilities tried to resist by sending out videos and stories, while others resigned. Some flight attendants and pilots refused to fly separated children without their parents. And faith-based organizations across theological and political lines strongly raised their voices against these policies, which defied their faith in Christ.[11]

The stark visible reality that these were just children was what seemed to reach and resonate with so many people, especially parents. It drew me back to another gospel text, where Jesus especially blesses the little children in Mark 10:13–16:

> *People were bringing little children to him in order that he might touch them; and the disciples spoke sternly to them. But when Jesus saw this, he was indignant and said to them, "Let the little children come to me; do not stop them; for it is to such as these that the kingdom of God belongs. Truly I tell you, whoever does not receive the kingdom of God as a little child will never enter it." And he took*

> *them up in his arms, laid his hands on them, and blessed them.*

The corollary to this teaching from Jesus is his warning in Matthew 18:5–6 about those who would harm a child or lead a child astray:

> *"Whoever welcomes one such child in my name welcomes me. If any of you put a stumbling block before one of these little ones who believe in me, it would be better for you if a great millstone were fastened around your neck and you were drowned in the depth of the sea."*

A deeper analysis of our political situation came from those who likened what was happening to these migrant families to what happens to people under fascism, mirroring what former secretary of state Madeleine Albright prophetically titled her new book, *Fascism: A Warning.* In a powerful column for the *New York Times* titled "First They Came for the Migrants," Michelle Goldberg made the comparison to the historic words of German pastor Martin Niemöller after World War II when he had been held in a Nazi concentration camp:

> First they came for the socialists, and I did not speak out—because I was not a socialist.
>
> Then they came for the trade unionists, and I did not speak out—because I was not a trade unionist.
>
> Then they came for the Jews, and I did not speak out—because I was not a Jew.
>
> Then they came for me—and there was no one left to speak for me.[12]

The oppression and violence of fascism always begins with the most vulnerable and waits to see who will protest before it goes after others. As Goldberg argues in her column, "We still talk about American fascism as a looming threat, something that could happen if we're not vigilant. But for undocumented immigrants, it's already here."[13] A big question for us will be for whom we are willing to protest or, in the Gospel's language, "Who is my neighbor?"

## THE MUSLIM BAN

Another example of public outrage to the new administration's policies came when the Muslim ban was issued by an executive order, first in 2017. And a Muslim ban it was—with all the implications of both race and religion involved. It had nothing to do with national security or honest public debate over confirming proper vetting procedures for refugees, or the bogus charges of such things as immigrant crime or loss of jobs, but it had everything to do with the ideology of white nationalism. I remember teaching my course at Georgetown the week after the Muslim ban was imposed, and the activism against it had already spread across the country, especially at airports, where both Muslim refugees and completely legal citizens were being unexpectedly and massively turned away.

Many of my students at the McCourt School for Public Policy were very upset. One woman, who was already a Harvard Law School graduate now studying public policy, shared with the class how depressed she was with what she saw at the airports. I asked her to tell us what she and other lawyers and law students were doing all weekend at airports across the country where people were arriving and being detained—and she told these amazing stories of what she and others had experienced helping and meeting the Muslim migrants and citizens coming to the United States. I responded, "So instead of lawyers and law students planning their lucrative careers, you were all waiting at airports to defend and serve those refugees and citizens who were being blocked from coming into America because of their race and religion? That doesn't depress me," I said to her, "but actually makes me very hopeful." She smiled, and the whole class agreed it was a great response to the very people we were discussing in class as modern-day "strangers" and "neighbors"—helping frightened Muslims who had been banned from the United States.

One of the clearest and best stories about the impact of welcoming and loving our neighbors comes from an extraordinary example from a little suburb outside Memphis, Tennessee, called Cordova, at a church called Heartsong, that took place in 2009 and 2010. Here's how Heartsong's pastor, Steve Stone, talks about his church's welcome and relationship to the congregation of a mosque that had come to town a couple of years earlier, in an article titled "Why We Opened Our Church to Muslims":

> Allowing MIC [Memphis Islamic Cultural Center] to use our Celebration Center for prayer was done in the context of our relationship with them. We had been talking with them from the moment we knew they were moving next door to us. These were not enemies or strangers but neighbors, acquaintances, and friends. When they asked us if they could use our space, we felt honored because we knew they

would never have dared ask us if they thought our answer might possibly be no. That spoke volumes to the quality of the neighborly love we had shared for almost two years.

They asked. So what do we do? How do we respond? On what basis? Our response has to be grounded in our love for Jesus and our commitment to follow only him. The first thing that came to me was the parable of the Good Samaritan. Jesus intentionally chose as the hero of that story one whom his hearers would most "naturally" have feared and hated. He said that the one they despised out of hand is the very one who was the neighbor—the very one who fulfilled the second commandment. And then, he told all who would hear to go and be that kind of neighbor. We heard.

Beyond that "no brainer" decision to love our neighbors was the question of how we would do so in the case of inviting them to use our worship space. No thought at all was given to the political ramifications of that decision, either regarding those among our flock who might disagree with it or anyone anywhere who might attack or applaud what we were doing. The decision was firmly based only on our understanding of the mission and nature of the church.[14]

In 2010, the infamous and fabricated "ground zero mosque" story that was created by the right-wing media dominated cable news coverage. The media discussions about the new controversy were terrible, full of falsehoods about the nature and mission of this Islamic cultural center, divisiveness, and outright hatred toward Muslims. I was in the middle of many of those ugly television conversations and was continually pleading with the networks to broadcast some positive stories of Christian-Muslim relationships around the country, many of which were positive but almost entirely not publicized.

But on a pivotal Sunday morning, CNN aired a segment on this relationship between an evangelical Christian Church and a group of Muslims in Tennessee. Here were two clergymen being interviewed together about the story of their meeting and how fellowship and friendship developed. You could tell by watching that these two clerics knew, respected, and liked each other. They even laughed together and were clearly friends now. The reverend and the imam told the story of how their communities had come together with still different faiths but had learned how to communicate and even minister together in the community. I watched the show that Sunday morning and was moved to tears after trying to speak into the heated and hateful media confrontations all that week.

Two days later, I tracked down and called pastor Steve Stone (who I didn't know then) just to thank him and his church and to tell him how proud I was to be a Christian that morning after watching the CNN story of Heartsong Church. Steve kindly thanked me for *Sojourners* and said that he and many in his congregation had been subscribers for years. "Can I tell you about a phone call I just had last night?" he asked me, and I was eager to hear some good news. "I got a phone call at two in the morning. 'Is this the pastor?' a voice said. 'Yes, this is Steve Stone,' I replied. Then the voice on the phone said, 'We are a roomful of Muslim men, calling from Kashmir, Pakistan [one of the most conflicted places in the world], and we saw the CNN segment. We were all silent for a long time afterward. Then one of us said, "I think God is speaking to us through that pastor." Another said, "How could we ever kill those people?" I must tell you what happened with another one of us because he can't speak English to tell you himself. He went out to the small Christian church near our mosque and washed it clean with his Muslim hands. Now we are all back together calling you. Pastor, please tell your congregation that we don't hate them, we love them. And from now on we will protect that little Christian church near us because of what you did.' "

In the town of Cordova there was no more hatred or violence expressed against Muslims because of what the Heartsong church did—they simply followed Jesus's teaching to welcome and love their neighbors.

## RELIGIOUS ISSUES, NOT POLITICAL ONES

We must keep emphasizing that these are religions issues and not merely political ones. Voices both liberal and conservative need to speak out because of faith and moral convictions, instead of lining up based on political ideology. Some conservative voices have.

Republican strategist Peter Wehner says, "Trumpism is not a political philosophy; it is a purposeful effort, led by a demagogue, to incite ugly passions, stoke resentments and divisions, and create fear of those who are not like 'us'—Mexicans, Muslims, and Syrian refugees. But it will not end there. There will always be fresh targets." Conservative evangelical Wehner contrasts that with the principles of Jesus, saying, "[A] carpenter from Nazareth offered a very different philosophy. When you see a wounded traveler on the road to Jericho, Jesus taught, you should not pass him by. 'Truly I say to you,' he said in Matthew, 'to the extent that you did it to one of these brothers of mine, even the least of them, you did it to me.' . . . At its core, Christianity teaches that everyone, no matter at what station or in what season in life, has inherent dignity and worth."[15]

Michael Gerson, a former speechwriter and top policy adviser to George W. Bush, and an originator of "compassionate conservatism," says,

> [O]ur faith involves a common belief with unavoidably public consequences: Christians are to love their neighbor, and everyone is their neighbor. All the appearances of difference—in race, ethnicity, nationality and accomplishment—are deceptive. The reality is unseen. God's distribution of dignity is completely and radically equal. No one is worthless. No one is insignificant . . . you can argue about the proper shape of our immigration system—but you can't support any policy that achieves its goal by purposely terrorizing children.[16]

The opposite of loving your neighbor is not always hating them, but just being indifferent to them.

In 2015, Pope Francis said to the world in his Lenten

message, "Indifference to our neighbor and to God also represents a real temptation for us Christians. Each year during Lent we need to hear once more the voice of the prophets who cry out and trouble our conscience."[17]

Instead of giving up chocolate or alcohol for Lent, the pope seems to want us to give up our indifference to others. In his apostolic exhortation titled *Evangelii Gaudium* (which means "The Joy of the Gospel"), Francis tells us that as a result of indifference, "We end up being incapable of feeling compassion at the outcry of the poor, weeping for other people's pain, and feeling a need to help them, as though all this were someone else's responsibility and not our own."[18]

Francis describes a phenomenon he calls "the globalization of indifference." Here is how he describes it: "[W]henever our interior life becomes caught up in its own interests and concerns, there is no longer room for others, no place for the poor. God's voice is no longer heard, the quiet joy of his love is no longer felt, and the desire to do good fades."[19]

Perhaps it is the "indifference" to our neighbor that allows our willingness to ignore their lives, their needs, and even their children. And if we are to be honest, we must admit that white privilege, and privilege of any kind, allows this indifference. It has been striking to me as I travel the country how oblivious many white people are to their own privilege. When you are used to white privilege, racial equality feels like a threat. Or as one young black man at a forum said, "If you can't see white privilege, you have it."

But the hopeful thing I have found is that many are hungry for a deeper conversation about what and who our neighbors are—with concrete action as a result. For example, I have always been struck how conversations between mothers about their hopes, fears, and dreams for their children are such bonding experiences (for dads too, but even more for moms). But when those conversations are not occurring across lines of difference such as race, religion, immigration status, and others, it is such a lost opportunity for learning how to be neighbors together. That kind of deep listening to our neighbors to whom we have been indifferent may be the most important spiritual discipline for us Christians (especially white Christians) going forward.

When we realize that the very heart of all religion and law is "Love God, love your neighbor"—particularly the ones who are different from you—it can literally transform our lives, our communities, and our world.

After teaching his parable about the Good Samaritan, Jesus said, "Go thou and do likewise."

# Chapter 3
# The Image Question

Then God said, "Let us make humankind in our image, according to our likeness; and let them have dominion over the fish of the sea, and over the birds of the air, and over the cattle, and over all the wild animals of the earth, and over every creeping thing that creeps upon the earth." So, God created humankind in his image, in the image of God he created them; male and female he created them.

—GENESIS 1:26–27

What is the image of God? What does it mean to be created in God's image and likeness? What are the implications and responsibilities of humanity's status as image-bearers? In many ways Jesus's incarnation as both fully human and fully divine, and his entire life and ministry, proceed directly from God's creation of human beings as bearers of God's image, as related in Genesis 1. That is to say that the radical love that Jesus embodies and teaches is a direct consequence of each and every person being a child of God in a very real sense—which makes us all siblings—as well as the love God showed us in taking on our form in Jesus Christ.

John the Apostle introduces Jesus Christ by saying, "In the beginning was the Word, and the Word was with God, and the Word was God. He was in the beginning with God. All things came into being through him, and without him not one thing came into being. What has come into being in him was life, and the life was the light of all people. The light shines in the darkness, and the darkness did not overcome it" (John 1:1–5).

How a society treats people is an essentially moral decision. It is also a theological matter. And it reflects our obedience, or not, to the Word of God. To make those personal and political choices about how we treat people, especially those different from us (as we have seen Jesus defining who our neighbor is), it is spiritually vital that we go back to the beginning. Jesus is called the Word of God, and the gospels make it clear that he was there at the beginning. Therefore, how we treat people and why will determine whether we are serious about reclaiming Jesus.

Christ was at the beginning. To be a disciple of Jesus Christ is to go back to the beginning, to the creation of the world in which Christ, the Word of God, was at the center. In the first chapter of Genesis (1:26–27) we learn, "Then God said, 'Let us make humankind in *our* [emphasis added] image, according to *our* likeness; and let them have dominion [i.e., stewardship] over the fish of the sea, and over the birds of the air, and over the cattle, and over all the wild animals of the earth, and over every creeping thing that creeps upon the earth.' So God created humankind in his image, in the image of God he created them; male and female he created them."

Therefore historically, when some people decide to have *dominion* over some other people, instead of stewardship *with* other people over the rest of creation, it literally is a sin against God's act of creation, and an overturning of God's original purposes in the world—from the beginning. Submission to racism, both explicit and implicit, is also disobedience to Jesus Christ, who came to announce a new kingdom of God in which all of God's children have equal dignity, value, and participation.

Going back to the beginning in John and Genesis is the theological foundation for how Jesus then teaches us to treat all human beings, since we are all the children and creations of God—created in God's own image and likeness. John anchors Christ in the very creation of the world and then identifies him as the "life" and "light" of "all peoples."

In other words, the foundation of all human rights, equality, and dignity is *all* of us being created in the image of God—*imago Dei.* This was a radical new paradigm that God introduced to the world with and through Jesus, and we are still experiencing the shock waves of this new way of viewing others two thousand years later. Seeing all people, no matter their race or ethnicity, gender, who they are, how they worship, or who they love as full image-bearers of God undermines any human attempt to build barriers or divisions between groups. Racial bigotry is, therefore, not only an ugly political appeal to racialized anxiety, fear, and hatred, but *a brutal assault on the image of God.* There is a deeply theological offense here, not just a political one.

This text is the theological undermining and biblical rebuke of not only white supremacy but also any ethnic claim to superiority by any group. In American history, one people deciding to have violent dominion over other peoples by saying they weren't fully human, to justify our greed in the ways we were treating them, was literally throwing away *imago Dei.* White people—white Christians—knew they couldn't do to indigenous people and kidnapped Africans what they were doing in taking free land, labor, and lives away from other human beings if they were created in the image of God, so we said they weren't—that they were less than human—not really made in the image of God. We even wrote their inequality into our Constitution as slaves counting as only three-fifths of a person.

Human beings tend characteristically toward prejudice, wanting to sort things out by our tribes that can be based on history; geography; families; territory; culture; and, almost always, skin color. But racism is prejudice with power; racism is prejudice made into a system to benefit, divide, and oppress. And that's what we did in America, with our racism based on the lie, myth, ideology, and idolatry against God that is white supremacy. It was and is a sin.

It was our big and founding and original sin, as I tried to describe in my most recent book, *America's Original Sin: Racism, White Privilege, and the Bridge to a New America.*

The deliberately racialized dehumanization of indigenous people for their land, and of stolen Africans to justify our greed in slavery, was America's original sin; any form of racial discrimination based on that original dehumanization—in policing and incarceration, voting rights, education, economics, housing, the despoiling of land, and more—further perpetuates that sin. The language of sin in regard to racism is crucial, requiring a response of repentance across all lines of political philosophy. As difficult and painful as it will be to act in repentance for the sin of racism, it is perhaps one of the most important decisions that could bring churches together. I am encouraged when I see black, white, and multiracial churches now studying these issues together.

*This is why it is always a good and necessary thing to go back to the beginning, to our creation, where and when all of us human beings were made in the image and likeness of God, and to remember that Christ was there. This is the best and truest way to reestablish the worth, dignity, and value of those from whom such things have been taken away.* And that is what we must do again now.

Therefore, the denial of equal education, economic opportunity, and racial fairness in policing and the criminal justice system are instances of theological disobedience—much more than mere political matters and partisan conflicts. They ultimately raise for those of us who call ourselves Christian whether we believe the scriptures that say Jesus Christ was central to the creation of the world, and that all human beings are created equally in God's image and likeness. We either believe that or we don't and, if we do, we must act accordingly.

For example, it is not just partisan politics for a party to deliberately and systematically seek to suppress minority votes; it is also a heretical denial of the biblical assertion of the image of God in every one of us that entitles us to equal dignity, equal rights, equal citizenship, and equal opportunity. The deliberate suppression of a single vote is an offense against the image of God found in every citizen who should have the right to vote. I remember a workshop at one of those endless interfaith leaders' conferences where we were asked to come up with ideas we could all agree on. My friend Barbara Williams-Skinner and I were in the same small group, and we reported two commitments: first, to honor the image of God in every human being; and second, to an interfaith campaign to protect the voting rights of those who were being targeted with deliberate and racially focused voter suppression campaigns. We said the two commitments were directly tied together, that faith must lead to action.

We said our theology should directly undergird our public commitments, but that theology means very little without direct practical applications. Out of that workshop and several other conversations, Sojourners and the African American Clergy Network started a new campaign called Lawyers and Collars, where pastors and local congregations work alongside lawyers, prior to and on election days, to protect vulnerable voters in key states where they were being targeted around the country—a new campaign rooted in the image of God. Church-led efforts to help register voters, educate voters, turn out voters, and protect voters exercising their hard-fought-for rights of citizenship—all in nonpartisan ways—are also rooted in seeing every citizen as made in the image of God.

Other groups of human beings also face current and historical vulnerability, marginalization, and persecution—including those persecuted for their faith, their gender or sexual identity, those vulnerable because they are still in the womb, and others—and are as equally made in the image of God as everyone else and therefore as worthy of dignity and protection. In the end, how we treat *all* other people, especially the most vulnerable, will demonstrate whether we believe that all human beings are made in the image and likeness of God—or not. Protecting the dignity of all of these groups of people will be explored in this book.

## THE ARC OF HISTORY

"You are bringing politics into the church!" That is a frequently heard comment when pastors and community leaders bring things such as the Reverend Dr. Martin Luther King Jr.'s birthday commemoration services into their churches. I asked the gathered audience at the Millbrook Christian Reformed Church in Grand Rapids, Michigan, if they had ever heard that before. I was honored to give the keynote address for their MLK Day 2018 service—which was filled with leaders and members from local and national Christian Reformed Churches, and students and faculty from Calvin College—all very white places. Heads were nodding yes throughout the congregation in response to my question.

The title for the evening was "Where Do We Go from Here?"—the same as the title of Dr. King's final book—and it was a question that brought a standing-room-only crowd to Millbrook CRC on a very snowy January night, perhaps in light of the political situation in which we now found ourselves. Where in the world do we go from here?

Often, MLK birthday commemoration days and events are a little vague. How can we be better people, have a better country, or perhaps do a day of service in honor of one of the greatest moral leaders in our nation's history? But not in 2018. You could feel the tension and the controversy in MLK events everywhere and in the media coverage of them because of the recently elected president.

A very sharp contrast was evident between Dr. King's vision for racial equity and healing, and the contrary words and behavior of the new president after his first year in office; in fact, many saw the White House as trying to move MLK's vision backward. Perhaps the most referred-to words on MLK Day 2018, apart from the inspirational words of King that were often quoted, were the president's words from a meeting in the Oval Office just days before—words that were both profane and hateful—denigrating and disparaging people of color.

On the plane traveling to Grand Rapids, I read an article in the *New York Times*[1] that came out of interviews with many black church members from across our country.

They said they saw America slipping into an earlier, uglier version of itself. When the president used crude words to describe Haiti and African countries ("s-hole countries"), while also saying he would like more immigrants from Norway, in an Oval Office immigration discussion, black church leaders reflected that the president was voicing what many white Americans were still thinking, even if it was something they no longer felt comfortable saying, *that America prefers white people.*

Many black Americans were continuing to feel deeply betrayed and traumatized by the 2016 election. And it was painfully clear how America's original sin still lingers in our systems, structures, cultural narratives, and even top-level meetings in the White House. From racialized slavery to the institutionalized continuation of white preference from the current president of the United States, that sin was felt at every MLK service around the country. And it hurt.

The biblical prophets were sometimes angry. And that prophetic anger is called for now in relationship to the divisive racial rhetoric from this president. Here is just some of what Americans of color and Christians of color in the United States have been forced to watch and listen to since the presidential campaign and election of 2016. Imagine how all of this has felt to brothers and sisters of color in the body of Christ.

The man now in the White House started his political career by promoting an utterly factless and racially inspired "birther conspiracy," saying that President Barack Obama wasn't really a genuine American citizen and therefore was not a legitimate president. And, despite being treated with exceptional grace by the outgoing president, the new president has had *nothing* good to say about the first black president ever since, but *always* has a nasty word of blame or accusation.

We now have the president of white backlash. He began the first day of his official candidacy by calling Mexicans criminals and rapists in his opening press conference. He has continued to demand a wall against immigrants coming to America because there are so many "Latin Americans" coming into the country, as he has said (a lie—as the number of Mexican immigrants is actually declining,[2] even with a humanitarian crisis of Central American asylum seekers exacerbated by "zero-tolerance" presidential policies), who are mostly dangerous criminals and gang members (another lie—immigrants commit fewer crimes than ordinary citizens)[3] and are "animals" who are "infesting" our country. The American president also told Europeans to keep immigrants out or they will destroy Europe's "civilization" (a not-at-all subtle way of saying "white civilization"). He once suggested that a Hispanic judge couldn't competently do his job because of his ethnicity (this was in a case examining the president's former bogus university). In the face of a national outcry against racialized policing, the man in the White House uncritically uses the coded language of "law and order" and never speaks of holding police departments accountable for fair community policing. In one of the most indefensible but clear signal-sending pardons in presidential history, the president pardoned legally convicted Sheriff Joe Arpaio of Arizona, of racial police brutality fame.

The president of a country of immigrants infamously banned primarily Muslim refugees, migrants, and travelers because he claimed our country couldn't be sure they weren't terrorists (another lie, as lengthy vetting procedures were already in place before he took office). The commander in chief attacked a Gold Star Muslim family who lost their son fighting for the United States in the 2003 Iraq War. After the violent white supremacist march in Charlottesville that killed one protester and injured many others, the president claimed that there were "very fine people on both sides." The white president continues to denounce black athletes and call for the firing of NFL players who take a knee to protest racialized police brutality, while falsely accusing them of protesting the national anthem, the flag, and veterans (again completely not true), as well as attacking other black sports figures who don't want to come see him in the White House, not to mention calling black athletes, black journalists, black legislators, and even a former black White House staffer "dumb," "low IQ," and even "that dog."

This is hard to write and certainly hard to see and hear over and over again. All of the above are statements of fact of what the president has said and done, not political exaggeration or rhetoric. Imagine how people of color in the United States feel when they see the president talking and acting like this. The fact that all of this ugly, vicious, lying, hateful, and shamelessly evil noise is coming from the president regularly should hurt and outrage us all—not just people of color. Does it? Official racism from the president weighs down our nation's soul and keeps us from focusing on all that is good, gracious, just, and beautiful about the diverse new nation that God is creating in our midst.

Yes, racism is and should be an intolerable deal breaker for followers of Jesus Christ.

But as I said to the gathered Christians in Grand Rapids, known for being a mostly white and Christian city in Michigan, the question is not just about what was in the president's heart, but about what was in ours. The issue is not whether his faith is real but whether ours is. The heart of the problem was not the president's characteristic cursing, but his consistent preference for white people over people of color, and his implementation of policies that support that preference.

The biggest question for the Christian community in the United States was whether the operative word in the phrase "white Christian" was "white" or "Christian." I asked that on the Monday night service, and the strong aspirational response from the congregation was that we want to be "Christian." I suggested that in the weeks and months and years ahead, that commitment would be put to the test.

In his 1963 letter from a Birmingham jail, Dr. King said, "We will have to repent in this generation not merely for the hateful words and actions of the bad people but for the appalling silence of the good people." As I spoke to that large group of Christians on MLK Day, I asked whether, in this present political moment, Dr. King might say, "We will have to repent not merely for the hateful words of the openly racist bigots threatening their violence in places like Charlottesville, but the silence of the white Christians who don't speak up for institutional racial justice and genuine racial reconciliation with both now at stake."

Clearly, what we need to do in moments like this is not to bring our *politics* into the churches, but to bring our *theology* into our churches, and into our politics, especially in regard to theological issues such as racism.

That is Dr. King's deepest legacy. Racism is, finally, a matter of theology. As I said in *America's Original Sin*,

> It's not easy to face the deep wounds of racism in our country and in our church. It will require self-examination and repentance. But just as Christ reconciled us to God, let us show one another the forgiveness, grace, peace, and mercy we have received. The church must be at the forefront of racial reconciliation and justice and healing in this country. It's nothing less than our calling.[4]

All the politicians who give their traditional lip service to Dr. King on his birthday must be called to a place where racism and our response to it are not identified as liberal or conservative issues. We need leaders across the political spectrum to stand up to racism, to address both explicit and implicit biases to keep moving our nation toward "a more perfect union" where freedom and opportunity exist equally for everyone.

The words of Dr. King that most came to mind for me in 2018 were ones we played that night in Grand Rapids and that speak directly to what so many of us were feeling. Dr. King concludes his 1967 "Where Do We Go from Here?" speech to the Southern Christian Leadership Conference with this:

> When our days become dreary with low-hovering clouds of despair, and when our nights become darker than a thousand midnights, let us remember that there is a creative force in this universe working to pull down the gigantic mountains of evil, a power that is able to make a way out of no way and transform dark yesterdays into bright tomorrows. Let us realize that the arc of the moral universe is long, but it bends toward justice. . . . Let us go out realizing that the Bible is right: "Be not deceived. God is not mocked. Whatsoever a man soweth, that shall he also reap." This is our hope for the future, and with this faith we will be able to sing in some not too distant tomorrow, with a cosmic past tense, "We have overcome! We have overcome! Deep in my heart, I did believe we would overcome."[5]

Dreariness and despair were indeed the feelings of many after the 2016 election, and we need to believe again that "the arc of the moral universe is long, but it bends toward justice," but that is a faith statement that will require a spiritual commitment of renewed belief in God's purposes at the very creation. Truth-telling about racism, across religious and political lines, will become increasingly vital in the days ahead.

## THE ELEPHANT IN THE ROOM

I named this often invisible giant beast in our political life in the previous chapter. Let me unpack what I mean a bit more here.

In the next few decades, a fundamental demographic change will occur in the United States. By the year 2045, the majority of US citizens will be descended from African, Asian, and Latin American ancestors, according to US Census Bureau projections.[6] For the first time in its then-269-year history, America will no longer be a white majority nation. Rather, we will have become a majority of minorities—with no one race in the majority. This could make the assumptions of white preference and privilege increasingly less assumed.

This will be a historical milestone, a fundamental demographic shift. Demographic changes are already affecting our nation's elections in many states, especially at the national level. But demographic shifts don't automatically translate into shifts in wealth, power, or governance—and the white "minority" will still retain economic and political dominance for a long time to come.

Nonetheless, the demographic shift in America, with a majority of its citizens being people of color, is both significant and dramatic for the culture, ethos, and politics of a new America. And the truth needs to be told that many, if not most, white Americans are simply not ready for that demographic change—especially older white Americans—which was made dramatically clear by the 2016 election.

The question becomes: Who will help navigate this fundamental demographic change? Who will provide the moral compass for such a transformation?

It's an important question to ask, because demographic shifts do not make positive change inevitable or easy. On the contrary, these great demographic shifts could simply lead to more and more conflicts; some even invoke the language of a second civil war that includes violence—which some white supremacist groups seem to be actively preparing for. For real and positive change to occur, choices must be made, and some people and groups have to provide leadership. The choices are between *collisions* or *community* or, as Dr. King's final book put it, between "chaos or community."

Fifty years after some of the great victories of the civil rights movement, but also Dr. King's dramatic reminder that Sunday morning at eleven o'clock was the nation's most segregated hour, most Americans still live most of their lives segregated from other races. It is the geography of race that continues to separate us, keeping us in different neighborhoods, schools, and churches and keeping us from talking more deeply together and developing the empathy and relationships that bring understanding, friendships, common citizenship, and even spiritual fellowship. And those relationships are critically necessary to change public spaces and public policy.

When you are not with other people, you simply don't know what their lives are like, what they are most concerned about, what their core values or top priorities are, and what they most want for their children—and we do connect when we learn that we all mostly want the same things for our children. You learn about other people when they are your neighbors, or parents of your children's classmates or teammates, or the fellow members of your religious congregation. This is why we focused on the question "Who is my neighbor?" in the previous chapter. Jesus has clear guidance for how to find and be neighbors.

This is one place where the churches can and must lead the way. The New Testament says in Galatians 3:28, "There is neither Jew nor Gentile, neither slave nor free, nor is there male and female, for you are all one in Christ Jesus" (NIV). If churches are just silos of people all like each other, we're simply not doing what we are supposed to do. We're supposed to be the ones who are demonstrating a diverse "beloved community," in Dr. King's words. Our theology of the image of God is really meant to trump our sociology—but it's usually the other way around: our racial geography trumps our faith.

At the beginning of the church, this was literally a declaration of the meaning of "the body of Christ," and Galatians 3:28 was used as a *baptismal formula* for Christian converts to the early church. Baptism was what made the new converts' faith public. That Galatians passage became the public baptismal text, telling both converts and the world about the new kind of community that people were joining. The usual divisive and oppressive factors are always used to fuel human conflicts, but now there was a new human community that would deliberately and publicly work to reconcile and unite human beings—from different races, classes, and genders.

Many Christians today don't know or fully realize that racial and cultural integration was an original and primary mission of the first disciples of Jesus. Galatians, and similar passages in the epistles of Ephesians and Colossians, were culminations of earlier biblical commands about how the children of God should always be welcoming to "outsiders."

The early church was making a public statement, because baptism was a public and not a private event.

This was the statement: In this community we will overcome the divisions between Jews and Greeks, men and women, slaves and free. If you don't want to be part of the kind of community whose purpose is to bring people together, don't join this community! Imagine churches in America making that kind of strong statement today. We need to reimagine that early church reality into being again. Clearly, with congregations being one of the most common institutions in nearly every local community, such a bold declaration and practice of racial inclusion would help lead America to a new multiracial future.

Creating this new reality is the job of the faith community, and central to our vocation: to show that this will really work, that this was God's design and dream from the beginning of the creation described in Genesis—as we have discussed. Instead of our becoming an illusory postracial society, the book of Revelation prophetically depicts the worship of God by countless numbers of people—*in their own diverse languages, tribes, and ethnicities* (Rev. 7:9). Our job right now in this country is not only to call out the racism we see, but also to *lead by example*—by getting our own houses of worship in order and using the power of our diverse churches and our multiracial congregational relationships to change public spaces and public policy.

Together we must get to the place where our racial and cultural diversity is understood not as America's biggest problem, but as our greatest gift. If our faith communities can help us do that, it will also be our best contribution to a world threatened as much by ethnic, racial, and religious conflict as by economic confrontation, violent clashes, and environmental catastrophe—and the spiritual conviction that we are all equally made in the image of God lies underneath the hope we have.

The consequences of not listening and not talking are too great to risk, while the rewards and potentials of racial justice and healing are too important to lose. And given the historic nature of the new America coming into being, the potential conflicts and dynamic hopes are now so important that leadership is crucial. It all goes back to who we believe is made in the image of God.

## "MALE AND FEMALE GOD CREATED THEM"

The first principle of our relationship to each other, to all others, and especially to those who are different from us is, again, that we are all image-bearers of God—no exceptions. All the other differences and distinctions between us are therefore secondary. To reconnect with Jesus, it is essential that we rediscover that. Jesus was there at the beginning of creation when all human beings were made in God's image and likeness. Therefore, another fundamental violation of the image of God is misogyny. We have gone off the course of Jesus's teachings in the mistreatment of women in all its forms—including social and economic inequality, workplace discrimination, sexual harassment and assault, rape, domestic violence, and more.

"Male and female God created them," Genesis says, and Jesus makes dramatically clear that nobody gets to place one over the other. As many women have noted over time, Jesus's positive and respectful treatment of women was completely out of place for his patriarchal time and our times since. Sharon Watkins, former head of the Disciples of Christ denomination, speaking at our Reclaiming Jesus service in May 2018, put it this way:

> Jesus saw women. Jesus talked theology with the woman at the well. Jesus changed his mind conversing with the Syrophoenician woman. Jesus commended women as examples, [like] the woman with two coins [and] Mary, who rejected so- called "women's work" in order to study with Jesus. On Easter morning, the first two evangelists trusted to carry the witness of a risen Christ were women.[7]

Misogyny is also an image-of-God issue, and this moment in our nation's history has revealed how much further we have to go. Our treatment of women has entered the public conversation in a deeper and more meaningful way since the beginning of the #MeToo movement, which came to the fore with the exposure of movie producer Harvey Weinstein as a serial sexual predator—and it exploded from there.

What has been revealed is the sense of powerful male entitlement to harass, abuse, or assault whomever and whenever they want, and by any means necessary, crossing political and ideological lines and infamously including the current president of the United States. From Hollywood, to the media, to Washington, to workplaces and college campuses and, yes, even to the churches—from Catholic priests, bishops, and cardinals, to famous and successful megachurch pastors—in our country and beyond, this male predatory behavior and assumption of male privilege is tragically and characteristically common.

Again, the issue here is an assault on the image of God, the denial of the dignity and worth of people God has created, and the use of women as commodities and property, like the use of racial minorities, at the pleasure and disposal of men.

Many male commentators say they are coming forward to speak out because "I have daughters"—as they point to their daughters, wives, sisters, and other women in their lives whose assault or abuse would directly affect them. Of course, they want them to feel safe; I also have a wife and three sisters and understand that perspective. But I also am committed to changing these horrible realities *because I have sons.* The toxic masculinity that infuses our culture encourages and excuses the abuse of male power. Parents and caregivers who want to raise boys into good men must be ready to challenge that toxic masculinity with one centered on a commitment to nurture and defend people of all gender identities. At its core, the issue is again treating people as children of God made in the image and likeness of God. As Aretha Franklin, the Queen of Soul (and from my hometown, Detroit) whom we lost in 2018, made beautifully and powerfully clear, the issue is RESPECT.

A cultural commitment to changing these inexcusable realities will take more than women speaking out. Women and all assault survivors have been leading and raising their voices for decades, now with movements like #MeToo and #YesAllWomen, to paint a picture of the daily abuse they encounter just in living their everyday lives. The onus shouldn't be solely on women to continue to prove this type of abuse exists—it does exist—and men need to take responsibility for creating and participating in this toxic male-dominated culture and commit ourselves to raising a generation of boys and young men who instead embody a nurturing masculinity committed to gender equity.

We need to teach our sons not only that sexual harassment and assault are never excusable, but also that it is their responsibility to step up and call out their peers when they act or speak in sexist ways. We need to understand and teach our children that sexism, sexual harassment, and sexual assault are all sequentially related to each other and on a continuum. Unchallenged sexism creates the permission structure for sexual harassment, which in turn creates fertile ground for sexual abuse and assault that violates the image of God—"Male and female God created them."

Male silence means sharing responsibility for these crimes against women. Accepting the legal systems that protect predatory men who settle sexual harassment or sexual assault lawsuits with agreements that require silence from the accuser keeps in place the power structure and culture that allows these crimes to happen in the first place. The fact that very few sexual abusers and predators are ever legally prosecuted is proof that we live in a culture that penalizes women for seeking justice and protects men who commit these crimes.

These offenses are deeply institutional in the patriarchal cultures where they take place. The necessary punishing of individuals who commit or cover up such horrendous acts isn't enough; the institutional and patriarchal systems that undergird and protect such behavior must be honestly addressed and changed. This will be a vital test throughout our society of whether we believe in the dignity of all people created in the image of God—or not. And the examples set by the most politically powerful houses and households in the country are critical.

We also need to acknowledge that breaking down our culture of toxic masculinity and gender inequity must include rejecting the commodification of women and the consumerization of sex. When women's bodies are seen as commodities, it can make "locker room talk" seem more acceptable. And embracing, excusing, or ignoring sexist talk makes sexual harassment and assault more likely to be excused or ignored by other men. Young women and young men must stand up to the student cultures of rating and ranking women. These have also become front-page White House issues with payoffs and secret agreements for male pleasure and privilege and, from a parent's perspective, it has become enormously negative role modeling behavior for our children.

Men need to take a stand against all of this. Young men can define a new, more human, and more Christian masculinity by objecting to that cycle all along the way. As the blogger Nora Samaran says, "The opposite of masculine rape culture is masculine nurturance culture: men increasing their capacity to nurture, and becoming whole."[8]

Men need to join women in speaking out about sexual violence and sexual harassment, everywhere from the dinner table to the pulpit. And the church must become a place where we need to see some hopeful signs on this front while admitting we have a long way to go. As Jenna Barnett, the Women and Girls Campaign coordinator at Sojourners when she wrote this, put it,

> Hear me now—the biggest liability to the church is not a person coming forward to say, "I have been wronged, violated, or abused." Jesus spent his ministry hearing and responding to those statements. No, the biggest liability to the church is the silence at the pulpit, the pastor using their power for sexual gain, and the church leadership that would rather follow the lead of a pastor who harasses instead of a Christ who liberates.[9]

Opposing domestic and sexual violence openly and explicitly, including providing practical resources for faith communities to combat this evil, is an essential element of faithful Christian witness. If we believe that how we treat the most vulnerable is how we treat Christ, we must be in deep solidarity with the women and men who experience domestic or sexual abuse at some point in their lives. If we believe that we are all created in the image of God, we cannot tolerate that only half of US pastors feel sufficiently trained to address sexual and domestic abuse in their congregations.[10]

If we believe that in Christ "there is no longer male or female," it's time for men to do their part in confronting and teaching their brothers and working in solidarity with their sisters to make that vision of God's love a reality in our churches and in the world.

## AREN'T WE ALL BELOVED OF GOD?

Perhaps the most divisive issue in our churches today, especially in America, is about the rights of LGBTQ people and their welcome, inclusion, and participation in the church.

I vividly remember when a freshman at the University of Wyoming, Matthew Shepard, who was gay, short, and slight of build, was tied to a prairie fence by two men on the night of October 6, 1998—then beaten, tortured, and left to die near Laramie, Wyoming. I remember feeling and saying at the time that, no matter their theologically different views on homosexuality, every Christian should have been standing between Matthew Shepard and his attackers. And we still belong there in all our theological diversity. Shepard's ashes were interred at the National Cathedral on October 26, 2018. For me, when Christians discuss issues related to LGTBQ people, what is not up for debate is that *all the initials of LGBTQ represent people made in the image of God*, and we need to start there.

LGBTQ persons are beloved of God and, as all human beings, are made in the image of God. Therefore, I believe that faithfulness to Jesus in respecting the image of God in all of God's children means affirming and protecting the dignity and civil rights of LGBTQ people in US society and around the world. I support the welcome, inclusion, and full participation of LGBTQ people in the church.

I also believe that we in the churches, regardless of our theological views or biblical interpretations on these matters, must seek to repent and repair the hurt and harm many of our churches have caused to LGBTQ people. Far too many LGBTQ Christians have felt crushed by the rejection they have experienced from the churches and faith families in which they grew up. And we must always lift up the particular love and care for marginalized people that Jesus has taught us.

I also respect Christians and churches who are at different theological places on what all that means for the churches: whether churches can ordain LGBTQ people and bless same-sex marriages, with different interpretations of complicated scripture surrounding these issues, which have deeply divided congregations and denominations. Given the complicated and difficult issues of biblical interpretation on the issues of church practice, I understand how Christians can come to different conclusions and believe that there are sincere biblically faithful Christians in different places on church matters.[11] However, the commitment to protection, civil rights, and justice for LGBTQ people should be universal among Christians.

I believe we should assert some common ground among Christians who theologically disagree. First, as above, we should affirm the image of God, dignity, and civil rights for all LGBTQ people, without exception. Marginalized people always need protection. We should also agree on the importance of covenantal marriage, which is a biblical and countercultural message in our society in both straight and gay cultures. It is important that organizations and individuals exist that continue to play a bridge-building role on these difficult issues within the church, working to encourage dialogue and understanding based on biblical perspectives and values and carried out with a commitment to respect, civility, and justice for all. It is appropriate and necessary to beckon fellow believers to what we think is right and best for the church, rather than to disrespect and even attack one another for theological differences or varying biblical interpretations. How to best apply scripture to our times and issues is always the hermeneutical task of the church.

Strong and sometimes strident voices regard denominational and local church decision-making on same-sex marriage and gay ordination as a theological "essential" in the life of the church—on both sides of the debate. But this is not the Resurrection. Some voices believe the churches should welcome and affirm LGBTQ Christians, which includes ordination and same-sex marriage. Other voices call for the protection and welcome of LGBTQ people into the church but are still conflicted on differing biblical interpretations on gay marriage, for example. And still too many Christians remain hostile and hateful toward people who are lesbian, gay, bisexual, transgender, or queer.

The particularly strident "Nashville Statement," released in 2017 and made by mostly white conservative evangelical leaders, determined that it was time to declare that agreement on issues of sexual orientation and identity is a litmus test for authentic Christian faith, while white evangelicals have been far less clear on issues of white supremacy and privilege. I believe this was a grave mistake of public discernment and helped create more polarized divisions that seriously damage any credible evangelical witness in today's culture. That one position on same-sex marriage and ordination was presented as *the* litmus test for true Christian faith, just weeks after the horrible and deadly white nationalist attacks in Charlottesville sent a clear message to many other Christian brothers and sisters of color.

Many Christians, including some other evangelicals and Catholics,[12] have been seeking to repent of the damage done to LGBTQ people by our churches, even if they still genuinely wrestle with theological issues around sexuality. In the Nashville Statement and others like it, there is none of that spirit—no repentance or humility for the church's harmful treatment of LGBTQ Christians. Rather, the spirit of certainty and judgment in rejection of LGBTQ persons is one of the reasons a new generation of believers is leaving the church—because of the way churches have treated their friends or family members who are LGBTQ. In great contrast, Jesus's radical call to love each other, our neighbors, those different from us, the most vulnerable, and even our enemies are all painfully missing from too many evangelical statements.

What's often missing in the hottest church debates is any attempt to find common ground, welcome deeper biblical conversations in faith communities, and find civil and compassionate ways to dialogue and even to honestly disagree over the meanings of biblical sexuality. Rather, the deliberate purpose of some in these pitched ecclesial battles seems to be to further divide the church on these very difficult theological and pastoral issues. The fact that few women signed the Nashville Statement was also indicative of the clear connection being made between the rejection of LGBTQ Christians and the overwhelmingly male evangelical signers' rejection of the equality of women and their leadership in the churches.

Instead we should be looking for common ground, compassion, protection of vulnerable people, civility, and consistency as we pursue and seek to discern the heart of God on these controversial questions.

Some of the common ground we should be able to affirm includes:

Sexuality is indeed part of the good creation of God, who intends for it to be lived in ways that are whole, holy, and within the framework of love, commitment, and marriage. For Christians, sexuality is meant to be covenantal instead of recreational, which indeed is the spirt of the age and critically needs healthier countercultural alternatives—perhaps with more leadership from faith communities.

We are still learning about sexual orientation and identity, so this calls us more to listening and humility than to certain judgment. Old cultural ideas about "choices" and "cures" have been undermined by evidence, and by our experiences of the people we love and are in relationship to. The vast majority of LGBTQ people have not made a choice to be who they are. And the churches have to deal with that. People are who they are, and our churches are trying to discern and live out what it means to accept the humanity and faith of our brothers and sisters. LGBTQ Christians are asking to be welcomed and accepted in the body of Christ, and people at various places on theological questions are trying to figure out what that means.

The Bible should indeed be central to how we decide hard questions, and the commitment to the authority of scripture should cross all our differences. But current biblical scholarship and reflection show that these issues are more complex than we have often thought. Biblical hermeneutics change over time and grow with history and experience, and that is certainly true for all of us on an issue such as slavery and the Bible, as with many on the best pastoral responses to the ongoing problem of divorce—with divorce rates in the church mirroring the larger society.

The three foundations of authority in the churches—scripture, tradition, and human experience, with each of these guided by the continuing work of the Holy Spirit—must be applied to all issues, including this one. Some credible, orthodox biblical scholars have now shown that the idea of committed Christian same-sex relationships was likely not something envisioned in biblical times. I believe it's understandable that biblically committed Christians, including evangelical Christians, can and do have different interpretations of scripture on the difficult and complicated issues of sexual orientation and identity—just as they do on many other important issues. Christians need to learn how to show respect, civility, and dialogue over schism, as well as learn the art of agreeing to disagree on some matters. This should not be seen as "losing" if done in the spirit of learning and love, despite what many leaders now say. When facing a same-sex committed Christian couple, churches with different theological traditions and pilgrimages will have to find some way to support these covenantal unions. If it isn't possible for people to change who they are or to remain celibate, which I believe is meant to be a calling and not a punishment, how should the church demonstrate Christ's love for same-sex committed Christian couples?

There is also the question of grace. Jesus actually didn't say anything about homosexuality. He did speak, however, to the issue of divorce. And many churches, including conservative evangelical churches, have accepted divorced and remarried people into their congregations and leadership. Having had a failed first marriage, I am personally grateful for that grace, and for the second chance I have had for a marriage and now a family. Why are some theologically conservative churches willing to accept people who have been divorced, with Jesus's statements against it, but not LGBTQ Christians, about whom Jesus had nothing to say?

I believe that a new generation of believers with practical relational experience and fresh thinking, led by their commitment to Christ, will ultimately resolve these issues in most churches. In the meantime, society is rapidly changing in regard to the constitutional rights and civil protections owed to LGBTQ people, and most younger people, of faith and nonfaith, agree with that.

How we talk and dialogue about these divisive issues will itself demonstrate the integrity of our Christian faith—whether we want to act like the followers of Jesus. Again, humility and civility are called for, rather than litmus tests of the right or left. A commitment to religious liberty on behalf of those with different opinions, based on their faith, is vitally important. The state should not impose its views—from the right or the left—on church ecclesial policy and practice. Theological and pastoral issues should be resolved over time with spiritual and biblical discernment within faith communities, not by state intervention and power. But both the churches and the government should protect dignity, civil rights, and justice for LGBTQ people. No matter their differing and evolving theological views, followers of Jesus should most be known by their compassion and empathy toward LGBTQ people.

Listening and not just pronouncing will be required of us all. And listening to those who have been made marginal by their society is especially important if we are listening to Jesus. My intuition is that the heart of Jesus, for example, would go out to the up to 40 percent of all homeless youth who are LGBTQ[13] because they were pushed out of their homes or even their churches, or to those LGBTQ people around the world who suffer terrible violence. I pray for prayerful discernment in the Christian community, mutual respect, and a spirit that invites people rather than marginalizes them. And the beginning of that discernment should be a common Christian conviction that every initial of LGBTQ is beloved of God.

## BRINGING THE IMAGE OF GOD INTO WHITE CHURCHES

I believe that reclaiming our obedience to Jesus will be tested by the issue of race more than by any other question in American life—given how our nation's original sin of racism violated the creation of all human beings in the image of God, with Christ there at the beginning. As I have said before, getting our houses of faith in order in regard to America's original sin is necessary if we are to be able to offer any helpful leadership to a nation whose very soul is now at stake in deciding who and what kind of country, culture, and society we want to be. So let's look at what getting our places of worship in order might begin to look like if we are really serious about reclaiming Jesus.

### 1. Pulpit

After Charlottesville, I recalled something Fordham professor and Catholic priest Dr. Bryan Massingale once told me that he always asks of his white students:

"Have you ever heard racism named and called a sin from the pulpits in your churches?" The answer is almost always *no.* I believe that Father Massingale's question should be asked from every pulpit in America. Our pastors should be challenged to call white supremacy a sin from each of our nation's pulpits, as just a beginning point for genuine repentance and transformation. We all could do the research to uncover whether our own churches or denominations have *ever* called racism a sin from the pulpit or in any other formal way. What a church-changing conversation and experience it could be if every American congregation decided to clearly and publicly call racism and white supremacy sins from their pulpits—especially in all of our predominantly white churches.

**2. Penitence**

What would be acts of penitence for our churches to take—not only to renounce but also to turn around (the true meaning of "repentance") from white supremacy and then take action against it? Serious and determined discernment in local congregations—again, predominantly white congregations—could and should be transforming around penitential acts of reading, listening, learning, and dialoguing with believers of color, accepting and joining black leadership in the churches and society, together identifying and embracing key issues of racial justice in the nation and in each of our local communities. As black pastors often remind me, repentance needs to take place in black churches too, for their own internalizing of white racism and culture and conforming to the affluent American church sins such as the "prosperity gospel," which is literally a biblical heresy. Repentance also includes reparations for past actions of support of and even profit from slavery and white supremacy.

### 3. Pastoral Care

All white people need pastoral care for being morally compromised, contaminated, and diseased by the sins of white supremacy, which has infected our hearts, minds, churches, systems, and structures—and it's time we made that a pastoral priority. Those angry and violent young white men whom we all saw marching without sheets at the "Unite the Right" rally in Charlottesville indeed need legal restraint, but also tough love and pastoral care, and not just our nonviolent confrontation. We need to develop comprehensive strategies for the pastoral care of white people trying to repent and to recover from the sins of racism; and a new generation is especially eager to do that.

**4. Prophecy**

All white people need to understand that white supremacy—as a myth and a lie, an ideology of racial difference and superiority, and an idol for the white church—is underneath everything in America and needs systematic and continual confrontation and transformation. And *the idolatry of white Christianity literally separates us from God*, as idols always do. All people need to understand that our nation, church, and world have a fundamental *imago Dei* problem in which people face oppression simply because of the color of their skin. Transforming the systems still based on white supremacy is a matter of prophetic urgency, and of the church finding the courage to use our prophetic voice when the image of God is at stake.

**5. Policy**

If religious changes in the faith community don't result in policy changes for racial, gender, and economic justice that uplift the common good, we have failed in our obligations to our society. Those systemic changes must be applied to every sector of our society, and this must be done intersectionally too.

How can the church, and our congregations in each of our local communities, become truthful, just, and healing balms to the wounds of such division and hate rising again in America? That is a question for the prayerful discernment of every church in the nation.

Until we see racism as a test of our belief in the theology of creation—that we were all made in the image of God—we will never go deep enough to overcome our sins against God's children. That theological assertion will be tested by our willingness to confront and change racially unjust systems in policing, law enforcement, and voting rights, which must be rooted in our commitment to creating genuine educational and economic opportunity for all of God's multiracial children.

## WHITE NATIONALISM IS ANTI-CHRIST

White nationalism. White supremacy. White power. These are words that too many white people—particularly too many white Christians—don't like to talk about; don't like to see and hear; want to put in the past; want to dismiss as applying to only a few white people; and refuse to see as systemic, structural, or still deeply embedded in our American history and national culture. Certainly, then, too many white people, including white Christians, need a theological lesson. If all human beings are made in the image of God, as is demonstrated biblically and spiritually, white nationalism as a political force against God's children of color—that discriminates against them, that tries to keep them out of societies, that commits violence against them and even kills them—is an evil political force that is disobedient to God and God's purposes in the world. And if Christ was there at the creation, as the scriptures say, then white nationalism is also anti-Christ. This must be clearly said from every pulpit and Bible study in America and around the world. And what also needs to be said is that too many white Americans don't want to acknowledge that white nationalism is now *the greatest terrorist threat to America's safety, and the greatest political threat to genuine democracy around the world. White terrorists inspired by white nationalism are the most dangerous terrorists in America, and their threat is spreading around the world.* Those are the facts now.

There's a clear pattern in the terrorist attacks and violence from Oklahoma City to Charleston to Charlottesville to Pittsburgh's Tree of Life Synagogue to Christchurch, New Zealand, to Norway and other places in Europe. White nationalism and the white supremacy underneath are a *movement*—and a growing one. White power has killed untold numbers of people of color in our history and is still taking the lives of people of color today, through both explicit and implicit violence. The facts now show it's currently the deadliest form of terrorism in the United States: white people who believe that their exclusive power and superiority is being taken away by the growth of more inclusive democracy.[14]

The New Zealand white-power killer, a twenty-eight-year-old white Australian man, murdered fifty Muslims while they were worshipping and injured fifty more in two deadly mosque shootings—the deadliest event of its kind in New Zealand's history. He cited as inspiration Dylann Roof, a young white American man who murdered nine African-American Christians while they were studying the Bible at Mother Emanuel American Methodist Episcopal Church, in Charleston, South Carolina, after they had invited the stranger into their Bible study.

White-power terrorist killings are on the rise in America and around the world, and our leaders are not showing any intent to address them. Here are the numbers:

- The Anti-Defamation League reports that in the United States, "right-wing extremists collectively have been responsible for more than 70 percent of the 427 extremist-related killings over the past 10 years, far outnumbering those committed by left-wing extremists or domestic Islamist extremists—even with the sharp rise of Islamist-extremist killings in the past five years."[15]

- While the United States spends a great deal of money countering radical extremists claiming the mantle of Islam abroad in military and intelligence actions, domestically the United States relies "almost entirely on the police to stop attacks like the one in Pittsburgh or jihadist-inspired attacks in Orlando or San Bernardino," according to Brookings senior fellow Eric Rosand.[16]

- Under the Trump administration, the small federal program that existed to partner with local efforts to counter all forms of violent extremism has been shifted away from considering how to counter white terrorism.[17]

- While precise numbers from the FBI's antiterrorism efforts aren't available regarding white-power violence specifically, it's instructive and disturbing that of 5,000 currently open terrorism investigations, only 900, or less than 20 percent, are focused on domestic terrorism.[18] This clashes with the recognition by ADL and many

> others that right-wing terrorism, especially of the white supremacist variety, is the most deadly terrorist threat in the United States.

As John Cohen, a former official at the Department of Homeland Security, said in March 2019:

> For those who subscribe to this white nationalism ideology, they feel a sense of empowerment when they hear elected officials in the U.S., Europe, Australia, and New Zealand promote their white extremist ideological viewpoints in mainstream political rhetoric. . . . Increasingly we have experienced a dramatic increase across the West in hateful rhetoric and targeted acts of violence by individuals who do so specifically in response to what they see as an attack on white society.[19]

Just days before the New Zealand terrorist murders, a detailed article by Adam Serwer appeared in *The Atlantic* titled "White Nationalism's Deep American Roots," showing how deeply American white nationalism is embedded in our history, tracing it from its roots to the present. It even demonstrates how Adolf Hitler was inspired and instructed by this history of white nationalism in America, which helped him to construct his racialized Nazism.

Serwer concludes his piece with a reality check about where the dangers to our nation historically have often originated, along with a stark warning:

> External forces have rarely been the gravest threat to the social order and political foundations of the United States. Rather, the source of greatest danger has been those who would choose white purity over a diverse democracy. When Americans abandon their commitment to pluralism, the world notices, and catastrophe follows.[20]

When it became public knowledge that the New Zealand killer had called Trump "a symbol of renewed white identity and common purpose" in his manifesto, reporters asked the president if he thought that the white nationalists were a growing threat around the world. Donald Trump replied, "I don't really. I think it's a small group of people that have very, very serious problems. It's certainly a terrible thing."[21] Clearly, Donald Trump is seeking to minimize the terrorist threat of white nationalism in America and around the world.

Let's be clear: I have heard nobody say that Donald Trump is personally responsible for the New Zealand tragedy. But, as many on all sides of politics have pointed out, words have meaning, and politicians, especially presidents, must be held accountable for their words and rhetoric as they have such impact on other people's thinking and behavior.

Donald Trump has *proved his identification with white nationalism* from his demonizing of immigrants to making his anti-immigrant lies the central message of his midterm election strategy, to deciding to make his symbolic wall the heart of his vision and legacy, to his anti-Muslim ban, to his expressed hostility and falsehoods toward the Muslim religion, to beginning his political career with championing the racialized birther movement seeking to undermine the citizenship and credibility of Barack Obama, the first black president of the United States—the list goes on.

The evidence of Donald Trump promoting and running on white nationalism, with all of the above and much more, is in.

In sharp contrast to Trump's anti-Muslim and anti-immigrant rhetoric and policies, former president George W. Bush unusually spoke out the same week as the Christchurch shooting in defense of immigration, and its role in making the United States the nation it is today, saying at an immigrant swearing-in ceremony, "Amid all the complications of policy, may we never forget that immigration is a blessing and a strength."[22]

So, too, immediately after the horrific 9/11 attack in a speech titled "Islam Is Peace," President Bush had the courage to defend both Islam and the dignity of Muslim-Americans saying, "America counts millions of Muslims amongst our citizens, and Muslims make an incredibly valuable contribution to our country. . . . Those who feel like they can intimidate our fellow citizens to take out their anger don't represent the best of America, they represent the worst of humankind, and they should be ashamed of that kind of behavior."[23]

Our current leaders should take note. Whether Donald Trump deeply believes in white supremacy or anything other than himself is a question about his soul that I won't try to answer. But it is absolutely clear now, if it wasn't to some before the election of 2016, that he is the most visible and powerful political leader of white nationalism, white supremacy, and white power. And his top allies and aides, like Steve Bannon and Stephen Miller and others, are all further proof.

This alarming report of the influence and danger of a growing white nationalism is in this chapter where it belongs—about the image of God. This, again, is not merely a political issue but a theological one. Let's be clear in conclusion: *white nationalism is a sin against God,* is an offense to the image of God in every and all of God's created human beings, *and is explicitly anti-Christ.* White nationalism must be named as the sin that it is and antithetical to the teachings of Jesus. This is an issue that must be called out from the church as disobedient to Christ. The sin of white nationalism must be called out even, or especially, during elections.

## THE CHOICE AMERICA HAS YET TO MAKE

In honor to and for the sake of fellowship with our brothers and sisters of color in the body of Christ, I believe that the greatest single test of whether white American Christians will embrace the image of God in all God's children comes back to us again and again around the questions of race. And there will be no reclaiming Jesus until that happens.

After the 2016 election, I said that, in the end, the election was mostly about race. I received much criticism for that, both from conservatives and liberals—almost entirely white conservatives and liberals. Some of the harshest criticisms, and hard conversations with friends, came from progressive whites who were most concerned about winning back the white voters that

Democrats had lost. "You talk about race too much," my white liberal friends would say, "and it will make white working-class people feel like we are calling them racists." Let me be clear: I am all for winning back white voters on the basis of their real economic interests, which are actually being ignored by the alleged populist in the White House. It's indeed time to lift a vision of America that is based on the common good that is indeed best for all. But as much of the polling data and other evidence clearly show, white racial attitudes and fears of "cultural displacement" were indeed central to the motivations of voters in the 2016 election, more than economics or other issues such as abortion, gay marriage, or even religion.[24] The data shows us this in retrospect, but it's also something that was clear to many of us from the day Trump launched his campaign.

I do not think we get to a better America by not talking directly about race or diminishing the importance of it in politics and elections. We will not solve America's greatest contradiction and continuing flash point of racism by going around it; we must go through it. What are the core issues this president ran on and has governed on ever since his election, and blatantly during the midterm elections? Immigration, crime, a wall, MS-13 gangs, and Muslims.

The president of the United States has replaced racial "dog whistles" with "bullhorns," regularly turning the deep implicit racism of the nation into explicit expressions and policy choices that Americans on both sides of the racial divide clearly recognize. It is not rhetoric or hyperbole to describe the use of racism by this administration as blatant and consistent. That is what this marketing expert turned political candidate has decided will work best for him.

Historically, we are at a decision point, a milestone moment, a choice for the nation to make. And this racialized presidential strategy has both revealed and clarified our choices. Every time there has been a change in the country's racial history, a step toward a more equal nation, it is *always* followed by a push-back—a doubling down on the nation's historic racism toward people of color by those whose identity is "white American."

When America finally ended slavery, requiring a brutal and costly civil war to do so, the era of Reconstruction that followed began to rectify the great injustice of a slave nation; and it was proving very successful, even electing former slaves to political office. And that's why Reconstruction was quickly ended in a political compromise between white politicians from both North and South. A new system of slavery, called Jim Crow, was then imposed legally and violently to enforce a system of racial separation and inequality. After many years of oppression signified most dramatically by the lynching tree, it took a monumental struggle before a black-led civil rights movement achieved a civil rights law and a voting rights act.

But the doubling down began again, with the Republican Party strategically playing its "southern strategy" by becoming the white party in both subtle and not-so-subtle ways. Now, as Michelle Alexander has demonstrated to the country, the new strategies of mass incarceration deliberately directed at people of color have created the "new Jim Crow" as the latest doubling down against racial progress. Bryan Stevenson says it well: "Slavery has never ended, it has just evolved." White resurgence has become a growing movement, with white nationalism and the "alt-right" among its many names. The election of 2016 became a consequence of that insurgence, and its victor a new cause for the white nationalist movement, which is international now as its leaders such as Steve Bannon, recently traveling through Europe with anti-immigration ideology, are so happy about. President Trump is not the cause but the consequence, not the reason for our continuing racial illness but merely a symptom—and a very powerful and dangerous one.

All this is what this candidate and now president saw as his opportunity and his base. An implicitly and explicitly racial argument could be made for his candidacy, *based entirely on fear.* The demographic changes in America are indeed significant and dramatic, especially over the past several decades, and many white people are afraid of losing *their* country, their culture, their preference, their power in a multicultural tsunami that will change the way America looks and is for the future. This is the latest doubling down on racism in America, and is at the core of the president's message, policy agenda, and political strategy. He is the president of white America and not the president of the United States—a multiracial "united" country that he is literally trying to prevent from happening. Most of his core issues are about diminishing the number and influence of nonwhite people in America.

Will America be a racist nation going forward, or a genuine multiracial democracy? Will our country continue to have a white preference, or will it ultimately see its diversity as a gift rather than as a threat? Is what we are now experiencing a "last gasp" or "death knell" of white supremacy, as some people like to say? Or is this period just another doubling down against racial equity and justice that we have seen and will continue to see over and over again in our nation and in the lives of all our children? Will there always be a "new Jim Crow"?

This is the choice that America has to make but still has not made. It is, of course, a deeply moral question, and a determinative one for the future of the county. Will the stated ideal of all our citizens being "created equal" become the goal we continue to choose, hopefully believing it will one day arrive for all of our children? Or will it continue to be the sign of the nation's ongoing fundamental hypocrisy? It has always been deeply revealing that the reference to the ideal in our founding documents says this about *how* people are "created equal"—"that they are endowed by their Creator with certain unalienable rights, including life, liberty, and the pursuit of happiness"—meaning that we all were created by God and in God's image. Therefore, the choice we must make as a nation will ultimately reveal more than our genuine fidelity to the civic covenant made at the foundation of the nation. Whether the overt white nationalist ideology and behavior of this president will be defeated in an election, these issues and moral choices will continue to be with us and test the soul of the nation.

In a spirit of Christian love and accountability, we must tell Christians who still publicly or privately support President Trump that his becoming a champion of white nationalism no longer makes that support possible. That support can no longer be justified by his appointment of federal judges the conservatives prefer. That support is no longer justified by his change of mind and politically convenient alliance with the Christian opposition to abortion. It is not justified by his alliance with evangelicals against same-sex marriage. It is not justified by his strong advocacy of religious liberty for Christians but not for Muslims, which is explicit hypocrisy.

I believe the Faustian bargain for power undertaken by the white evangelical religious right must be exposed and opposed on the basis of Donald Trump's support for white nationalism, which is in direct disobedience to the reconciling gospel and person of Jesus Christ. Even some political and media leaders, both Republican and Democrat, are now saying that Donald Trump's life and behavior is a direct contrast to the Beatitudes, Sermon on the Mount, and Matthew 25.

I am asking why the white evangelical leaders of the religious right haven't drawn a moral line in the sand on the racial idolatry of white nationalism and supremacy that is directly and distinctively anti-Christ—as they have with issues like abortion and same-sex marriage. That choice not to draw a moral line sends a clear signal to people of color around the world in the body of Christ as to what is a political deal breaker for American white evangelical Christians and what is not.

Donald Trump has become an evangelist of white nationalism and white supremacy, and therefore his message must be rejected on grounds of faith by responsible Christians around the world and here in the US. And the bargain for power made by the white evangelical leaders who unquestioningly support Donald Trump must become a debate within the American church—the integrity of our commitment to the gospel of Jesus Christ is clearly now at stake.

Ultimately this is not about the political history and issues of race; it is about what the Bible says in the first chapter of Genesis, and how Jesus was there at the beginning as the Word of God. How we respond to the resurgence of racism in America at this critical moment of America's demographic history is not a matter of politics, and certainly not a matter of left or right. Rather, it reveals our obedience to God: whether white people of faith in America really are people of faith more than just white Americans. And whether white Christians are going to decide to be followers of Jesus. Our nation's identity and our religious identities are both at stake here. And Jesus cannot be reclaimed if we don't make the choice to live by the radical truth that all people are equal image-bearers of God.

# Chapter 4
# The Truth Question

And you will know the truth,
and the truth will make you free.
—JOHN 8:32

In John 18:38, Pontius Pilate famously asks Jesus, "What is truth?" just before he washes his hands of any responsibility for what he is about to do to him. Pilate may have meant the question rhetorically, to imply that there is no such thing as objective truth, but we need to ask the question earnestly and literally. Earlier in John's gospel, at 8:32, Jesus says, "And you will know the truth, and the truth will make you free." That assumes there is something called the truth, and there are choices we have to make about it, and what those decisions are will determine whether we are truly free. How do we answer Pilate's question today? And what can we learn from prophets, both ancient and modern, about how to speak truth to power?

The opposite of what Jesus said is also true—without the truth we are easily held captive to claims and assertions that are indeed untrue and can eventually enslave us into false ideologies or narcissistic lies that demand belief. These untruths depend on not being exposed to what is genuinely true. *Jesus clearly connects the truth with freedom*, and that is key here both in our personal lives and in any test of the health of the body politic. Truth sets us and keeps us free, but lies will finally enslave us. If you care about freedom, you had better care about the truth.

The key gospel texts on "truth" are almost entirely found in the gospel of John. After reading them carefully, we will see that for Jesus the meaning of truth is linked with relationship—in fact, with our very relationship to God. Truth is more than factual or propositional; Jesus sees it as relational. And that makes the concept of truth much deeper and more important than merely litigating the facts, though, as we will see, nothing in the gospel message allows us to ever ignore or obfuscate truthful facts:

- "And the Word became flesh and lived among us, and we have seen his glory, the glory as of a father's only son, full of grace and truth." John 1:14
- "The law indeed was given through Moses; grace and truth came through Jesus Christ." John 1:17
- "And you will know the truth, and the truth will make you free." John 8:32
- "You are from your father the devil, and you choose to do your father's desires. He was a murderer from the beginning and does not stand in the truth, because there is no truth in him. When he lies, he speaks according to his own nature, for he is a liar and the father of lies. But because I tell the truth, you do not believe me. Which of you convicts me of sin? If I tell the truth, why do you not believe me? Whoever is from God hears the words of God. The reason you do not hear them is that you are not from God." John 8:44–47
- "Thomas said to him, 'Lord, we do not know where you are going. How can we know the way?' Jesus said to him, 'I am the way, and the truth, and the life. No one comes to the Father

except through me. If you know me, you will know my Father also. From now on you do know him and have seen him.' " John 14:5–7

- "If you love me, you will keep my commandments. And I will ask the Father, and he will give you another Advocate, to be with you forever. This is the Spirit of truth, whom the world cannot receive, because it neither sees him nor knows him. You know him, because he abides with you, and he will be in you." John 14:15–17

- "Sanctify them in the truth; your word is truth. As you have sent me into the world, so I have sent them into the world. And for their sakes I sanctify myself, so that they also may be sanctified in truth." John 17:17–19

- "Pilate asked him, 'So you are a king?' Jesus answered, 'You say that I am a king. For this I was born, and for this I came into the world, to testify to the truth. Everyone who belongs to the truth listens to my voice.' Pilate asked him, 'What is truth?' " John 18:37–38

Notice how relational all these texts are. Truth in the Johannine texts is about much more than "just the facts." In these texts *truth* is manifested as faithfulness, obedience, and loyalty to God; so truth is about the choices we make that determine our spiritual lives—who we believe and follow.

Professor of New Testament Andreas J. Köstenberger compares John's Gospel to the Synoptics:

> In John's Gospel, where the importance of "truth" is underscored by 48 instances of the *aleth*-word group in comparison with a combined total of 10 in the Synoptics, the notion of truth is inextricably related to God, and to Jesus's relationship with God.
>
> In John, then, truth is first and foremost a theological, and perhaps even more accurately, a Christological concept. Rather than merely connoting correspondence with reality, as in Greek philosophy, or factual accuracy, as in Roman thought, truth, for John, while also being propositional, is at the heart a personal, relational concept that has its roots and origin in none other than God himself. As the psalmist (Ps. 31:5) and the prophet (Isa. 65:16) call God "the God of truth," so John's Gospel proclaims that God is truth, and that therefore his Word is truth. Jesus, then, is the truth, because he is sent from God and has come to reveal

> the Father and to carry out his salvation-historical purposes. For this reason the only way for us to know the truth is to know God through Jesus Christ (8:31; 14:6; 17:3).[1]

That is very significant. Our deepest concerns as people of faith, as followers of Jesus, is not just the accuracy of the news, or whether the facts being told correspond with reality. Our understanding of and our obedience to the truth are bound up in our spiritual identity and welfare, our personal relationship to God in Jesus Christ, who is identified as "the truth, the way, and the life," as the "Son of God," son of the "God of Truth." This is the God who is and embodies the truth. I like how Köstenberger and other commentators distinguish the Greek and Roman concepts of the truth from the Christian one. There is no "knowing" of the truth unless that truth changes your life, which is also, of course, closer to the Jewish conception of the truth. And not being impacted by what is true will also affect your life—even your relationship to God.

Köstenberger shows how all of the many references to the truth in John's Gospel "set the stage" for Jesus's dramatic encounter with Pilate: "Jesus's mission is summed up as bearing 'witness to the truth' (cf. 3:11, 32; 7:7; 8:14); everyone who is of the truth listens to

Jesus; and Pilate is dismissive of, or at least indifferent to, the truth."[2]

Jesus's answers to Pilate's question about Jesus's kingship show that the "kingdom" Jesus came to bring has not to do with "political exploits but with the truth." Pilate's rhetorical question "What is truth?" is simply a way to dismiss the truth Jesus came to bring, to make the truth relative and defined in many ways—especially by those in power, as I would say we now experience daily. Pilate is losing the debate with Jesus about truth, so he gives up and tries to distract the debate by giving up on the truth and saying there really is none, or that we will never find it. When autocrats say there is no truth but what they say, they do so because they want nothing or no one else to be believed but them. The gospel commentator concludes,

> In the end, therefore, Pilate is a tragic figure who fails to realize the momentous significance of the present encounter. His curt dismissal of the larger question of truth will have eternal personal consequences, and he can ill afford to brush aside the issue as glibly as he does. *In fact, through Pilate, the evangelist teaches us something quite profound about the connection between Jesus and truth, namely, that the more one knows who Jesus is (who*

> *is the truth), the more one must become apathetic about the issue of truth itself if one is to continue rejecting Jesus*[3] [emphasis added].

Theologian Miroslav Volf seems to agree:

> Trials are supposed to be about finding out what happened and meting out justice. In Jesus' trial, neither the accusers nor the judge cared for the truth. . . . The judge scorns the very notion of truth: "What is truth?" he asks, and uninterested in any answer, he leaves the scene of dialogue. . . . For both the accusers and the judge, the truth is irrelevant because it works at cross-purposes to their hold on power. The only truth they will recognize is "the truth of power." It was the accused who raised the issue of truth by subtly reminding the judge of his highest obligation—find out the truth.[4]

The relationship between truth and power is central here. I am writing this chapter the day before political primary elections across the nation in 2018. Politicians so often want to use "the truth," deny the truth, manipulate and manage the truth, and seek to discredit any notion of the truth that is a threat to their power.

But indeed, that is the very nature and purpose of the truth in our public life—to hold power accountable and even transform politics with an appeal to deeper and higher realities, to the things God cares about, to the common good. And that is why the truth indeed is a "threat" to power and why the current administration in the United States is so afraid of the truth.

Followers of Jesus must also be very wary of the way that political leaders pit power against the truth, and our vocation is to pit the truth against worldly power. As Köstenberger says, "Truth is pitted against power, and 'the truth of power' is pitted against 'the power of truth.'"[5] We are the ones who do more than just tell leaders to get their facts straight. At a deeper level we must bear witness to the truth of love over hate, to service and sacrifice over domination, to what is the "common good," best for all, and not just the few in power, for our neighbor (as defined by Jesus as the one different from us, which we discussed in chapter 2) over just our tribe, and to nonviolence over violence for what is truly redemptive.

Think of the many examples of redemptive truth revealing the falsehoods of official power: Dr. King and others leading children against the clubs, dogs, and water cannons of Sheriff Bull Connor in Birmingham,

Alabama; Congressman John Lewis and the other voting rights foot soldiers crossing Edmund Pettis Bridge on "bloody Sunday" in Selma, Alabama; the students who stood up for democracy in Tiananmen Square in China; East German Christians marching in prayer against the Berlin Wall; South African young people giving their lives at Sharpsville; Parkland teenagers standing up to the gun lobby after their classmates were killed.

It's also worth noting that pitting the power of truth against the truth of power usually entails risk and even self-sacrifice because of how entrenched the truth of power is. Truth is dismissed or denied by power, and the power of truth is then crucified by the powers that be—with Jesus and Pilate being the ultimate example.

But as Köstenberger concludes,

> Truth has a power of its own, a power that in the long run proves stronger than the usurped authority of institutional power. Jesus embodies this hope, the hope of the ultimate triumph of truth in the reign of his kingdom. It is this hope to which he bore witness in his "good confession" before Pontius Pilate. May you and I bear witness to this truth, the gospel, which is found only in Jesus, and may we, by our words and our lives, give a clear,

distinct, and irrefutable answer to Pilate's question, "What is truth?"[6]

In contrast to being a continual liar, being a truth-teller clearly is the best thing for us. As Simone de Beauvoir put it, "Defending the truth is not something one does out of a sense of duty or to allay guilt complexes, but is a reward in itself."[7]

## TRUTH VS. "ALTERNATIVE FACTS"

Kellyanne Conway, the president's senior communications adviser, told *Meet the Press* in 2017 that the White House has "alternative facts." Rudy Giuliani, the president's lawyer, told *Meet the Press* in 2018, "Truth isn't truth." Pontius Pilate, the Roman governor, asked in his debate with Jesus, "What is truth?"

What does that mean in a time when the truth itself is politically manipulated, managed, and deliberately undermined, when people are encouraged to choose their own facts, and the truths we don't like to hear or want to hide can be eliminated by screaming "fake news!," or when a free press is called "the enemy of the people"? Bob Woodward's influential 2018 book, *Fear*, claims that the president of the United States has engaged in a "war on truth." What is most dangerous is when people finally don't even believe there is truth anymore, or just stop trying to look for it. That is indeed what leads us to the controlled media of authoritarian states and the resultant loss of freedom.

When you can no longer even count the lies of the current president,[8] who seemingly makes his own "truth" as he goes along, and who continues to subject us to social media tirades that much of America sees before the press has the opportunity to fact-check them (and some media outlets are determined to report whatever the president says as true), our lack of freedom becomes normalized. Multiple reputable accounts document the several thousand false claims and statements President Trump has made since his inauguration, which have now become a normal expectation for a president's behavior—for our country, our culture, and especially for our children.

I have had specific conversations with pastors, especially megachurch pastors who tell me how they can no longer compete with the "truths" of cable news, news websites, and social media; as well as how rumors and lies quickly spread on their congregational email lists and message boards. Some pastors tell me they have to look through those false or distorted online posts, try to correct them, and encourage people not to spread the ugly rumors and even conspiracy theories that go around their church. One megachurch pastor told me, "I only have our people for two hours per week, if I am lucky, and Fox News has them 24/7."

Because of the central importance of the truth in our personal and public lives, an honest, hardworking, and informed press is critically important to genuine freedom in a democracy, and we see some of the best reporters at work right now in America—despite being under continual attack. But I believe faith communities also have the responsibility to speak truth to power, especially given the political independence we are supposed to have in any society. Therefore, the prophetic role for faith communities is not only necessary for our own integrity, but also for the health and balance of the society in which we exist.

## JUDGING OTHERS WITH A LOG IN OUR OWN EYE

But these very serious issues go deeper than just telling the truth. Let's go back to the gospels.

> *"Do not judge, so that you may not be judged. For with the judgment you make you will be judged, and the measure you give will be the measure you get. Why do you see the speck in your neighbor's*

> *eye, but do not notice the log in your own eye? Or how can you say to your neighbor, 'Let me take the speck out of your eye,' while the log is in your own eye? You hypocrite, first take the log out of your own eye, and then you will see clearly to take the speck out of your neighbor's eye."* (Matt. 7:1–5)

This is one of those very tough gospel passages. It is almost an everyday occurrence to see and hear people criticize others for the very things they are also guilty of, sometimes in much greater ways. But they don't even see how their hypocrisy undermines their credibility and genuine pursuit of the truth. Such hypocrisy is a way of life in Washington, DC, and politics everywhere in our nation. Indeed, accusing others of things you have also done, and sometimes even worse, has been normalized in American political life for many years now.

Here is what Matthew Henry's *Concise Commentary* says about this passage:

> We must judge ourselves, and judge of our own acts, but not make our word a law to everybody. We must not judge rashly, nor pass judgment upon our brother without any ground. We must not make the

> worst of people. Here is a just reproof to those who quarrel with their brethren for small faults, while they allow themselves in greater ones. Some sins are as motes, while others are as beams; some as a gnat, others as a camel. Not that there is any sin little; if it be a mote, or splinter, it is in the eye; if a gnat, it is in the throat; both are painful and dangerous, and we cannot be easy or well till they are got out. That which charity teaches us to call but a splinter in our brother's eye, true repentance and godly sorrow will teach us to call a beam in our own. It is as strange that a man can be in a sinful, miserable condition, and not be aware of it, as that a man should have a beam in his eye, and not consider it; but the god of this world blinds their minds. Here is a good rule for reprovers; first reform thyself.[9]

Sound familiar? While "reform thyself" should be the starting point for any calls to public reform, it is often passed over completely. How can we ever act upon the truth to change our public life when we deny or ignore that same truth in ourselves or don't even see it? Humility is always a prerequisite for truth-telling. Otherwise, we can easily become blind to the meaning of the truth we claim to be for.

My friend Richard Rohr describes the "plank in your eye" as "embracing the shadow." And he shows how much of our lives are lived in the shadows. Indeed, the shadows become the working and even living space for too many of our political leaders, but also for some church leaders and, of course, in our own lives, because it is harder to see or recognize the truth in the shadows.

> Jesus' phrase for the denied shadow is "the log in your own eye," which you instead notice as the "splinter in your brother's eye" (Matthew 7:3–5). Jesus preceded modern psychology's shadow work by two thousand years. His advice is absolutely perfect: "Take the log out of your own eye, and then you will see clearly enough to take the splinter out of your brother's eye" (7:5). Jesus does not deny that we should deal with evil, but we'd better do our own housecleaning first. If you do not recognize and name your own "log," it is inevitable that you will project and hate it elsewhere. In political campaigns, hateful candidates invariably accuse others of being hateful, and angrily attack others for being angry. People with little self-knowledge usually do not see this clear pattern, but instead join with them in their attacks.

> Jesus' genius is that he wastes no time on repressing or denying the shadow. In that, he is a classic prophet; he does not merely expose the shadow, but attacks the real problem, which is the ego and the arrogance of people misusing power. Once you expose the shadow for what it is, its game is over. Its effectiveness entirely depends on costume and pretense. The true seer knows that "the angels of darkness must disguise themselves as angels of light" (see 2 Corinthians 11:14). As C. S. Lewis taught, if the devil were to succeed in England, he would need to wear a three-piece suit and speak with the Queen's English, and surely never appear as a red demon with horns and a pitchfork. It is the same today. . . .
>
> Immature religion creates a high degree of "cognitively rigid" people, utterly dualistic thinkers, and often very hateful and crusading people, invariably about a single issue where they focus all their anger. "Those who live by the sword will die by the sword" (Matthew 26:52) takes on a whole new meaning.[10]

To seek the truth, to live the truth, to be accountable to the truth, and certainly to do truth-telling toward others, especially in powerful leaders and systems, require us to come out of the shadows—both personally and politically—and walk into the light.

The Reverend Dr. Martin Luther King Jr. said this in a sermon called "Splinters and Planks." He knew and he learned as he went along about the vital relationship between truth-telling and one's own honesty and transparency. To see the weaknesses in others while ignoring or even covering up the weaknesses in yourself is a formula for moral disaster. That applies to the huge contrasts between truth-telling and slavery and racial discrimination, as Dr. King pointed out, for example, but also to all the moral contrasts between our "talk" and our "walk"—both in our public lives but also in our personal lives in ways that undermine us and the movements in which we participate.

> Why do you note the Splinter in your brother's eye and fail to see the plank in your own eye? (Matt. 7.3) This figure of speech used by Jesus might seem for the moment quite exaggerated. But if we stop for the moment and analyze human actions with a disinterested eye, we will find that this contrast is not big enough, for it is a common human trait to see the weaknesses of others and never see one's own weakness.

> The splinter and plank scandal has presented itself throughout human history. In colonial Virginia a man could be sent to jail for failing to attend church twice on Sundays, while at the same time the slave trade went on with the sanction of the church and religions.[11]

There is often a relationship between the sins we see in others and the sins within ourselves. We increasingly see biases all around us, including the systematic biases in cultures, structures, and systems. But we often miss or are even blind to the personal and social biases we have in ourselves and don't even notice. To ignore and even deny the parts of the truth that challenge or disrupt our narrow cultural or personal self-interests can prevent us from seeing the truth in people and things. Such blindness to our blind spots, as they are often called, can prevent us from ever seeing or finding the truth. And often a willful blindness blocks our view of the truth.

Another friend, Brian McLaren, writing in *Sojourners* in 2008, warns of just this issue:

> [This] seems to reflect a belief that many religious rhetoricians share: that others are trapped within a

> "worldview," while they themselves are privileged to speak from a position of pristine objectivity and/or absolute truth. When in this way religious leaders are unwilling (or unable) to apply the same scrutiny to their own assumptions that they apply to the assumptions of others, they need to be held rhetorically accountable.[12]

How many times have we heard the president or other political leaders launch their attacks on others while completely avoiding acknowledging their similar sins, which are sometimes much greater than those of the political opponents they attack? But as we listen, it is important to recognize when and where many of us do that very same thing. This is a problem for church leadership as well as political leadership.

Brian is especially right about how our "worldviews" shape our views and perspectives of what is a true reflection of reality. When we do this we can so easily miss the truths that would challenge our preconceived views of the world, which reflect our own experience, history, and privilege. If we always look to the top of society for the truth, we will never find it at the bottom. If we only really listen to the voices of people who look like us, we will never hear the voices that we need to if we are ever to learn or understand the truth.

## A LEGION OF LIES

But it is indeed stunning how, since becoming president, Donald Trump—both directly and through his top aides—has made a virtual legion of demonstrably false statements. Rather than backing away from these statements when confronted with the truth, he and his team have doubled and tripled down on claims that defy reason, logic, evidence, and just common sense.

The first ridiculous example of this behavior came the day after the inauguration, when the president and his press secretary both made wildly inaccurate and provably false assertions about the size of the crowd that attended and watched his inauguration, particularly in relation to the number of people who attended Barack Obama's first inauguration, in 2009. It quickly became a highly sensitive thing for the new president, a source of personal insecurity and embarrassment that significantly more people attended President Obama's inauguration.

On *Meet the Press*, Chuck Todd challenged the president and Press Secretary Sean Spicer's falsehoods in a conversation with Kellyanne Conway, one among the president's innermost circle of advisers, during which she said Spicer had presented "alternative facts," a phrase that quickly went viral due to its Orwellian overtones. Alternative facts lead to alternative truths, and alternatives to the truth are more accurately called lies.

The new president also began to propagate the false claim that three to five million undocumented immigrants ("illegals," he calls them) voted illegally for his opponent—another very sensitive subject for him, considering that he lost the popular vote by almost three million. There was absolutely no evidence for any claims of voter fraud. However, in what has proved to be a dangerous precedent, the new administration began to put the force of government behind his hurt feelings, vowing an "investigation" into alleged voter fraud, as a rhetorical foundation for voter file purges and other efforts that were already under way to diminish and even suppress the votes of minority voters—again a racial motivation. The special commission the president subsequently created to investigate alleged voter fraud and justify voter suppression was later disbanded due to lack of evidence and a visibly corrupt process.

Of course, anyone can get things wrong; many presidents have gotten things wrong. Lying must also contain intent. And behind the current president's continual falsehoods is intent: replacing the facts with "alternative facts" and conspiracy theories that support him, his agenda, and his brand. In a *New York Times* op-ed David Leonhardt made this distinction: George W. Bush thought that Iraq had weapons of mass destruction and was wrong; Barack Obama thought people would be able to keep their current health insurance program if they wanted, under his new Affordable Care Act, which also turned out to be wrong:

> They made careless statements that proved to be false (and they deserved much of the criticism they got). But the current President of the United States lies. He lies in ways that no American politician has before. He has lied about, among other things, Obama's birthplace, John Kennedy's assassination, Sept. 11, the Iraq War, ISIS, NATO, military veterans, Mexican immigrants, anti-Semitic attacks, the unemployment rate, the murder rate, the Electoral College, voter fraud, and his groping of women.[13]

Very alarmingly, most of the readers of this column, and probably even their children, could easily add many more Trump lies to the list: the size of his inauguration crowd, the size of his victory, the size of his wealth, the size of his business successes, and insults his opponents and anyone who dares to challenge him—as Trump has made a habit out of bullying his way through life.

A unifying theme of all of the president's outrages and threats is his brazen assault on the very concept of truth and objective, knowable facts. Amid everything that's going on, consuming and interpreting the news each day is considerably more exhausting than it should be because it has never been more difficult to sort fact from fiction. While this isn't entirely the president's doing, his almost daily falsehoods have the large platform and weight of the presidency to prop them up and pound the American people with persistent and pervasive lying.

The news cycle was thrown into turmoil for more than a month by the president's evidence-free allegations that his predecessor, Barack Obama, had illegally wiretapped Trump Tower during the campaign. The president lied, accusing his predecessor of a serious crime with no justification or evidence. Rather than retracting it and apologizing, the president tasked his administration and the intelligence community with finding any shred of evidence to retroactively justify his lie. It is also worth remembering the context in which the current occupant of the White House emerged as a political figure. Though already famous due to his real estate deals and reality TV show, he perversely gained much of his credibility with the GOP primary base by feeding their hatred of the country's first African-American president with racist lies about Obama's birthplace that clearly sought to delegitimize him.

His presidential campaign was also largely built on lies, including the claim that Mexico was going to pay for his "big, beautiful wall." Then there are the many facts that the president refuses to disclose, such as his tax returns. And, of course, with the facts of his financial life hidden, he can create his own facts to protect his personal financial interests—even if they conflict with the national interest. The president and his team have also consistently repeated that he and they have nothing to do with Russia, have no serious business interests or history there, had no relationships with Russian foreign operatives who tried to influence the American election in his favor, and that the Russians had no impact in their interference in the 2016 US election. The president has often said, "Russia is fake news." Trump never revealed that he was actively pursuing his financial dream for a Trump Tower in Moscow before and during his candidacy, and then lied about it.

In Special Counsel Robert Mueller's investigation, what struck me the most about the initial downfall of those such as his ex-campaign chairman Paul Manafort; national security adviser Michael Flynn; foreign policy adviser George Papadopoulos; and Trump's personal attorney for a decade, Michael

Cohen, who were charged with crimes, was that it was all about their *lying*—lying to Congress or to federal officials about money, and lying about contacts between representatives of the Russian government and representatives of the presidential campaign. And that doesn't even get into the lies and money deployed in the service of lies surrounding the president's affairs with adult film stars and nude models by both the president's former personal lawyer and "fixer" Cohen and the president himself, all done to prevent news that could have changed the result of the election, timed as it was mere days before and with such a close race.

As Leonhardt suggests, there is a need for more than journalistic fact-checking. Deeper moral reflection is required. "He tells so many untruths that it's time to leave behind the textual parsing over which are unwitting and which are deliberate—as well as the condescending notion that most of Trump's supporters enjoy his lies," Leonhardt writes. "Trump sets out to deceive people. As he has put it, 'I play to people's fantasies.' "[14] The man who is now the president of the Unites States has spent his whole public life trying to deceive people—and little could be more alarming than that.

A narcissistic personality makes some leaders incapable of acknowledging their own unpopularity. More deeply, these lies and the determination to stick to them show a leader who is obsessed with the image of his own legitimacy as president, despite having won an electoral victory by the rules in an election that experts and authorities across the political spectrum cannot prove was tainted by major fraud. Of course, the more we eventually find out about the extent of Russian efforts and the president's personal involvement in concealing allegations of marital infidelity just days before the election, the more his insecurity about the result makes sense.

## TAKE A KNEE

I also find it very interesting how lying by people in power is often related to further oppressing those who are already suffering and making them into villains instead of *victims*. Perhaps the presidential lie that bothered me the most and is one of the clearest examples of that destruction of the truth is the president's attacks on NFL football players who took a knee during the national anthem before their football games to specifically and clearly protest police violence that is disproportionately against people of color—thus using their local and national platforms as black athletes to stand up for those who have no platforms, often young black people suffering from racialized policing. Those protests were *never* against the national anthem, the flag, our military veterans, or patriotism—but in fact the reverse, by pointing to the ideals that those things should stand for—but the black athletes are continually attacked by the president with outright lies about what they were really trying to do.

He said in a speech in Alabama:

> Wouldn't you love to see one of these NFL owners, when somebody disrespects our flag, to say, "Get that son of a bitch off the field right now. Out! He's fired!" You know, some owner is going to do that. He's going to say, "That guy disrespects our flag; he's fired." And that owner . . . they'll be the most popular person in this country.[15]

This was clearly racial, and many commentators named it a further example of the hostile "culture wars" by which the leader of the White House was trying to further inflame in the country. But Adam Ericksen, who blogs for the Raven Foundation, says,

*We're not so much in a "culture war" as we are in a search for cultural truth. And here's the truth: Trump's whole cultural narrative is based on a hostile lie, or what mimetic theory calls a "myth." His weekend spat with the NFL is just one example of Trump's mythical narrative* [emphasis added]. According to mimetic theory, "myths" are stories we tell that silence the voice of the victim. The victim cries out for justice, which makes those in power uncomfortable. So the powerful start telling a mythical story that dehumanizes the victim. In the ancient myths, victims are (mis)understood to be monsters that threaten our community. Those in power control the cultural narrative by telling the myth that gets the majority of people to believe the lie that the victim is a guilty monster. The majority unite and pounce on the victim, whose voice is silenced by banishment or sacrifice.

Donald Trump attempts to push this mythical narrative on almost every minority: Muslims, Mexicans, African Americans, journalists, immigrants, the transgender community—and now we can include professional athletes in the long list of Trump's scapegoats. The mythical narrative (i.e., the lie) he espouses is that these minorities pose a significant threat to American values.

Trump accuses NFL players who kneel during the national anthem of being unpatriotic, and are thus a threat to the United States. That's the narrative he is trying to sell the American people. . . . When anyone seeks to silence another person's voice, when they start dehumanizing them or calling them unpatriotic, you know that they are creating a myth. You know that they are caught up in a swirl of lies.

The president is caught up in a swirl of lies.[16]

## LYING TO DECEIVE

We are not seeing the first political leader who has trouble with the truth, nor is he the first with an overwhelming and sensitive ego. It's something that almost all public figures have to deal with, even the wisest among them. But clearly our current leader is on the extreme end of the narcissism scale and, reportedly, spends a great deal of his time watching television to see how he is being covered.

I believe there is much more at stake here than just self-absorbed personality; this president had already shown himself to be a lifelong autocratic leader before he took office. Historically, the most autocratic and unpopular political leaders around the world often feel compelled to prop up their legitimacy with falsehoods, and actually try to change the political narrative by lying about it. I don't think we should comfort or delude ourselves into treating this consistent lying simply as comedic or sad because of an ego that is so fragile. And the president knows that a certain percentage of Americans, especially many of his most loyal followers, will believe anything he says and will dismiss those, especially in "the media," who dispute his claims.

This president is the ultimate marketer—with his own brand as his moral measure of life. Perhaps the lying isn't just personality, but also purposeful. The liar in chief may not be an intellectual or someone who reads books or understands policy issues well. But he is smart and a savvy marketer and ran his campaign that way. Sometimes marketers lie to deceive, for the sake of their own agenda and brand. Perhaps this lying is ultimately intended to change the political conversation such that the narrative is no longer accountable to the facts. If you are successful in delegitimizing fact-checkers and truth-tellers, pretty soon nobody knows what the truth is—and the strongest and most powerful voices, especially the one controlling the highest bully pulpit, get to define the truth as they see it.

As I mentioned above, a good example of the purpose behind the lies is the way the president and his allies use lies and deception to advance a false narrative that voter fraud is a major problem. Their clear goal is to provide the justification and political cover to institute voter suppression on a massive scale to disenfranchise low-income and minority voters who are less likely to support the president and his party allies. Those Republican allies have already been caught trying to use the myth of voter fraud to disenfranchise African-American voters with "surgical precision," as a federal court described Republican voter laws in North Carolina. Lying almost always has a purpose.

## GRAVE SPIRITUAL DANGER OF ITCHING EARS

Our national conversation about the brazen and shameless use of blatant falsehoods for personal and political reasons needs to go far beyond politics.

This assault on truth should concern us spiritually as Christians. As evangelical and Republican Michael Gerson has noted, conservative Christians in particular are in "grave spiritual danger" during this presidency. Gerson's reasons—the need to reject racial nativism, the fact that religious freedom needs to be applied equally to Christians and Muslims, and the dangers of faith aligning itself with the power of the state—are all important.[17]

White Americans in particular, including white Christians, are especially subject to untruths told about immigrants, refugees, Muslims, African Americans, and other minorities. Timothy's second epistle warns about people who "having itching ears, they will accumulate for themselves teachers to suit their own desires, and will turn away from listening to the truth and wander away to myths." Those myths and lies can lead to justifications for practices and policies against "the others," which is a principal fear now about this administration—especially among people of color. That fear has shown itself to be entirely justified time and time again. White Americans who call themselves Christians have an absolute obligation to stop, pray, and honestly ask themselves the deep questions that come from this Timothy text: Do we as white people have "itching ears" to hear the lies of "teachers to suit their own desires" and racial assumptions? Do we "turn away from listening to the truth" about our nation's racial history and current realities? Do we easily "wander away to myths" that justify our own privilege and the status quo?

The volume and brazenness of the president's lies

have metastasized outward from him and infected much of his administration, many of the Republicans in Congress, and a distressing number of white Christians who both voted for and continue to support him. The moral compromises by Christians to justify supporting the president were already immense before the election, but the unwillingness of so many to stand up for truth now further corrupts their witness, and frankly, their integrity.

The disregard for what is true, and the cynical spreading of blatant falsehoods, do indeed present grave spiritual dangers to those who might acquiesce to or embrace these tactics. Christians are called many times in the scriptures to be truth-tellers and to reject falsehoods, from scriptural commandments against bearing false witness to Paul's exhortation in Ephesians 4: "We must no longer be children, tossed to and fro and blown about by every wind of doctrine, by people's trickery, by their craftiness in deceitful scheming. But speaking the truth in love, we must grow up in every way into him who is the head, into Christ. . . . So then, putting away falsehood, let all of us speak the truth to our neighbors, for we are members of one another."

As the book of Proverbs (12:22) puts it, "Lying lips are an abomination to the LORD, but those who act faithfully are his delight."

Christians who are comfortable with a loss of the truth are sending a clear and dangerous message about how seriously they really take their faith to younger generations of believers and potential believers. This is how Courtney Hall Lee, a black attorney and theologian, puts it:

> Truth is an essential part of Christianity: the Ten Commandments told Moses and his people not to bear false witness; in the Gospel of John, Jesus calls himself the way, the truth, and the light. And in Revelation 21:8, we read a very serious condemnation of liars: "But as for the cowardly, the faithless, the polluted, the murderers, the fornicators, the sorcerers, the idolaters, and all liars, their place will be in the lake that burns with fire and sulfur, which is the second death." It is fair to say that a value for truth is completely woven into our theology. So it's curious that in our culture of "fake news" and "alternative facts," so many Christians seem comfortable with a loss of truth.[18]

It does not reflect well on loyalty to God to defend a lying earthly ruler instead of defending the truth. And the consequences are hardly abstract.

What will happen to a nation's freedom when its

people don't know the truth anymore? What happens when the political leader of the nation lies day after day? Under this White House, the repetitive lying has become normalized. What will the effect be on our children when even they can see that the president regularly lies? Will that make it harder for parents to tell them to always tell the truth? How does it affect a nation's credibility when the president's supporters say that nobody should take what he says literally? What does it do to the nation's moral fabric when intelligence and justice officers tell us that there is no proof behind the president's numerous claims? And what does it mean when the president refuses to accept any responsibility for his mountain of deceptions?

According to Stanley Hauerwas, German theologian Dietrich Bonhoeffer taught us that politics "can never be divorced from truth." Indeed, Hauerwas maintains that Bonhoeffer believed that "cynicism is the vice that fuels the habits to sustain a politics that disdains the truth."[19] The cynical use of blatant falsehoods, as well as using facts in incredibly misleading ways, were both hallmarks in the president's 2016 campaign, and have continued virtually every day of his presidency.

This cannot be a political or partisan issue for people of faith. Truth-telling is a matter of faith for us and a fundamental principle of how we hold politics accountable. We cannot let our knowledge of both objective scientific facts and deeper spiritual truths become casualties of this administration. The free press has a critical role to play in protecting the truth—but so do people of faith and conscience.

The perpetual and seemingly pathological lying of the president is now more than a political issue, and certainly more than a partisan one; it is a moral and a religious crisis. And it is time for the faith community to defend the truth. Pastors should preach truth from the pulpit. Teachers and parents should clearly point out when the president is lying and teach children what the truth is. We can all use social media to confront lies with facts. The truth will indeed set us free, but the unwillingness of the faith community to speak truth to power could push us toward political bondage.

For the sake of the nation's soul, we must now see clear consequences to lying. We need to acknowledge how the normalization of lying is creating a society for ourselves and for our children in which truth no longer matters—and we must correct course. That is, if we truly want to reclaim Jesus.

# Chapter 5
# The Power Question

"The kings of the Gentiles lord it over them; and those in authority over them are called benefactors. But not so with you; rather the greatest among you must become like the youngest, and the leader like one who serves. For who is greater, the one who is at the table or the one who serves? Is it not the one at the table? But I am among you as one who serves."

—LUKE 22:25–27

What does leadership look like in the world today? What should it look like? Does it matter? What does Jesus teach us about leadership and wielding power? What responsibility do power and leadership confer on those who have them? "Who is the greatest?" is a question Jesus's disciples asked him as one wished to step ahead of another. His answer was clear and world-changing, as the scripture above from Luke 22 demonstrates.

The contrast here could not be greater—between the way of "the kings of the Gentiles" (meaning the way of the world) and Jesus's way. Think about traditional political leadership and what its dominant values are; then compare those values with the transformative ethic of servant leadership that Jesus is offering to those who would follow him. The first shall be last—those who want to lead will be those who take care of the others. In other words, *the leader won't be the first in the lines for safety and help, but the one who helps everyone else get into the saving lines.*

Let's take a closer look at the other gospel texts that deal with leadership. What we first notice is how these leadership discussions rose out of "disputes" and "arguments" about who would be most important. It caused Jesus's disciples to bicker among themselves and even to see their parents involved advocating on behalf of their children over others (anyone had any experience with that?).

Jesus turns everything about leadership completely around by reversing the dominant, traditional, and conventional wisdom about how to become and be a leader. In the sharpest contrast to what we live with in Washington, DC, and the everyday news cycle, Jesus says, "[W]hoever wishes to be first among you must be your slave; just as the Son of Man came not to be served but to serve, and to give his life a ransom for many" (Matt. 20:27–28). Jesus's call for "servant leadership" changes everything, even for those who want to exercise their leadership for a great cause—as Jesus's disciples clearly did, and many in politics often feel compelled to do too. Indeed, this was a lesson Jesus had to teach his disciples multiple times over the course of his ministry, as in addition to Luke 22 and Matthew 20, similar passages also occur elsewhere in the gospels (Lk. 9:46–48 and Mk. 9:33–37).

Conservative Southern Baptist pastor Steven J. Cole reflects on the fact that in Luke 22 the disciples are once again having this argument at what would turn out to be the Last Supper, which shows how difficult the practices of humility and servant leadership are to live by:

> [I]n spite of these repeated lessons, here they were again, right on the eve of the Lord's death, arguing over which of them was the greatest! This shows us that although we can have this lesson in our heads,

> it takes a while to put it into practice. We just think that we've learned it once and for all when someone does something to bug us and we think, "I'm a better servant of Christ than he is!" Although we may not get into a verbal debate, the thought of our heart is, "I'm greater than he is!" So we all have to keep coming back to this fundamental lesson: The greatest in God's sight are those who humbly serve. This is a lesson that all who are actively serving Christ must continually apply.[1]

Here is a commentary on these extraordinary texts of Jesus from none other than John Calvin, a Protestant Reformation leader:

> Jesus describes worldly leadership, where the top man lords it over others but then demands the title of "Benefactor"! But then He states, "But not so with you" (22:26). Worldly leadership is not a model for biblical leadership. Biblical leadership does not lord it over people, even though at times it must exercise authority (1 Pet. 5:3; Titus 2:15). Biblical leadership does not demand recognition and status. It does not pay attention to titles. It does not use its position for personal advantage at others' expense. In all these areas, worldly leadership models selfish

> men seeking selfish advantage. Biblical leadership models servanthood, even at personal sacrifice or inconvenience.[2]

These texts of Jesus's teaching are among the most radical—and they obviously affect us all, along with Jesus's original disciples. It really is about our motivations and purposes: Why do we do what we do? Are we always looking to see and worried about what our role will be, what our place is, how much we are going to be valued, looked up to, and rewarded for our good work? Jesus provides radically different starting and ending points. The one who leads, in this new order of the kingdom of God, will be the one who first and foremost learns how to serve—who literally puts others first. The older I get, the harder I realize this is; younger ambition covers over a lot of leadership issues, as we also see with the earliest disciples.

As nineteenth-century British nonconformist Baptist preacher Alexander MacLaren says in his *Expositions of Holy Scripture,*

> Jesus lays down the law for His followers as being the exact opposite of the world's notion. Dignity and pre-eminence carry obligations to serve. In His kingdom power is to be used to help others, not to

glorify oneself. In other sayings of Christ's, service is declared to be the way to become great in the kingdom, but here the matter is taken up at another point, and greatness, already attained on whatever grounds, is commanded to be turned to its proper use. The way to become great is to become small, and to serve. The right use of greatness is to become a servant.[3]

## WASHING FEET—REALLY?

One of the most powerful examples of Jesus's "servant leadership" is revealed in John 13, in the text of Jesus washing the feet of his disciples before the Last Supper. Just before his death, sitting at table with his disciples, Jesus dramatically demonstrates what he means by servant leadership. Doing so, the master washing the feet of the disciples, puts into action the servant leadership Jesus called for earlier. This last reminder was so important, as the disciples were still competing with one another. This time the question and dispute were about who would be the one to betray Jesus, to turn him over to the authorities. "Not me, Lord, certainly not me!" *But who is it?* the disciples wondered, gazing around the table:

*Now before the festival of the Passover, Jesus knew that his hour had come to depart from this world and go to the Father. Having loved his own who were in the world, he loved them to the end. The devil had already put it into the heart of Judas son of Simon Iscariot to betray him. And during supper Jesus, knowing that the Father had given all things into his hands, and that he had come from God and was going to God, got up from the table, took off his outer robe, and tied a towel around himself. Then he poured water into a basin and began to wash the disciples' feet and to wipe them with the towel that was tied around him. He came to Simon Peter, who said to him, "Lord, are you going to wash my feet?" Jesus answered, "You do not know now what I am doing, but later you will understand." Peter said to him, "You will never wash my feet." Jesus answered, "Unless I wash you, you have no share with me." Simon Peter said to him, "Lord, not my feet only but also my hands and my head!" Jesus said to him, "One who has bathed does not need to wash, except for the feet, but is entirely clean. And you are clean, though not all of you." For he knew who was to betray him; for this reason, he said, "Not all of you are clean."*

> *After he had washed their feet, had put on his robe, and had returned to the table, he said to them, "Do you know what I have done to you? You call me Teacher and Lord—and you are right, for that is what I am. So if I, your Lord and Teacher, have washed your feet, you also ought to wash one another's feet. For I have set you an example, that you also should do as I have done to you. Very truly, I tell you, servants are not greater than their master, nor are messengers greater than the one who sent them. If you know these things, you are blessed if you do them." (John 13:1–17)*

This is the transformative idea. For the world's culture and politics, leadership is based on talent, skills, hard work, discipline, fame, wealth, success, overall attractiveness, influence, and, in the end, power. While all of those qualities can be useful, *or not*, to a society—and not just the individual—what makes leadership "great" for Jesus is when leaders are being servants to others, even to the point of self-sacrifice. And think about it: the few leaders in world history whom many of us would call great are not so just because of their intelligence, judgment, oratory, charisma, or even their personal character; they become great when they decide to give their lives, even literally, for others. They put other things and other people ahead of themselves.

St. Thomas Aquinas says Jesus's action in the foot washing was meant to show the disciples an example in deed of what Jesus had taught them in words about what it means to serve each other, and how they should make that their future standard for measuring leadership:

> He said the reason I did this was to give you an example; **so you also ought to wash one another's feet**, because that was what I intended by this action. For when we are dealing with the conduct of people, example has more influence than words. A person chooses and does what seems good to him, and so what one chooses is a better indication of what is good than what one teaches should be chosen. This is why when someone says one thing and does another, what he does has more influence on others than what he has taught. Thus it is especially necessary to give example by one's actions.[4]

This goes to a familiar theme of Jesus and directly counter to what we see in Washington, DC: not just talking the talk, but also—and much more importantly—walking the walk, as we say. Jesus saved some of his strongest condemnatory language for hypocrisy, which in its simplest form is precisely the act of teaching or saying one thing but doing the opposite in one's own life and conduct.

The cultural context of foot washing and therefore its symbolism and resonance for the disciples when Jesus performed this act of service are worth noting, as Rodney A. Whitacre points out in his commentary on the gospel of John:

> For the love that is evident in the laying down of life at the crucifixion is also demonstrated in the laying down of life in humble service in the footwashing. In the footwashing we have "an acted parable of the Lord's humiliation unto death" (Beasley-Murray 1975:154; cf. D. Wenham 1995:15).
>
> It is extremely important to realize that Jesus is going to wash the feet of one who is considering betraying him. Judas has not yet given in to the temptation (cf. v. 27), but the devil has prompted him, or more literally, "put it into his heart."
>
> Having taken off his outer garment (himation), Jesus was left with his tunic (chiton), a shorter garment like a long undershirt. Slaves would be so dressed to serve a meal (cf. Lk 12:37; 17:8). Jesus

tied a linen cloth around his waist with which to dry their feet, obviously not what one would expect a master to do. A Jewish text says this is something a Gentile slave could be required to do, but not a Jewish slave (Mekilta on Ex. 21:2, citing Lev 25:39, 46). On the other hand, footwashing is something wives did for their husbands, children for their parents, and disciples for their teachers (b. Berakot 7b; cf. Barrett 1978:440). A level of intimacy is involved in these cases, unlike when Gentile slaves would do the washing. In Jesus's case, there is an obvious reversal of roles with his disciples. The one into whose hands the Father had given all (13:3) now takes his disciples' feet into his hands to wash them (cf. Augustine In John 55.6). . . .

The cleansing and the further footwashing are symbolic of the revelation that Jesus gave of the Father, and thus the disciples are called upon to embody this same revelation. The disciples are to pass on the same teaching that he, their teacher and Lord, has done by conveying as he has, both in word and deed, the selfless love of God (cf. Barrett 1978:443; Michaels 1989:241–42). The community Jesus has brought into being is to manifest the love of God that he has revealed through serving one another with no vestige of pride or position. **There**

**will be recognized positions of leadership within the new community, but the exercise of leadership is to follow this model of servanthood** [emphasis added].[5]

One contemporary story of foot washing that caused a stir was when a new young college president, named Will Jones, did just that after he became the incoming leader of Bethany College in Lindsborg, Kansas, a small, racially diverse school in red rural America. At his first opening convocation, to signal a new day of racial reconciliation; to show the importance of showing hospitality across traditional boundaries of race, national origin, and power dynamics; and to demonstrate the value of servant leadership, the new young white president washed the feet of a black student and encouraged the student body and faculty to then go outside and wash each other's feet in the nearby fountain. All of this was captured in photos by the local media, which in turn caused a group of white supremacists from the surrounding area to vandalize the school with the messages "Make Lindsborg white again," with a chalk outline of a body with the message "rest in peace my friend" next to it. The perpetrator even went so far as to make calls to Will taking credit for the vandalism and confirming that he and his group were upset about the racial diversity at Bethany and in Will's own family (Will and Amy have six children, two of whom are adopted and biracial).[6]

I had hired and mentored Will early on in his career and found him to have great ambition—but one that turned into an ambition to serve. Will came from a poor white family in Appalachia, with no inside toilets in his house, and was the first in his family to go to college. Social justice became his calling and, especially, to serve those who had been left out and behind, like his own people had been. When I asked him what he wanted to do with his life, while interviewing him for his first postcollege job, he said he wanted to do his best to emulate the life and leadership of the Reverend Dr. Martin Luther King Jr., who was his personal hero. That put Will on the path to help provide education for others who didn't have it and to accept leadership of a small, racially diverse Christian college with financial troubles in the midst of an overwhelmingly white and conservative small town. After the foot washing at the convocation drew the racist vandalism and threats against Will and his family, the campus and surrounding community came together. The city council passed a unanimous resolution supporting the values of diversity and inclusion, and Will rallied the community in a widely shared Facebook post, which read in part:

Hurtful, racist actions are not "activism." Hate language is not blunt talk. Think about what you post and share online or the jokes you tolerate. Use your imagination to walk a mile in someone else's shoes, kicks, or sandals. Do the simple thing and treat all people the way you want to be treated.[7]

The convocation's foot washing, those incidents it caused, and the community's response to them provided a moment of real revelation and transformation in both the local community and the region.

This all happened in September 2016, just a couple of months before the presidential election. In its wake, Will has repeated the foot washing tradition each year at the opening convocation. And in the two years since, the college's enrollment has increased by 24 percent.[8]

These teachings of Jesus represent the model of servanthood in the development of leadership and are really at the root of the ethics of what we call public service or public interest. Public service is not supposed to be for personal reward, but rather time set aside for the common good—a rich and deep tradition, especially in many of our faith traditions. It is also a foundation of all the checks and balances our founders put into our Constitution and system of government, with three branches that are intended to be accountable to each other, to help guard against the leadership ethic of domination.

The contrasts between Jesus's ethic of leadership and what we now see every day out of the White House are overwhelming. When power becomes the goal over service, self-interest over public interest, conflicts of interest over the common good, winning and losing over mutuality and compromise, and personal narcissism over shared benefit, we are headed for deep trouble. Autocratic behavior becomes more acceptable and even admired by people who are already subject to anxiety and anger. And before long, the road to authoritarian rule is a threat to freedom.

I find it very interesting and significant that Jesus literally washes his disciples' feet and invites his followers to follow in his steps—again, not only for their good but also for the common good of other people and the places in which they live. *Service vs. tyranny is the moral fight over the nature of leadership in our time, in which we will have to recognize and make the right choices.*

## THE UNEXPECTED LEADER

It is undoubtedly true that those in the highest levels of power often set a tone for the style of leadership that gets reflected in our cultures, our politics, and even among our schoolchildren. What are some of the most current better examples of different styles of leadership to which disciples of Jesus might point? In your lives, your history, and your community, who reminds you of the ethics of servant leadership—well-known people or those just known to the people they served?

One of the things I like most about the gospel is how Jesus continually surprises people and their expectations. And God keeps doing that. We all can see how Jesus's lessons about servant leadership have been violated not only by political power but also by hierarchal leadership in the churches when authority and power prevail over serving. Who would have thought that one of the most dramatic and powerful examples of Jesus's leadership ethic of servanthood would come from an earthly church that is perhaps most prone to embody the opposite? The profoundly new leadership of Pope Francis seeks to change the Roman Catholic Church from *closed and judging* to *open and encountering.*

After his selection, praises for the new pope were soon flowing around the world, commentary on the surprising pontiff was on all the news shows, and even late-night television comedians were paying humorous homage. But only a few of the journalists covering the pope were getting it right: Francis was just doing his job. The pope is meant to be a follower of Christ—the Vicar of Christ.

Isn't it extraordinary how simply following Jesus can attract so much attention when you are the pope? Every day, millions of other faithful followers of Christ do many of the same things. They often don't attract attention, but they help keep the world together.

The remarkable acts of kindness and grace we have seen with Pope Francis are natural responses from a disciple who has known the kindness and grace of Christ in his own life. The pope's moments of Christ-like compassion, love, and service point not to "a great man," but rather point to Jesus. He is not asking us to follow him, but inviting us to follow Christ by being a servant.

In each story we hear, we are really seeing the beauty of the kingdom of God, where human beings are treated as wonderfully loved as they are. All the narrations of the things the pope has done remind us of the Christ who said the greatest will be the one who serves.

Despite being flawed and imperfect like the rest of us, so much of what Pope Francis has done reminds us of Jesus, calling us again to a deeper relationship with Christ. When he invites homeless men to have breakfast with him on his birthday or when he kisses the feet of Muslim prisoners or offers to baptize the baby of a woman who was pressured to abort it, he reminds us of Christ. When he asks, "If someone is gay and he searches for the Lord and has good will, who am I to judge?"[9] he reminds us of Christ. When he embraces a disfigured man, he reminds us of Christ. When he chooses a simple place to live and simple clothes to wear, or drives around Washington in a little Fiat, or when we hear rumors of his going out at night in disguise to minister to the homeless, he reminds us of Christ.

What sorts of values motivate such behavior?

Perhaps my favorite story about Francis is that first encounter he reportedly had with his guard after becoming pope. As I have heard it, Argentinian cardinal Jorge Mario Bergoglio had just spent his first night sleeping as Pope Francis. In the morning he went outside of his new simple guest room and discovered a Swiss Army guard, who traditionally protects the pope. "Who are you?" Francis asked. "I am your guard" came the reply. "Where is your chair?" asked Francis. "My commandant says we must stand while we guard." Then Francis told the guard there was now a new commandant. "How long have you been here?" asked Francis. "All night," replied the guard. The pontiff told the guard to wait a minute, then came out with a chair for him to sit on. When Francis asked him if he had had something to eat, the guard started to say, "My commandant . . ." then trailed off. "Wait a minute," said Francis again, then came back with a sandwich, and the two sat and ate together. *A closed and judging church was trying to become an open and encountering church.*

Christ's kingdom is meant to change everything, and Pope Francis reminds us of that, by drawing the attention not to himself but to Christ and his way of servant leadership.

One of the other things I most love about Francis is the kind of shoes he looks for on the feet of his priests—a practice we are told that goes back to his time as an archbishop in Buenos Aires. He always looked for dirty shoes, as they were a sign to him of a priest who was serving the people in poor places with lots of mud. That became a telling sign or test of servant leadership to the man who would later become pope. Here's what Francis says about the theology of dirty shoes:

> We see then that the task of evangelization operates within the limits of language and of circumstances. It constantly seeks to communicate more effectively the truth of the Gospel in a specific context, without renouncing the truth, the goodness and the light which it can bring whenever perfection is not possible. A missionary heart is aware of these limits

> and makes itself "weak with the weak . . . everything for everyone" (1 Cor 9:22). It never closes itself off, never retreats into its own security, never opts for rigidity and defensiveness. It realizes that it has to grow in its own understanding of the Gospel and in discerning the paths of the Spirit, and so it always does what good it can, even if in the process, its shoes get soiled by the mud of the street.[10]

Of course, Pope Francis is flawed, as all human beings are. And the most painful signs of that and of remaining Church hypocrisy to the servant ethic of Christ has been the abuse of young people, including children, by priests, bishops, and cardinals. Pope Francis has been slow in dealing with that as directly as he has other things, and is only now beginning to call for fundamental change and is still too slow to implement the fundamental policy changes that would end the patriarchal cover-ups of such horrible abuses.

"Preach the Gospel at all times, and if necessary, use words" is a quote widely attributed to St. Francis of Assisi. It also seems to be the motto of Pope Francis and should be ours as well. Instead of just talking about abstract doctrines, Pope Francis is living out his beliefs in public ways that have grabbed the world's attention and embody the model that Jesus sets for his disciples in

John 13. His example of humility, compassion, and authenticity resonate as so contrary to the world of Washington, where cynicism is rampant, pride remains even after the proverbial falls, and an ideology of extreme individualism has overtaken our politics.

## THE THEOLOGICAL CASE FOR DEMOCRACY

"The right use of greatness is to become a servant," MacLaren's *Expositions* noted earlier in this chapter. That says it all. Obviously, these leadership issues have become extreme in the nation's capital. The contrast between the way of Jesus and the way of the benefactors has become more dramatic than anyone can remember. Of course, none of us would compare presidential leadership with the way of Jesus. But normally there is some accountability to the language of "public service" over private gain, and at least lip service given to wanting to serve the country and others. That has disappeared since the 2016 election.

Communities of faith don't expect Christlike service from their political leaders, but they do reasonably expect honest efforts at public service over personal self-interest and corruption. Democracy is a commitment that derives from the need for service over tyranny and serves as a way to hold public officials accountable to prevent authoritarian autocrats from replacing the public interest. Let's look at the theological case for democracy.

Here is what C. S. Lewis wrote many years ago:

> I am a democrat [i.e. a believer in democracy] because I believe in the Fall of Man. I think most people are democrats for the opposite reason. A great deal of democratic enthusiasm descends from the ideas of people like Rousseau, who believed in democracy because they thought mankind so wise and good that everyone deserved a share in the government. The danger of defending democracy on those grounds is that they're not true. Whenever their weakness is exposed, the people who prefer tyranny make capital out of the exposure. I find that they're not true without looking further than myself. I don't deserve a share in governing a hen-roost, much less a nation. Nor do most people—all the people who believe advertisements, and think in catchwords and spread rumors. The real reason for democracy is just the reverse. Mankind is so fallen that no man can be trusted with unchecked power over his fellows.[11]

In 1944, American public theologian Reinhold Niebuhr wrote in *The Children of Light and the Children of Darkness*, "Man's capacity for justice makes democracy possible, but man's inclination to injustice makes democracy necessary."[12]

Dr. Vincent Harding, one of my personal elders and a close associate of the Reverend Dr. Martin Luther King Jr., said this from his civil rights, black church, and Mennonite roots: "Democracy is not a static thing. It does not stand still. If we don't keep finding ways to expand and deepen democracy, we will see it diminish."[13]

Almost every week is stunning now regarding the kind of leadership we see modeled at the top of the political order, and it seems to reinforce the points of the commentators above of both the importance of democracy and of its fragility. In 2017, in the midst of FBI director James Comey's firing, Nancy Gibbs, then editor of *TIME* magazine, summed up the situation well, in words that seem as relevant in 2019 as they did at the time:

> The firing of FBI Director James Comey shook an already rattled body politic even more profoundly. At a moment of deep division and broad dis-

> trust, the machinery of justice matters more than ever—and when the Chief Executive monkeys with that machinery, well, that's why the founders built a Constitution that checks Executive power. We are learning in real time how resilient our institutions will be when facing, among other threats, a foreign power intent on undermining them. . . . During past political scandals and even constitutional crises, the messy, miraculous contraption of checks and balances and freedoms and duties constructed by the founders somehow carried us to safe, common ground. We are testing our instruments again, the world is watching, and as exhausting as the journey has been so far, it appears it is only just beginning.[14]

As I write this book, our own political and institutional crisis unfolds every day—and where it will lead is still very unclear. When the ethos of servant leadership and even the moderated ethics of public service are trampled each day, the future of democracy itself is now in genuine jeopardy.

The kind of political leadership we are now experiencing from the top of political power in Washington, DC, stands in the sharpest contrast to what we read in the gospels. It is, indeed, "the exact opposite" of the model that Jesus was consistently laying out for his disciples. The "greatest," the "biggest," the "richest," the "strongest," the "best," the "only one who can do this" are the constant self-described language of the leadership that we now see and consistently hear from the Trump White House. Many point to all the lying, as we described in the previous chapter, as foundational to the leadership style of the current president, along with the many things he says both about himself and others whom he clearly doesn't intend to serve but rather to constantly disparage.

Perhaps the incident, the picture, the example that best encapsulates the leadership ethics of the man who is now the president of the United States was what President Trump did in front of the whole world to Dusko Markovic, the prime minister of Montenegro, at the NATO summit in 2017. He literally pushed him out of his way to walk in front of him. At his first major meeting with international leaders, the leadership ethos of the "leader of the free world" was to physically push aside the leader of one of the world's smallest countries and stride past him. Apparently this is what it means to the president to be great and to "make America great again."

## MONEY, SEX, AND POWER

We are facing a spiritual reckoning that is more than just politics. Christians have traditionally rejected the worship of money, sex, and power. Do we still? The alternative to servant leadership, in service to others and in service to God, is a different kind of obedience—to the classic human objects of self-worship: money, sex, and power. And that is exactly what we are facing now.

Many traditions in the history of Christianity have attempted to combat and correct the worship of these three things. Catholic orders have for centuries required "poverty, chastity, and obedience" as disciplines to counter these three idols. Other traditions, especially among spiritual renewal and revival movements through the years, have spoken the language of simplicity in living, integrity in relationships, and servanthood in leadership. All our church traditions have tried to provide authentic and more life-giving alternatives to the worship of money, sex, and power—which all can be understood and used in healthy ways when they are not given primacy in one's life.

But Donald Trump alarmingly exemplifies the ultimate and consummate worshipper of money, sex, and power. American Christians have not yet reckoned with the climate he has created in our country and the spiritual obligation we have to repair it. As a result, the soul of our nation and the integrity of the Christian faith, as we have continually said, are at risk.

President Trump's adulation of money and his love for lavish ostentation (he covers nearly everything in gold) are the literal worship of wealth by someone who believes that his possessions belong only to himself, instead of that everything belongs to God and we are its stewards. In 2011, before his foray into politics, the future candidate said, "Part of the beauty of me is that I'm very rich."[15] And in his 2015 speech announcing his candidacy for president, he said, "I'm really rich. . . . And by the way, I'm not even saying that in a braggadocio—that's the kind of mind-set, that's the kind of thinking you need for this country."[16] Later, during the campaign, he suggested that our country must "be wealthy in order to be great."[17]

Then there's sex. Before Trump, Republicans liked to suggest that theirs was a fairly puritanical party of family values with high standards for its candidates (despite many and enormously embarrassing exceptions). But their candidate's, then president's, boastful sexual treatment of women—including bragging in a video about grabbing their genitals and the ability of celebrities like him to do that—along with his serial infidelity and habitual adultery are clear evidence of his idolatrous worship of sex. And it no longer seems like his is a unique case. And yet, according to a poll taken just before the 2016 election, 72 percent of evangelicals now say that "an elected official who commits an immoral act in their personal life can still behave ethically and fulfill their duties in their public and professional life," though only 30 percent of evangelicals thought so a mere six years ago.[18] That's a 70/30 percent turnaround!

And when it comes to power, we have already discussed the president's overwhelming will to it. Week after week, we see a leadership that is always and only about one person: *him.* Not the people, the country, or even his party—and certainly not about morality. The conflicts among his money, power, and governing are always resolved in the same way—by his selfishness, by whatever happens to appeal to him, and only him, at that moment.

All leaders struggle with these temptations, and public figures must wrestle with them the most. Christians, rightly enough, have never expected perfect leaders—just those who can keep up their end of the moral struggle. But for some leaders, there is no moral struggle. I would suggest that Donald Trump is not immoral—knowing what is right and wrong, and choosing the wrong—he rather seems *amoral*: lacking any kind of moral compass for his personal or professional life. That's why the Christian compromise with this antiservant leader and his ilk has put faithful Americans at such serious risk.

Central to the health of our society is rescuing an authentic, compassionate, and service-oriented leadership from the clutches of personal abuse, narcissistic corruption, and the idolatry of money, sex, and power.

As the "Reclaiming Jesus" declaration says, "*We support democracy, not because we believe in human perfection, but because we do not. The authority of government is instituted by God to order an unredeemed society for the sake of justice and peace, but ultimate authority belongs only to God.*"[19]

For us, that is not merely a political issue but also a theological one—one I hope and pray that the nation's faith leaders will make clear to the nation's top political leaders and self-described "strongmen" such as the current president. Differences in policy and rigorous debate are essential to democracy; but the behavior of leaders who do not respect their opponents, the rules of the political process, the protections of the Constitution, and the limits of power are a definite threat to democracy.

This president doesn't show any respect for those checks and balances, or even the rule of law. He seems to believe that government agencies that have traditionally operated with more independence from the political leadership of the executive branch, such as the Justice Department and the FBI, should serve him instead of holding him accountable to the law. Even more important, as the Constitution lays out, it is absolutely vital that the three branches of our government—executive, legislative, and judicial—operate effectively in a coequal manner. These checks and balances of power are essential to our democracy. Nobody can be above the law in a democracy, but this president seems to believe he is.

When you are a leader, everything cannot be about you—but for President Trump, everything is indeed about him. That is not only a complete reversal of the ethics of Jesus (and the president's religious supporters must pay attention to that); it is also a fundamental danger to democracy that is not merely politically alarming but is also a theological violation of the proper role of government, which we will deal with in chapter 7, "The Caesar Question."

To hold up the ethos of servant leadership, translated into the ethics of public service, is a prophetic obligation of the faith community's response to political leaders. And because of the dangers of human nature with unchecked power, we should also always be the defenders of democracy—its values, protocols, and balances of power. *And when it comes to the dangers of political autocracy and the rise of authoritarian behavior, people in the faith community must be among the first to raise the challenge.*

Our "Reclaiming Jesus" declaration concludes its proposition on our commitment to "Christ's way of leadership" with this commitment: "*We believe authoritarian political leadership is a theological danger threatening democracy and the common good—and we will resist it.*"

# Chapter 6
# The Fear Question

But he saith unto them, It is I; be not afraid.

—JOHN 6:20 (KJV)

For God hath not given us the spirit of fear;
but of power, and of love, and of a sound mind.

—2 TIMOTHY 1:7 (KJV)

What is fear? When is fear necessary and even useful, and when is it harmful and destructive? What does it mean to live and act in a spirit of fear? What does it mean to have a sound mind, and how do we cultivate that? Who are we told to fear? What does

Jesus really mean when he tells us, over and over again, "Be not afraid"?

"Be not afraid" occurs eight times in the New Testament. In fact, the assurance of "do not be afraid" is the most often repeated command in the Bible: 365 scriptures command us to not fear or be afraid in reaction to the world, to people, to the events around us, to the storms on the sea or in our lives. That's enough for one reflection for every day of the year!

The "do not fear" language was used by the angels who announced the birth of Christ to the shepherds, told to Mary and Joseph as well as Elizabeth and Zechariah about what was going to happen to them with two new babies named Jesus and John the Baptist, and when Jesus's frightened disciples were in a rocking boat on a roiling sea, among other examples. They saw him coming toward them and saying, "It is I; be not afraid." The God of the Bible keeps telling us, again and again, not to be afraid or, going deeper, how not to live in fear.

Perhaps this is because our human nature makes us fearful. We are naturally afraid. Yet God is proposing a radical contrast to a life of fear, and the scriptures say that "God hath not given us the spirit of fear; but a spirit of power, and of love, and of a sound mind" (2 Tim. 1:7, KJV). Paul also tells us that perfect love casts out fear (1 John 4:18). Psalm 23 even says, "Yea though I walk through the valley of the shadow of death, I will fear no evil; for You are with me" (NKJV). There are many valleys in this life with many dangers there, but we are encouraged not to be ruled by fear, because we are not alone.

> *When evening came, his disciples went down to the sea, got into a boat, and started across the sea to Capernaum. It was now dark, and Jesus had not yet come to them. The sea became rough because a strong wind was blowing. When they had rowed about three or four miles, they saw Jesus walking on the sea and coming near the boat, and they were terrified. But he said to them, "It is I; do not be afraid." Then they wanted to take him into the boat, and immediately the boat reached the land toward which they were going. (John 6:16–21)*

I vividly remember this story from Sunday school. We imagined how frightened the disciples must have been. The sea was tossing a relatively small boat in big waves, we were told. They were scared, as all of us kids would have been scared in their situation. Then they saw Jesus walking toward them. Just seeing him would have been a relief, it seemed to me. Then he spoke to the ones he loved: "It's me," he said, "so you don't need to be afraid." They were quite happy to invite him into their boat and when they did, the seas were calmed. What a great story. And the lesson was clear: Invite Jesus into your boat, especially when you are in a storm. He will calm the storm and help you get to where you want to go. The key here was that the presence of Jesus would overcome your fear and make you safe. That, of course, is a continuous message of the scriptures—how the fear of danger can point us to the presence of God.

On John 6, Rodney Whitacre says this:

> The story of Jesus' walking on water alludes to several Old Testament passages, which builds the case for Jesus' divine identity. It is said of God, "he alone stretches out the heavens and treads on the waves of the sea" (Job 9:8). Psalm 107 speaks of those who "went out on the sea in ships" (Ps. 107:23) and were caught in a great storm. They should "give thanks to the Lord for his unfailing love" (Ps. 107:31) because "he stilled the storm to a whisper; the waves of the sea were hushed. They were glad when it grew calm, and he guided them to their desired haven" (Ps. 107:29–30). The poetic imagery of these passages is reenacted on a historical level in the actual

> event John is describing. . . . So John continues to witness to Jesus' identity and his gracious activity. The feeding (of the five thousand) shows that Jesus is able to provide even when our resources are very small. *The rescue on the sea shows that he can protect and guide in the midst of great adversity, when we have no control over the forces of chaos* [emphasis added]. In both cases the physical realm reveals his identity and his loving care.[1]

As a pastor, I have been beside many sickbeds and deathbeds, and Psalm 23 always comes to my mind, heart, and lips:

> *The Lord is my shepherd;*
> *I shall not want.*
> *He makes me to lie down in green pastures;*
> *He leads me beside the still waters.*
> *He restores my soul;*
> *He leads me in the paths of righteousness*
> *For His name's sake.*
> *Yea, though I walk through the valley of the*
> *shadow of death,*
> *I will fear no evil;*
> *For You are with me;*
> *Your rod and Your staff, they comfort me.*

*You prepare a table before me in the presence of*
*my enemies;*
*You anoint my head with oil.*
*My cup runs over.*
*Surely goodness and mercy shall follow me*
*All the days of my life;*
*And I will dwell in the house of the Lord*
*Forever.* (NKJV)

This Psalm became one of my favorite and memorized texts as a small boy and I keep going back to it, as it so often feels like the most needed thing to say—and the response from fearful persons and their families always confirms that. It is the promise of the presence of God that calms the spirit and the storm.

Honestly, I often turn to it myself, now as an older man in moments when I am afraid. I recall times when I have been in conflictual and violent situations, trying to help reduce those conflicts, both in countries at war and in urban places called war zones, when this psalm has come to mind. I remember reciting this psalm with others as mortar bombs were flying over our heads in Nicaragua, as I have watched armed police and soldiers square off against unarmed people in poor countries and in our own cities, or as I confront my own fears and feelings of inadequacy in not knowing what to do in difficult or dangerous situations. "Yea, though I walk through the valley of the shadow of death, I will fear no evil." The lesson for us is to bring God into our fears, our boats, and the valleys in our lives.

That word of comfort goes right back to the announcement of Jesus's birth to the shepherds; to Mary, the woman who would bear him; her husband, Joseph, who was very confused; and to her relatives Elizabeth and Zechariah, who also had surprising things happening to them. The familiar Nativity narrative tells us what the shepherds experienced:

> *In that region there were shepherds living in the fields, keeping watch over their flock by night. Then an angel of the Lord stood before them, and the glory of the Lord shone around them, and they were terrified. But the angel said to them, "Do not be afraid; for see—I am bringing you good news of great joy for all the people." (Lk. 2:8–10)*

It is significant that the announcement of the birth of Jesus first came to shepherds, people who were near the bottom of the social order, looking after herds of animals. Many Christians like the story of the wealthy wise men better, who brought their gifts to the new king! But shepherds were also central to Jesus's stories, perhaps more than the wise men, as his parables of their going after the lost sheep were central to explaining his own mission. They were poor, with tough jobs to do, but they were the ones to whom the angels first appeared; they were the ones who heard the words "Do not be afraid." There is good news to tell, especially for people like you.

Then there was the primary role of a young, poor peasant woman who was actually homeless when she finally gave birth to the Christ child. I think that Mary, the mother of Jesus, was perhaps the one who understood the meaning of her son's coming better than anyone else did in her remarkable prayer, Mary's Magnificat:

*He has shown strength with his arm;*
*he has scattered the proud in the thoughts of their hearts.*
*He has brought down the powerful from their thrones,*
*and lifted up the lowly;*
*he has filled the hungry with good things,*
*and sent the rich away empty.* (Lk. 1:51–53)

Mary was the first to really get what the coming of Jesus Christ was all about. But at first she was afraid, as all the rest of us would be (Lk. 1:24–33), as were Joseph (Matt. 1:18–21) and Zechariah (Lk. 1:12–14) when angels appeared to them. In each case, there were good and understandable reasons for all their confusion and for their fear, from a very human perspective. But in each situation, an assurance was offered—"Do not be afraid" and "The Lord is with you"—telling them not to fear because a relationship between the fearful person and God was being strengthened.

What is clear from the texts is that the feeling of fear is not the problem for human beings, even for those who believe they have a relationship with God. The issue is never just the fear; the problem is living in the "spirit of fear." Again, it is natural to be afraid, but living in the spirit of fear is like living in a spiritual prison. The apostle Paul explains in his second letter to Timothy:

> *For God hath not given us the spirit of fear; but of power, and of love, and of a sound mind. (2 Tim. 1:7,* KJV*)*

> *Ellicott's Commentary* says this on 2 Timothy 1:7:

> **For God hath not given us the spirit of fear.**—Or better, perhaps, *the spirit of cowardice*—that cowardice which manifests itself by a timidity and

> shrinking in the daily difficulties which the Christian meets with in the warfare for the kingdom of God (Comp. John 14:27, and Revelation 21:8.). . . . It is a grave reminder to Christians of every age and degree that all cowardice, all dread of danger, all shrinking from doing one's duty for fear of man's displeasure, proceeds *not* from the Spirit of God.[2]

There is an assumption here that in following the Christian faith, there will be things that happen or are threatened that can make you afraid, cause you to be timid in "the warfare for the kingdom of God."

> **But of power, and of love, and of a sound mind.—** Instead of rendering the Greek word by "a sound mind," it were better to substitute the translation *self-control.* The Holy Spirit works, in those to whom it is given, power, or *strength,* to fight the fight of God, power, not only patiently to endure, but also to strike good blows for Christ—the power, for instance, of steadfastness in resisting temptation, the strong will which guides other weaker ones along the narrow way "of love." It works, too, in those to whom God gives the blessed gift, that strange, sweet love for others which leads to noble deeds of self-surrender—that love which

> never shrinks from a sacrifice which may benefit the friend or even the neighbour. And lastly, the Spirit works in us "self-control"—*selbst-beherrschung*—that power which, in the man or woman living in and mixing with the world, and exposed to its varied temptations and pleasures, is able to regulate and to keep in a wise subjection, passions, desires, impulses.[3]

Not succumbing to fear allows us to seek and find peace of heart and mind. The deepest contrast to the anxiety that fear creates is joy. The alternative to the anxious life is the joyful life. Like we have seen in the definition of who our neighbor is and what the truth is, in the end, this is all relational.

Living with the "spirit of cowardice," always experiencing the "dread of danger," is what "shrinks" our humanity. Only the power of love can counter that along with a "sound mind" or "self-control." Thinking and loving become the goals here in overcoming fear. What turns our anxiety into joy is giving thanks to the God we know, with whom we feel a relationship.

Philippians 4:4–7 is a deeply moving description of how our relationship to Jesus Christ can liberate us from the spirit of fear and bring us "peace beyond understanding":

> *Rejoice in the Lord always; again I will say, Rejoice. Let your gentleness be known to everyone. The Lord is near. Do not worry about anything, but in everything by prayer and supplication with thanksgiving let your requests be made known to God. And the peace of God, which surpasses all understanding, will guard your hearts and your minds in Christ Jesus.*

In his commentary on the letter to the Philippians, Gordon D. Fee explains how important joy is to Paul and should be to Christians, and how rejoicing in the Lord can give us peace even amid challenging, fearful, and oppressive circumstances:

> Joy, unmitigated, untrammeled joy, is—or at least should be—the distinctive mark of the believer in Christ Jesus. The wearing of black and the long face, which so often came to typify some later expressions of Christian piety, are totally foreign to Paul's version; Paul the theologian of grace is equally the theologian of joy. Christian joy does not come and go with one's circumstances; rather it is predicated altogether on one's relationship with the Lord and is thus an abiding, deeply spiri-

tual quality of life. It finds expression in "rejoicing," which is an imperative, not an option. With its concentration *in the Lord,* rejoicing is *always* to mark individual and corporate life in Philippi. They who "serve by the Spirit of God" (3:3) do so in part by *rejoicing in the Lord,* whatever else may be their lot. In this letter "whatever else" includes opposition and suffering at the hands of the local citizens of the Empire, where Caesar was honored as "lord." In the face of such, the Philippians are to rejoice in *the* Lord *always.*" (See further comment on 1:18; 2:2, 17–18; 3:1.)[4]

Nowhere does the text or the commentary suggest that Christians will not experience fear, but it does suggest that turning to God in fearful times and focusing on our joy and gratitude can help us get through those times. All this is confirmed by both therapists and spiritual directors who tell us how gratitude is what most releases our anxieties and calms our fears. Remembering what and whom we are grateful for is a better way than the worrying and blaming that come too easily to us and that keep and squeeze us into the spirit and downward spiral of fear.

## FEAR IS NATURAL AND HUMAN, BUT LIVING IN FEAR CAN MAKE US LESS HUMAN

Fear is universal among human beings and is completely bipartisan. But fear is not wrong, it is natural. Rather, it is our response to fear that is most important and becomes a matter of faith. Let's be clear: it is entirely and necessarily human for people to fear. In fact, we are wired biologically to fear things that could harm us. Ever since our ancient days, humans have responded instinctually to real dangers that we confront and that do indeed threaten us. To react to those genuine dangers is built into us to protect us and is often integral to our very survival. So to fear is to be human.

But living in a spirit of fear is not healthy and can actually dehumanize us if we submit to fear's control. Fear can lead us into saying and doing things to others that can be very destructive. In a sermon on fear that my sister, Marcie Rahill, preached to her home congregation and shared with me, she describes how fear can create a "spiritual amnesia" where we forget God—forget who God is and forget God's promise to always be with us. That very presence of God seems to be what scripture promises us we can rely on to help overcome our fear, but fear can easily cause us to lose our trust in it. And the hate that often comes from fear causes us to forget the power of love to transform our fear.

Marcie pointed out that whenever we humans enter into fearful situations, God doesn't cease to be God or fail to keep loving us. Indeed, it is often at those times when we most need to turn to God as we encounter fearful and sometimes genuinely dangerous circumstances. Our scriptures keep reminding us that God is indeed love and continues to love us in fearful situations.

Therefore, if fear is natural to us and not inherently wrong, the question is not how to avoid fear, because we literally can't as human beings. It is rather how we respond to fear that brings faith, life, common sense, and hope instead of dysfunction, despair, destruction, and even death. Faith is finally believing in love instead of fear, and believing that fear can be overcome by love—especially by the perfect love that Jesus teaches us.

Jesus's words "Be not afraid" therefore do not mean to be fearless. To be fearless may be a cultural goal, especially in societies that continually lift up violence to save us. But we can't and shouldn't try to be fearless, because that's just not how we're built. Rather we can learn to respond to genuine valleys of evil with real dangers by being less fearful, having more courage, and having more faith. Fear may always be with us and around us, but fear does not have to consume or control us.

Timothy's second epistle describes the choices we have—of fear versus the power of love, and panic versus a sound mind and self-control. Fear itself is not sin, but it can lead us to sin if we lose control (a sound mind) and act out of our fear in ways that hurt others. Fear is part of how we are made, but it must not be allowed to gain control of our hearts and minds, which is why we seek God and depend on God to be with us. In fact, when fear is in control, it pushes us away from God.

Could fear be a reminder, even a friend, when it causes us to trust and lean in to God? Storms can always be scary, in our weather or in our lives or in our society, but they can and do indeed turn us to God. I love the story of the disciples being afraid, fighting the storm on the Sea of Capernaum as fishermen are trained to do. But in their fright, they see Jesus coming to them. He sees their fears, but says, "It is I; be not afraid." And *they invite him into the boat.* They decide to trust him, to invite him into their boat. Jesus stands outside of all our boats of fear. Whether we will invite him in is always the spiritual question before us.

## TOUCHING FINGERS BETWEEN FENCES

Fear can lead us to do terrible things to others, because being afraid of "others" who are "different" than we are seems to be a common human fear. And that fear can be easily, brutally, and horrifically used by political leaders to engage in discrimination and violence against the people who are different from "us." Trappist monk and mystic Thomas Merton said it well: "The root of war is fear."

All too often, political leaders use and manipulate fear to turn people against their opponents and enemies for their own political advantage. One of the most graphic and grotesque uses of fear against others is what the current administration has done in the deportation of immigrants and the brutal treatment of asylum seekers coming to this country. "I was a stranger, and you welcomed me," said Jesus. Later in the same Matthew 25 gospel scripture, Jesus warns of the inverse: "I was a stranger, and you didn't welcome me." Jesus identifies with those who are hungry, thirsty, naked, strangers, sick, and in prison. "It was me," Jesus says, "As you have done it [or not done it] to one of the least of these, you have done it to me." Compare that Matthew 25 instruction to his reassurance that his followers need not fear him: "It is I; be not afraid," Jesus said to his disciples in a boat on a stormy sea.

Just before Christmas 2018, I was at the US-Mexico border between San Diego and Tijuana for a *posada* (shelter) liturgy. The US-Mexico border version of this centuries-old Advent liturgy is called La Posada sin Fronteras, or Shelter Without Borders, and that year was its twenty-fifth anniversary. The service was a powerful experience for me, as we joined in the liturgy with hundreds of ecumenical, bilingual, and multiracial pilgrims on both sides of the border—singing to each other the lovely words of Mary and Joseph asking for shelter from innkeepers, who keep refusing them until the last one welcomes them in. We sang Christmas carols and recited the names of migrants who have died, as crosses and prayers were lifted. This liturgy on the border makes friends of people who can be turned into enemies; the love and relationship deliberately counteract the fears that others use to divide people.

We began a short distance from the border with a press conference with faith leaders from both the United States and Mexico, with many members of the California and Mexican media present, calling for more compassionate and humane policies toward those whom Jesus called us to welcome. We then made a three-mile pilgrimage to the border—a hike that was both focusing and taxing over mostly thick sand on the beach along the ocean, which gave us just a very small notion of what tens of thousands of refugee families experience each day for many months as they journey with their children and belongings over thousands of miles from Central America to this border.

In many past posadas over this quarter century, pilgrims have been allowed to touch each other's fingers through the fences, throw candy to children over the fence, and even pass tamales back and forth to celebrate a meal together as part of the tradition. In 2018, the scene was much more militarized, as those of us on the US side were kept far away from the fence, with Border Patrol trucks slowly driving between us and the fence. But being able to sing back and forth, with the words of the posada liturgy coming across the fence, was a very moving moment for me and for all of us.

When these kinds of actions become controversial and divisive matters, it is indeed important to reflect on these political issues theologically and relationally, as we have done with questions such as "Who my neighbor?" and "What is truth?" In this situation we need to ask, "Who are we being made to be afraid of and why? And, as the gospels remind us, bringing the presence of God into our divided communities helps to heal the fears that some seek to put in our hearts and in our public policies.

It has been heartbreaking to watch the president, his administration, and his party allies deliberately and directly pursuing policies of fear in relation to asylum seekers, immigrants, and refugees. "Be afraid!" they proclaim. The president campaigned almost entirely on fear again during the 2018 midterm elections, governs on fear, and makes immigration policy based on fear. We've seen this play out strategically: propagating rhetoric aimed at stoking fear of immigrants and treating asylum seekers so brutally—even separating children from their parents or putting whole families in prison detention centers as an attempt to deter immigrants of color from coming to America.

Jesus says, "welcome the stranger." But this president, in great contrast, enacts policies that inflict trauma, pain, danger, and even death on the ones Jesus tells us to welcome. I don't know any immigration advocates who don't recognize the importance of upholding just immigration laws and protecting our borders, and migrants have a legal right to seek asylum and pose less criminal danger to other Americans than American citizens do. Beyond the letter of the law, as people of faith we are called to uphold the higher law of *imago Dei*, that we are all made in the image and likeness of God, and the command of Matthew 25, that we treat the most vulnerable as we would treat Christ himself.

## A WALL OF FEAR

As Christians all over the world were preparing to celebrate the birth of Jesus in December 2018, the president of the United States shut down a big chunk of the federal government, forcing eight hundred thousand public servants to work without pay or putting them on essentially involuntary unpaid leave, just in time for Christmas. The shutdown was entirely a function of a debate over funding President Trump was seeking to build his promised border wall.

The president's wall was the signature issue of his political campaign and administration, and people on both sides of the aisle have long recognized that the wall has almost nothing to do with border security. Instead, the wall has everything to do with Trump's central message: You should fear people who aren't white. If built as Trump pitched it during the 2016 campaign, the wall would be a twenty-two-hundred-mile monument to fear and to hate, which is what naturally grows from fear. Both parties believe in border security, despite what the White House says. But Donald Trump has made his campaign, his presidency, his central message, and his vision for America about one thing: his wall.

Of course, the proposed wall for sealing off the southern border would do nothing to increase border security. The wall would not protect the United States from terrorism; according to our own government's State Department, terrorists don't come into America by crossing the southern border. A 2015 government study indicated that the bulk of illegal drugs that enter the United States comes hidden in trucks through established border checkpoints, so a wall wouldn't keep drugs out of the country, as the White House claims.[5] The wall fantasy will not stop criminality from coming into America, as Trump claims; immigrants commit fewer crimes than citizens.

Yet, despite the facts, the fear of the "other" is raised and manipulated, with fear leading to hate. What the wall is entirely about is a racially divisive message that appeals to an angry and fearful white political base. The wall says we must be afraid of nonwhite people coming to America, and this will keep them out of "our" country. Hate can lead to violence. The wall is just a symbol, a monument, a testimony to the worst of American fear, hate, and white racism.

A rough estimate of the total cost of the wall and the number of miles of wall that would be built suggests that Trump's wall would cost about $30 million *per mile.* A top government official who knows the budget line by line detailed to faith leaders in late 2018 all the programs that effectively assist low-income families that would need to be cut to pay for Trump's wall.

The communities most impacted by border crossings—those closest to the border—understand that the wall makes no practical or moral sense: there isn't a single member of Congress that represents a district on the US-Mexico border who supports building a wall.

In seeking the presidency in 2016, candidate Trump became the chief tempter of America's original sin, as some of us have named the racism that has been endemic to the United States since the first slaves arrived in the New World. As president, Trump has become the chief defender of America's original sin. Trump's wall is not just "medieval," as some have called it; it is also "evil," as biblical faith would call it.

Pope Francis made this point in stark terms in February 2016: "A person who thinks only about building walls, wherever they may be, and not building bridges, is not Christian. This is not the Gospel."

## THE CARAVAN OF FEAR

Right after the midterm elections, two of our Sojourners staff traveled to Mexico to hear the stories and walk alongside the group of Central Americans traveling together for safety as they fled violence and poverty in their home countries and sought asylum in the United States. This "caravan," as President Trump, his allies, and the media took to calling it, was used to weaponize xenophobia and racism in one of the most craven, transparent, and dangerous election tactics we've ever seen. Trump's overtly racial appeals to the politics of white grievance and white identity caused many people, such as retirees in Florida, to fear an "invasion" of an immigrant "caravan" that would bring leprosy, smallpox, and violent criminals into America. Trump appealed to racial resentment, fear, and even hate because he thought it would work. And it did work in some of the most politically conservative states in the country (but it worked significantly less well in the states that actually share a border with Mexico). We saw the tactic do what it was intended to do—use fear and hate to drive the president's base to the polls to vote for his political party.

As *The Washington Post* put it shortly before the election,

Trump's messaging—on display in his regular campaign rallies, tweets and press statements—largely avoids much talk of his achievements and instead offers an apocalyptic vision of the country, which he warns will only get worse if Democrats retake control of Congress.

The president has been especially focused in recent days on a caravan of about 5,000 migrants traveling north to cross the U.S. border, a group he has darkly characterized as gang members, violent criminals and "unknown Middle Easterners"—a claim for which his administration has so far provided no concrete evidence.[6]

The suggestion that some, even many, of the people journeying might be violent criminals, terrorists, or even carriers of diseases such as leprosy or smallpox was made by the president and his allies repeatedly and without evidence, to drive fear into people's hearts and to directly override the feelings of neighbor love that ought to be there for people who claim to be followers of Jesus.

Invoking leprosy doesn't seem like an accident, as it's a disease we seldom hear about today. It was declared to be "eliminated as a public health problem" by the World Health Organization in 2000, just as smallpox was declared eradicated in 1980.[7] But leprosy *is* a disease we read about in scripture. In my view, the goal of raising "leprosy" was to spark fear among the white evangelical members of Trump's base, of the migrants as a threat of biblical proportions.

The irony is that even an elementary reading of the Bible would suggest a very different treatment of people afflicted by leprosy than Trump was proposing. Jesus did not call for Roman legions to keep people with leprosy away from him and the rest of the Judean populace. Rather, Jesus directly related and ministered to people with leprosy and many others who were marginalized, cast out, feared, and hated by the society of his day.

President Trump even dispatched nearly six thousand soldiers to the border to "welcome" the tired, hungry, and desperate families fleeing violence, a move with absolutely no national security justification and one that actually kept many of these servicewomen and servicemen from spending Thanksgiving with their families.[8] Two retired colonels angrily called this the use of "toy soldiers" for a shameless political purpose.[9]

Unfortunately, an anecdote from a colleague whose family goes to a mainline church in a deeply red area of a southern state suggests that the spreading of false fears of a coming migrant caravan was effective. Shortly before the 2018 elections, at the end of a church choir practice and before the Sunday service, the choir director offered a prayer for the upcoming worship, as she always does. "O Lord, please protect us from that caravan of drugs and disease, of leprosy and smallpox, and terrorists and criminals coming to put us in danger. And we pray for the army soldiers who are being sent to protect us from this invasion." She is not normally a "political person" but had become so afraid that she felt she should pray for God's protection from the violent criminals and dangerous disease-carrying caravan approaching the southern border, still far away from their church members, and pray for the army to stop them. Fox News was setting prayer agendas, the lies were getting through to the public, and the fears they were falsely fomenting were very real—even for people who believed they were followers of Jesus.

## FEAR LEADS TO HATE, WHICH LEADS TO VIOLENCE

We continue to see presidential rallies that are hard to watch, and tweets that are hard to read, but what they clearly and significantly reveal is a political strategy of fear based on continual and unapologetic lying, which deliberately evokes racial resentment and hatred. And as we have now painfully seen, such hatred and fear lead to violence.

Just days before the 2018 midterm elections, the world reacted with shock, mourning, and fear at the horrific and murderous attack on the Tree of Life synagogue in Pittsburgh. Eleven congregants were killed while observing the Sabbath in the deadliest attack on the Jewish community in US history.

That this evil act of anti-Semitic terrorism should take place here in the United States was deeply shocking. Yet both US and world history teach us that the poison of anti-Semitism is very real and has deadly consequences. Anti-Semitism is one of the oldest and most persistent forms of bigotry alive in the world today, and Christians—who believe all human beings are created in the image of God—have a duty to name anti-Semitism and confront it at every turn, particularly given the shameful complicity of so many Christians in the Holocaust and other oppressions and killings of Jewish people.

This hate crime capped off a horrific week of violence inspired by white supremacist ideology, in which racist propaganda and conspiracy theories were openly promulgated on the campaign trail and amplified by prominent voices in right-wing media and dark web spaces. The attempted murder of critics of the Trump administration by mailing them pipe bombs, the killing of two African Americans—Vickie Lee Jones and Maurice Stallard—in a grocery store after a failed attack on a black church, and the massacre of Jews in their synagogue all were carried out by well-armed white supremacist nationalists, who have become the greatest terrorist threats in America today. These killings were reminiscent of the sequence of fear, to hate, to violence in the words spoken by Dylann Roof in his explanation of why he brutally murdered nine African-American Christians during a Bible study at their Mother Emmanuel AME church in Charlotte, North Carolina, now four years ago. It also painfully reminded many Americans of the angry words of the white nationalist protesters and their fear- and hate-spewing in Charlottesville, Virginia, which also turned to lethal violence, taking the life of Heather Heyer, with the president commenting afterward that "there were fine people on both sides," giving additional legitimacy and empowerment to the white supremacists who initiated the violence.

Throughout his campaigning for his allies in 2018, the president continually and unashamedly used a political strategy of fear and hate. The violence we have seen cannot be disconnected from the bigoted and hateful words of political rhetoric, especially at the presidential level. When the president proudly called himself "nationalist" amid such hate and violence, the white nationalists, white supremacists, and anti-Semites felt supported and emboldened.

Our hearts were broken as we reached out in love, care, and solidarity to our Jewish friends, colleagues, fellow believers, and citizens. Our faith was offended by these assaults, which directly contradicted the biblical commands to love and protect our neighbors, and especially to focus on "the other," who is often under attack. Our conscience was seared again by the hateful politics that likely will lead to more violence. *Words matter, and hateful words lead to violence.* At such times of moral crisis, we as people of many faiths must publicly and passionately demonstrate that we live and love side by side.

I felt a similar deep sense of sadness, mourning, and grief in March 2019 after the horrific shootings in Christchurch, New Zealand. We grieved for the fear we knew this atrocity would spread among Muslims all over the world. People of all faiths have the right to worship without the threat or fear of violence or retribution. Mosques are holy spaces, and this evil act damaged the sanctuary and security of those holy spaces. Millions of Muslims around the world questioned whether to go to prayers in the immediate wake of these shootings.

Just as in the Charleston and Pittsburgh massacres, attacking people of faith in their holy spaces is one of the most unconscionable acts imaginable.

Even as so many of us stood in solidarity with our Muslim brothers and sisters as they mourned the loss of so many beloved family and community members, I couldn't help but think about the twenty-eight-year-old white killer's assertion in his manifesto that he considered Donald Trump "a symbol of renewed white identity and common purpose." White nationalism, white supremacy, and white power are evil ideologies that depend on spreading fear and hatred of nonwhite people, with predictably deadly consequences in every nation and historical period where they have gained influence.

## THE SPREAD OF FEARFUL CONSPIRACY

We now see the growing spread of fearful conspiracy over the internet and social media. My own family was stunned when a pizza place called Comet Ping Pong, in our neighborhood on the same block as our favorite bookstore, was portrayed as the center of a child sex-trafficking ring run by top Democrats such as Hillary Clinton, prompting a man with a high-powered rifle to travel from North Carolina to Washington, DC, on a misguided rescue mission, enter the establishment, and fire his weapon before being apprehended by the police. "Pizzagate" was thoroughly debunked in every major media outlet, but the fractured, polarized, and compartmentalized nature of information and entertainment consumption in the United States today makes conspiracies such as this one extremely tenacious and resistant to fact-checking. More broadly, these information access and consumption dynamics create a fertile ground that ensures future conspiracies will take root and bear poisonous fruit.

Indeed, the perpetrators behind the massacre at Mother Emmanuel AME, the attempted pipe bombings of top political and media figures, and the killings at the Tree of Life Synagogue and in Christchurch, New Zealand, were all radicalized online by conspiracy theories designed to stoke fear and convert it into hate. Given the access to the vast number of high-powered firearms that Americans uniquely enjoy, it is all too easy to convert that fear and hate into violence. As I write this chapter, two more synagogues in California have been attacked by gunmen, resulting in deaths and casualties.

When fear can be used and spread with no accountability to any facts, it increases the "spirit of fear" of which our scriptures warn, because such fears do seed the ground for hate, which sets the motivation for violence. We see where the spirit of fear leads.

In such a time, the conviction that the spirit of love can overcome the spirit of fear must be in action, confronting the false fearmongers in our media, our politics, at our dinner tables, in our lives, and even in our congregations. For the health of the nation, a "sound mind" must be made to flourish—we must think and love without fear. This is such a time of fear in our country and around the world. Overcoming that dangerous spirit of fear becomes a central commitment if we are going to reclaim Jesus.

# Chapter 7
# The Caesar Question

Render therefore to Caesar the things that are Caesar's, and to God the things that are God's.

—MATTHEW 22:21 (NKJV)

This famous teaching of Jesus inspires some logical follow-up questions. What belongs to Caesar, and what belongs to God? How do we discern what belongs to whom? What level of allegiance, loyalty, or obedience do we owe government? When does obedience to God demand disobedience to government? These are all very important questions, since the texts we have from Jesus's teachings, and the ones in the epistles that later treat the subject of our obligations to governmental authority, have often been misinterpreted and even abused by those who want to put the power of the state over the power of faith.

Right after Jesus entered Jerusalem, to bring the kingdom of God into the rule of Caesar, he went to the temple to confront the authorities of his day, which, like many other times in history, were political, economic, and religious. Jesus's entry into the capital city on a donkey was perceived as a political event, not just a religious one. The donkey symbolized the humility, simplicity, and nonviolence of the kingdom of God, entering by the east gate of the city; while the horses and chariots of Roman governor Pontius Pilate, entering by the west gate at the same time, symbolized the arrogance, domination, and violent power of the empire.

These were two very different kingdoms side by side, representing two different and sometimes contrary orders and values. Some make the mistake of saying the new kingdom has nothing to do with politics—it is just personal and spiritual, really just private, and therefore Christians should always submit to the power of the state over politics and even faith. But that is not what Jesus said, or meant, at all. On the contrary, he suggests that his followers have choices to make in regard to what belongs to Caesar and what belongs to God—and when there is a conflict, there is no doubt where our ultimate allegiance and loyalty lies—with God and not with Caesar.

## OVERTURNING THE TABLES

One of the first and most famous confrontations that Jesus has with the existing authorities is the story of his cleansing of the temple in Mark 11:15–18:

> *Then they came to Jerusalem. And he entered the temple and began to drive out those who were selling and those who were buying in the temple, and he overturned the tables of the money changers and the seats of those who sold doves; and he would not allow anyone to carry anything through the temple. He was teaching and saying, "Is it not written, 'My house shall be called a house of prayer for all the nations'? But you have made it a den of robbers."*
>
> *And when the chief priests and the scribes heard it, they kept looking for a way to kill him; for they were afraid of him, because the whole crowd was spellbound by his teaching.*

Wes Granberg-Michaelson, general secretary emeritus of the Reformed Church in America and one of the "Reclaiming Jesus" elders, explains the significance of this dramatic event. Just days after Jesus's "triumphal entry," he moved directly to the temple—a place of both religious and political power:

> Jesus makes clear who he is, and what it means to come "in the name of the Lord." He attacks the corruption in the temple, disrupting its operation by overturning the tables and driving out the animals of those religious leaders controlling a sacrificial system that made them rich, while oppressing the poor—particularly poor women. In other words, this Jesus wouldn't tolerate unjust economic power in the temple, the heart of Jewish life. . . .
>
> Beyond that, the exclusivism of the temple's rules and practices brought forth the condemnation of Jesus. It's not just that Jesus characterized those in control as running a "den of thieves," but he declared that the temple was to be a holy "place of prayer for all the nations," and not just for those in a protected cultural and religious enclave.
>
> But there was far more. The ruling religious authorities, including the family of the High Priest, and the Sadducees, were the religious aristocracy of that day, controlling the temple and holding their grip on political and religious power. And they

compromised and even betrayed the heart of the Jewish tradition by supporting the oppressive rule of Rome. Their complicity with Roman power was the trade-off that kept them in power. And Jesus was steadfast in his rejection of all corruption of faith for the protection of oppressive injustice, through an unholy alliance between religious authority and Roman power. Jesus not only attacked those making money unjustly in the temple, but he predicted the destruction of the temple itself. He wanted to make clear that God's holiness was not wedded to religious practices in the temple which had become self-righteous and poisoned by the protection of power and privilege.[1]

InterVarsity Press commentator Rodney A. Whitacre, in his book on the gospel of John, says that the temple incident is fundamentally about a clash between conflicting authorities—those that come from God and those that come from the politics of religion and the demands of the marketplace. The confrontation in the temple is both Jesus exposing the hypocrisy and injustice of religion making money, but also proclaiming the very identity of Jesus and his relationship to God, thus making it clear that his authority supersedes that of worldly political, economic, and religious authorities, all of which are corruptible:

> The confrontation in the temple (2:13–16) culminates in Jesus's words: Get these out of here! How dare you turn my Father's house into a market! (v. 16). Jesus's authority and his identity are revealed in this statement. As the Synoptics tell the story, Jesus quotes Scripture at this point, combining Isaiah 56:7 and Jeremiah 7:11: "It is written," he said to them, " 'My house will be called a house of prayer,' but you are making it a 'den of robbers' " (Mt 21:13, with slight differences in Mk 11:17; Lk 19:46). Jesus is obviously exercising some sort of authority in the Synoptics, but perhaps this sense of authority is heightened in John since Jesus speaks in his own words. This authority is based on his identity. Instead of contrasting God's house of prayer with a den of robbers, as in the Synoptics, he contrasts my Father's house with a market. Here is the first use outside the prologue of the term Father, the single most important designation for God in Johannine literature. Equally significant is the implication that Jesus is God's Son: he refers to my Father's house. Jesus's provocative act is based on his relation to God as his Son.[2]

## CIVIL OBEDIENCE AND DISOBEDIENCE

The particular question of paying taxes was what led to the famous quote from Jesus about the choices we need to make regarding what belongs to Caesar and what belongs to God. What I have always found so interesting is the way the gospel writers describe this situation as both a "trap" and a "test," not unlike the trap and, indeed, test in which many of Jesus's followers in institutional Christianity today have also found themselves in relation to the state. The way Jesus avoids the trap and clarifies the choices Jesus's followers have to make is very instructive for us today, as related in Matthew 22:15–22:

> *Then the Pharisees went and plotted to entrap him in what he said. So they sent their disciples to him, along with the Herodians, saying, "Teacher, we know that you are sincere, and teach the way of God in accordance with truth, and show deference to no one; for you do not regard people with partiality. Tell us, then, what you think. Is it lawful to pay taxes to the emperor, or not?" But Jesus, aware of their malice, said, "Why are you putting me to the test, you hypocrites? Show me the coin used for the tax." And they brought him a denarius. Then*

> *he said to them, "Whose head is this, and whose title?" They answered, "The emperor's." Then he said to them, "Give therefore to the emperor the things that are the emperor's, and to God the things that are God's." When they heard this, they were amazed; and they left him and went away.*

Professor of Theology and Spirituality Min-Ah Cho relates the brilliance of Jesus's response to the authorities' "trick question," and how Jesus's response actually undermines imperial power:

> The beauty of Jesus's answer to the trick question posed in the text from Matthew is that while it looks like an endorsement of the census tax (verse 21), it actually subverts the emperor's power. To those who are able to see the kingdom of God as being beyond Caesar's territory, Jesus puts the imperial claim to rule in perspective: Render unto Caesar what is Caesar's, but remember who owns the world. "[God is] the Lord and there is no other," says the prophet Isaiah (Isaiah 45:6). Which side will you stand on when Caesar tries to usurp divine authority?[3]

Another important article on the larger biblical case for civil disobedience, based on the example of Jesus in particular and that will be helpful for these times, comes from Ched Myers and is called "By What Authority?"

> The singular model for civil disobedience for the Christian is of course the ministry of Jesus, much of which can be understood as calculated confrontation with the structures of socio-political power of his day. . . .
>
> Mark's narrative of Jesus's first mission around the region of Capernaum (Mark 2:13–3:6) presents us with a Jesus who systematically assaults the social order of first-century Jewish Palestine. Jesus takes on the rigid social caste system of clean and unclean by calling a tax collector into his discipleship community and underscores the point by sharing table-fellowship with a variety of outcasts. By touching a leper, recorded in the first chapter of Mark, Jesus was already considered impure; by eating with "sinners," Jesus defies the Pharisaical codes of ritual purity. . . . Jesus assaults the symbolic center of synagogue Judaism, the sabbath, by transgressing sabbath laws and boldly asserting, "The sabbath was made for man, not man for the sabbath" (2:27). . . . Jesus again breaks the sabbath law by healing a man's hand (3:1–6). The response

to these acts by the local Galilean authorities is a commitment to do away with Jesus.

Most importantly, Jesus's confrontation had a directly political thrust: his campaign was finally directed at the center of power, Jerusalem (Luke 9:51–56). . . . Luke's account of the Jerusalem section of Jesus's ministry is another sequence of highly symbolic and politically crafted actions. It begins with a messianic entry into the city, and a lament over Jerusalem's imminent demise (Luke 19:28–44). Then comes perhaps the most dramatic and provocative of Jesus's actions, the "cleansing" of the temple (19:45–48). . . .

Jesus is portrayed as deliberately choosing a prophetic style of confrontation with authority, at virtually every level of law and custom in society, in order to underscore the new authority of the kingdom of God. It is inevitable that he would meet the cross, a form of capital punishment reserved by the Romans for political dissidents, and that the Jewish authorities would work in close collaboration with Rome to secure his condemnation.[4]

A classic article from Mennonite professor Willard Swartley that ran in *Sojourners* in 1979 did a lot of the exegesis of key passages that are used to defend subjecting oneself to the state, in both the gospels and Romans 13. These issues of civil obedience and disobedience are very complicated and will become more important, in my view, in the times ahead. Therefore, they deserve some careful and detailed discussion.

In "Answering the Pharisees," Swartley analyzes Jesus's answer to the Pharisees' question in Matthew 20:

> [I]n our effort to derive contemporary moral guidance from this text we must be careful that we do not simply adopt the position of the Pharisees that law is the final word on moral issues. Significantly, Jesus's reply pointed beyond the rights of Caesar to the rights of God. God's claim and Caesar's claims must never be put on the same level. The text may not be interpreted in such a way as to equalize God's and Caesar's rights.[5]

As far as the apostle Paul's teaching on the payment of taxes, the commentator goes on to quote Romans 13:6–7: "For the same reason you also pay taxes, for the authorities are God's servants busy with this very thing. Pay to all what is due them—taxes to whom taxes are due, revenue to whom revenue is due, respect to whom respect is due, honor to whom honor is due." But Swartley then suggests:

> If, as various commentators have suggested, Paul modeled his counsel after Mark 12:17 [give to Caesar the things that are Caesar and to God the things that are God's], Paul apparently understood Jesus to say that taxes are due Caesar. But Paul's statement also recognizes the need for discrimination in making such a decision, a principle also dependent upon Jesus's statement.[6]

In other words, Paul's counsel in Romans can be read as quite contrary to a call for blind obedience, and viewed rather as a more radical call to discern how much tax, revenue, honor, and respect the authorities are *due*, and pay them that, as opposed to how much they ask for.

Swartley concludes, "Further, the call to be subject to the governing authorities (Romans 13:1) is not a command to obey the authorities. Obedience (*hupakouo*) is reserved for God alone (Acts 5:29). The text asks for subjection (*hupotasso*), which allows for disobedience when God's command contradicts the government's requirements. In that case, subjection means that the person disobedient for conscience's sake accepts the punishment."[7]

The points Swartley makes above take on a new resonance when in 2018 the presidential administration blatantly used and abused Romans 13 to justify its abhorrent and illegal policies toward immigrant families on the southern border.

## THE ABUSE OF ROMANS 13

This question came up often when I spoke about "Reclaiming Jesus." Following the signing of the declaration, multiracial elders from across traditions—including evangelical, mainline Protestant, Roman Catholic, and African-American churches—spoke out about the horrific border crisis. We spoke out because the presidential administration was abusing scripture to justify abusing migrant children and their families. We said the separation of immigrant children from their parents was not "biblical," as the administration shamelessly claimed.

Faith communities across the country rose to speak against this utter lack of compassion—especially when Attorney General Jeff Sessions, backed by Sarah Huckabee Sanders, tried to call child detention "biblical," citing Romans 13. The elders responded:

> This is yet another misuse and violation of the Word of God to defend a morally indefensible policy. This is a line of demarcation that political power must not be allowed to cross. If Jesus is Lord, we are called

to love our neighbors in every circumstance, and to even love our enemies. In Matthew 22, Jesus puts loving God and loving your neighbor at the heart of everything. "On these two commandments hang all the law and the prophets." In Matthew 25, Jesus commands us to welcome the stranger.[8]

From the Catholic bishops, from across denominations (including Sessions's own United Methodist Church), from the National Association of Evangelicals, to the Southern Baptists, faith leaders said no. As the broad "Reclaiming Jesus" elders' call said, this cruel policy that destroyed families was clearly *unbiblical* and showed why.

The elders' statement says in part:

> The apostle Paul, in Romans 13, does not say that cruelty is a justifiable tool or role of government. Rather, Paul says the government's role is meant to be "God's servant for your good"; government exists to be the protector of the good and to guard people from evil. Romans 13:3 says, "For rulers are not a terror to good conduct, but to bad." In cruel contrast, the new family-destroying policies of the administration are the reverse of the proper

role of government described in Romans 13: These actions by our government are a terror to families and an infliction of evil on children.

These family separation policies are directly contrary to the test of love laid out later in the same chapter of Romans (verses 8–10):

"Owe no one anything, except to love one another; for the one who loves another has fulfilled the law. The commandments, 'You shall not commit adultery; You shall not murder; You shall not steal; You shall not covet,' and any other commandment, are summed up in this Word: 'Love your neighbor as yourself.' Love does no wrong to a neighbor; therefore, love is the fulfilling of the law."[9]

The continued separation of children was blocked by the moral outrage of the society, and parents in particular, and really for the first time, the administration had to retreat. It was a great affirmation for moral conscience that provided some hope for the future.

But the administration doubled down on their hard line against immigrants—even using the word "infest" in reference to undocumented immigrants coming to America. Yet many Christians, including those who supported the president for other reasons, condemned such morally indefensible and "unbiblical" language and the zero-tolerance policies toward immigrants.

There are myriad examples of faith-based organizations who did and continue to do important work on the border to provide help, comfort, and kindness in the face of the government's cruelty. One such example is Sister Norma Pimentel, who houses and feeds immigrant families as part of her work with Catholic Charities. Given the way the law is defined by the administration and others, many of these acts of Christian compassion and ministry could be defined as "illegal," such as taking care of undocumented people in medical clinics or "transporting" them to church. But nobody has the courage to arrest Sister Norma!

There are many other inspiring examples of people resisting family separation and deportation in the ways that they were able. Airline attendants refused to work flights that were transporting immigrant children separated from their parents, and several airlines temporarily stopped booking flights for use with immigration authorities.[10] A man working for the Montana Department of Labor quit his job after he was asked to process subpoena requests for Immigrations and Customs Enforcement.[11] An employee at one processing center quit after receiving instructions to not allow siblings to hug one another.[12] People who work in detainment centers took pictures and videos of the children and sent them to advocates and press on the outside. Some people *did* refuse to be complicit in this atrocity, and we should all examine the ways that we are called to resist in such unjust situations.

Sojourners executive director Adam Taylor described the moral atrocity of the administration's zero-tolerance policy, and laid out why he, I, and ten other faith leaders decided to get arrested outside the White House gates while engaging in nonviolent civil disobedience:

> [A]s church leaders in South Africa taught me many years ago, Kairos-like moments occur when our current reality becomes so fraudulent and egregious that the status quo is no longer acceptable. It is these moments when people of faith and conscience feel called to engage in increasingly bold and sacrificial action.
>
> Today, Sojourners president Jim Wallis and I will be joining the Poor People's Campaign and other faith leaders in a nonviolent civil disobedience action in front of the White House to protest this zero-tolerance policy and the family separation

> crisis at the border. We will declare that the violence of policies against children cannot be tolerated.
>
> We have no illusions that this direct action on its own will change the hearts and minds of the Trump administration. But we hope and pray that our prophetic witness will ignite even greater public awareness, create more pressure, and inspire increasing political courage.[13]

A recent *New York Times* article reporting from Mount Pleasant, Iowa, puts this in perspective regarding how different churches are facing the debate. The piece reports on a local pastor getting into an impassioned argument on his Facebook page with an administration supporter who declared our immigration laws "good and Godly" and used the often-invoked Mark passage about "rendering unto Caesar the things that are Caesar's."

The pastor, Troy Hegar, is a Texan who spent four years in the marines before attending a Presbyterian seminary. He responded, "Which Scripture do we obey?" He answered himself: "The one from Jesus to 'Do unto others' is what we choose." The marine-turned-pastor expressed his frustration. "The nationalistic politics and theology goes hand in hand now," Mr. Hegar said. "It drives me crazy when we don't practice what Jesus preaches because of the mix of religion and national politics."[14]

I believe history will look back on this moment of how we treat immigrants in our country as a test of faith for which we will all be accountable and that will shape the meaning of faith and the response of a new generation in our future.

The *Times* story reports on a church meeting when Hegar spoke and "paused after each line to let Dina Saunders, who teaches English as a second language at the middle school, translate into Spanish."

"I am tired," the pastor said.

*"Estoy cansado."*

"I am tired of people talking about my neighbors breaking the law, when our country is breaking our own laws. By dividing up families. Separating women from children. Treating people seeking a better life like criminals.

"My church—"

*"Mi iglesia."*

"—is your church."

*"Es su iglesia."*[15]

## WAS JESUS A REVOLUTIONARY?

One of the most dramatic confrontations in history was between Jesus and Pontius Pilate—the Roman governor (recounted in Luke 23:1–25, John 18:28–19:16, Matthew 27:1–26, and Mark 15:1–15). The discussion takes place between the most powerful ruler in Jesus's home territory and the prisoner he has humiliated, flogged, and seemingly would like to disregard because Jesus seemed to worry the Roman ruler; but ultimately Pilate crucifies Jesus as a revolutionary. The topics they discussed were the biggest ones, namely who is king and what is truth. While politically subordinate to Rome's representative, Jesus was clearly morally in charge and even told the political leader that he really had no ultimate power over him.

Jesus's prophetic style of civil disobedience culminates in his arrest, trial, torture, and execution at the hands of the Roman state and the Jewish high authorities. The gospels portray Jesus as unbowed, unafraid, and in several instances uncooperative with his questioners, declining to answer many of their charges, or answering indirectly in ways that undermined the moral authority of both the Jewish and Roman officials who were interrogating him. For example, in Luke 23:3, rather than directly affirm or deny Pilate's question ("Are you the king of the Jews?"), he responds, "You say so," which avoids the sin of lying had he said no, yet also does not offer an unqualified yes because to do so would be to declare himself a direct revolutionary in the political sense and thus a challenger to Caesar's rule. Yet even in seemingly initially assuaging Pilate's fears (as verse 4 implies), Jesus's answer also denies Pilate the evidence he feels he needs to condemn him. Similarly, in verse 9, Jesus declines to answer any of Herod's questions. In John's account, Jesus takes a similar approach, declining to directly implicate himself in the way the chief priest and Pilate want him to, without denying the underlying truth of who he is. In fact, in John 19:11, Jesus tells Pilate directly, "You would have no power over me unless it had been given you from above," meaning not just that Pilate's power derives from the emperor, but also that the authority of governments comes only and ultimately from God and is subordinate to God's greater authority.

Those who seem oblivious to the need for Christian choices when it comes to political power or any confrontation with governmental authority need to answer the question "Why was Jesus killed?" It's important to ask that not only as a theological question but as a historical and political one. The death and Resurrection of Jesus Christ are key to our salvation, but why Jesus was killed in his historical context is important to understand. I asked the question once at a Christian college and the answer I received was "To save us from our sins." After that there was silence in the room and I asked the chapel audience to consider what might have been on Pilate's mind. (It was likely not "We need to crucify this Jesus to save American evangelicals from their sins.") Jesus was clearly killed because he was perceived to be a *threat*, a threat to the existing authorities. And he was accused of being a threat to the empire. Also, how do we deal with the fact that Paul wrote four of his epistles (Philippians, Ephesians, Colossians, and Philemon) while incarcerated in Rome?

Swartley points to biblical scholar Oscar Cullmann's reflections (which are some of my favorites on this subject) on the issue of whether Jesus's assertion that the laws of God superseded Roman law amounted to identifying himself with the revolutionary Zealot cause, which sought to expel the Roman regime from Palestine by violence. "Cullmann says: (1) Throughout his entire ministry Jesus had to come to terms with Zealotism; (2) He renounced Zealotism, although he also assumed a critical attitude toward the Roman State; (3) He was condemned to death as a Zealot by the Romans."[16] Swartley reflects:

> The crucial instruction that this insight gives us in our day is that we must be willing to be understood by others in a less favorable, more revolutionary way than we understand ourselves. In our relationships to political authorities, this is a difficult matter. Whether in conscientious objection to war or war tax resistance, we must accept the liability that political forces will brand both our resistance and nonresistance as revolutionary. But it might well be that such discrepancy between their perception and our self-understanding is the critical test of our faithfulness to the ethic of Jesus.[17]

It's significant that while the Bible only mentions the deaths of Judas and James, Christian tradition has long held that all but one of Jesus's twelve apostles were killed for spreading the gospel, most by the power of the state. There was a reason the Romans came to view Christianity as a threat to be stamped out, just as the Pharisees and Sadducees had viewed Jesus. Clearly, the power of the name of Jesus, and of his teachings, to upend the status quo maintained by oppressive rulers and assert the primacy of God's law over Caesar's continued decades after Jesus's death and Resurrection. We need to reclaim the Jesus who gave such pause to unjust and oppressive regimes.

Is Jesus a revolutionary? First, while Jesus did reject the violence of the Zealots, the way of life Jesus called for is indeed revolutionary in relation to the values of the status quo, and by asserting a whole new order whose values intend to turn the world upside down. Second, the direct threat to political power comes with the followers of Jesus always having, at best, a conditional obedience to governing authorities, depending on the choices they are asked to make, but always putting their allegiance to God at a much higher level than their obedience to whoever their Caesars are. Third, both as individuals within all of society's institutions and as communities of faith that defy the social norms and oppressive divisions of their society (as we described in chapter 2), they are to exemplify the "beloved community" of which the Reverend Dr. Martin Luther King Jr. spoke, with all the resulting transformation of society that such a community can demonstrate and inspire. And fourth, as individual leaders and as part of local communities and congregations, the followers of Jesus have often helped to start and sustain movements for social change—such as the antislavery abolitionists in both England and America; anticolonial movements in the global South; civil rights and freedom movements in the United States, South Africa, and around the world; human rights, justice, and peace movements in many countries; and countless movements to protect migrants, refugees, and victims of war, and to oppose trafficking and genocide. Such movements, if they are effective, will always include the religious and nonreligious, but they are often inspired and supported by people of faith—acting upon the way of Jesus, whom they believe to be calling them to a revolution of love and justice.

## POLITICALLY HOMELESS

Many followers of Jesus are feeling politically homeless in the United States and around the world, but that might be the way it is supposed to be. If we properly understand Jesus's instruction that our loyalty to God must supersede our loyalty to any earthly ruler when the two loyalties conflict with each other, that logic certainly also applies to loyalty to political parties. Our two parties are not morally equivalent in their failures, but both fall short of the values that come to us from following Jesus. Yet voting is very important, especially for the protection of those Jesus calls "the least of these."

The Republican Party has too often disregarded the best values of principled conservatism: fiscal integrity and responsibility, an allegiance to truth and honesty, genuine profamily values, national security through global engagement, the commitment to opportunity for all, the value of empathy for those in need, and the worth and equality of every person under the law. Instead, too many Republicans have substituted a moral relationship to the presidency with a transactional one, a Faustian bargain, perhaps, by ignoring Trump's consistent mental, emotional, and moral incompetence while accepting his fearful and hateful racial divisiveness—all in exchange for judicial appointments focused on the single issues of abortion or economic and environmental deregulation, and tax cuts that support the greedy demands of their wealthiest donors. And ultimately it seems that they will accept any behavior from the White House for its ability to appoint an antiabortion conservative judiciary that will also roll back racial, gender, and economic equity. All this also makes many conservatives with Christian and other moral values feel politically homeless.

The Democratic Party, on the other hand, has lost its historic relationship to working-class people around the country, and has indeed become dominated by cultural elites who have little connection to ordinary families and the many pressures on their lives. Democratic Party rhetoric doesn't appeal to the values of many people who care most about poverty and racism. For many election cycles, Democratic consultants have replaced the word "poor" with the words "middle class," and the party is no longer perceived as one that cares nearly enough about the needs of people on the margins of life in America. The text from Matthew 25 that draws many Christians into engaging in politics does not say, "As you have done to the middle class, you have done to me." Rather, it has Jesus saying to us, "As you have done to the least of these, you have done to me." It's a biblical text many Democratic consultants seem not to have read or to have forgotten.

Despite being dependent on African-American voters, the Democratic Party has often taken them for granted instead of courageously addressing the realities of institutionalized racism, and instead of investing in organizers, mobilizers, and candidates in African-American and Latino communities. And millennial voters of color who lead such new movements as Black Lives Matter are now asking Democratic leaders what they will actually do for young citizens of color who vote for them.

Unfortunately, the Democrats are also no longer a faith-friendly party. Voters with religious faith are often ignored or even dismissed without serious outreach or respectful dialogue. I have fought religious fundamentalism for most of my life, but the secular fundamentalism that controls some of the left and the Democratic Party at the national level can be equally ideological, irrational, and divisive—too often even seeming to attack religion itself.

It is hard to resolve an issue as complex as abortion when both the lives of women and the potential lives in their womb are so vulnerable (more on that in chapter 9), and the denial of a moral conversation about it within the Democratic Party continues to alienate many people of faith. Even language of "pro-life Democrats" or a party that can at least agree on the goal of "reducing" abortions is not acceptable to strong voices on the left with great influence on party control.

Similarly, the central importance of marriage, family, and parenting for the common good of society is not a central topic in Democratic Party language and policy. Why is the discussion of family values—for every type of family, both straight and gay—so absent from conversations on the left when we know that this is a vital part of critical solutions to both raise children and to overcome poverty? Voices advocating for strengthening families are too often not heard.

Third parties have not been a successful way forward in the American system of politics. But perhaps a "third way," or better yet a "moral movement," to revive and renew American politics, on both sides of the aisle, may be the way forward for people of faith; they put the poor and vulnerable, the consistent dignity of all human life, strong families *and* gender equality, the central priority of racial and economic justice, a foreign policy of peacemaking, and the urgent need for the environmental defense of the planet at the center of their faith-based political convictions. Our loyalty to Christ above all earthly rulers means that our support for candidates and parties should never be unconditional and always based on which candidate's character and policies will do more to advance God's kingdom "on Earth as it is in Heaven."

It is past time for a new moral conversation about politics. And as this book has argued, reclaiming Jesus is a starting place for those of us who call ourselves Christians.

## I WAS ARRESTED WITH YOU

When I spoke at Calvin College in Grand Rapids, Michigan, on the subject of my book *America's Original Sin,* the moderator introduced me with something that isn't in my official bio: "Our speaker today has been arrested twenty-two times." I was quite surprised when this conservative white evangelical audience of young people responded with enthusiastic applause!

*Things may be changing,* I thought. Indeed, the first question my thirteen-year-old son asked me the night of the 2016 election was, "Dad, how long until you get arrested?"

Jack's expectations were correct. The arrest record is up by two more now, after some of us faith leaders were arrested in December 2017 in the Hart Senate Office Building for reading biblical passages about poverty to protest the GOP tax plan, which disproportionately favors the rich (more on that below), and then again outside the White House gates in the summer of 2018, as mentioned earlier in this chapter, as we brought the message to the president that separating children from their parents at the border is the antithesis of the gospel.

As those twenty-four arrests imply, we have a long history of civil disobedience at Sojourners. Here is one example that ended up making a very significant political difference. In late 1983, on the heels of the Reagan administration's invasion of Grenada, church leaders in Nicaragua called me and pleaded with us to help stop the invasion of their country, rightly fearing that the United States could target Nicaragua next, and having received some intelligence to that effect. We asked ourselves, *What can we do?*

After much prayer and discernment, and in collaboration with many allies in the Christian peace movement, we launched the "Pledge of Resistance," wherein Christians across the United States pledged to fill the offices of their members of Congress in massive civil disobedience if Nicaragua were invaded. Eighty thousand people eventually signed the pledge. Most of the signers were prepared to be arrested and go to jail if necessary—all activated by a "phone tree" in the days before the internet. Within twenty-four hours of giving the signal, eighty thousand people could be reached and called to act.

Our hope in creating this pledge was to increase the domestic cost of a US invasion—and we used that language with the White House and the State Department—with a credible promise to mobilize tens of thousands to engage in principled nonviolent civil disobedience all over America, with Catholic nuns being carried away in their habits and pastors and priests removed in their collars—hoping that might make decision-makers reconsider. It worked. In the end, the United States did not send troops to directly invade Nicaragua (the Iran-Contra scandal and the US-paid mercenaries had also hurt the case for direct intervention). But we later got very reliable information that the Pledge of Resistance was a significant factor in the White House decision not to invade. Church leaders in Nicaragua expressed great thanks to American Christians for our solidarity.

Civil disobedience is just one tactic in the toolbox of social change, and it exists along a continuum of protest. It should be something we are willing to undertake when the stakes are high enough to demand such action and other tactics have been exhausted.

Civil disobedience on occasion has been the culmination of broader movements around particular justice and peace commitments. For example, for decades Sojourners helped lead faith-based national campaigns to stop and reverse the Cold War nuclear arms race. We focused on bringing needed biblical and theological reflection to the public debates, including producing nuclear study guides that were used by hundreds of thousands of people in churches across the United States. Our writing, speaking, and acting engaged Christians across the country, so that when Congress debated dangerous first-strike nuclear weapons in 1983, we were ready to respond with what at the time was the largest civil disobedience action in Washington since the Vietnam War, as 242 of us were arrested for singing and praying in the US Capitol.

People often come up to me and say, "I was arrested with you!" Many who have joined Sojourners in civil disobedience have learned that it can indeed change history, but it can be deeply transformational on a personal level as well. Especially when middle-class white people find themselves inside a jail cell for the first time, on the wrong side of the law they were raised to obey, it can be an emotional and life-changing experience. Of course, many people of color have had those experiences throughout their lives, and civil disobedience actions conducted by people of color are often treated in much more brutal ways. Consequently, when white people choose to engage in civil disobedience, they need to do so while fully recognizing their privilege and commit to using that privilege constructively. Getting arrested together is sometimes a good idea.

From protests at the nuclear weapons test site in Nevada and arrests at the South African embassy to oppose apartheid, from actions at the State Department against US wars in Central America and torture and blocking illegal evictions of low-income people in our own neighborhood, we have learned a great deal over the years about faith, justice, and the law.

## THE BIBLES ARE EVIDENCE OF THE CRIME

On November 30, 2017, several national faith leaders were arrested by Capitol Police during a nonviolent, faith-based civil disobedience action in response to the proposed tax bill. Faith leaders publicly read the Bible and prayed for the nation in the Hart Senate Office Building atrium. Because the treatment of poor and vulnerable people is lifted up in the Bible more than two thousand times, we began to read all those verses—but we didn't get very far.

According to Pew Research, 91 percent of the members of Congress profess to be Christian. The faith-based action served to remind senators of their biblical responsibility to the poor and to raise the nation's moral conscience to stop the attack on society's most vulnerable people. The new tax legislation will determine social outcomes for many years to come and signals a shift in the social safety net.

Here is the scripture that I read to open up our time at that Senate office building. It's from Isaiah 10:1–3 (NIV):

*Woe to those who make unjust laws,*
*to those who issue oppressive decrees,*

*to deprive the poor of their rights*
*and withhold justice from the oppressed of my*
*people,*
*making widows their prey*
*and robbing the fatherless.*
*What will you do on the day of reckoning,*
*when disaster comes from afar?*
*To whom will you run for help?*
*Where will you leave your riches?*

As faith leaders across the political spectrum, we had lobbied against this bill, talked to senators, made statements, had press conferences, and our people had called Congress from all over the country—but finally, in the end, when you've done all that you can possibly do, it may be a time to do nonviolent, prayerful civil disobedience. And what we did was very simple: we took our Bibles to the Senate and just began to read from scripture. We named this tax bill for what it would do to the poor, and then said the Bible's God of the poor speaks against doing such things to the most vulnerable.

The Capitol Police captain I spoke with before the action clearly would rather not have arrested these faith leaders. He asked how long it would take for us to read our scriptures in the Bible about the poor and how we should treat poor people. When I told him there were two thousand verses on this subject in the Old and New Testaments, he replied, "I think that would take too long."

As we continued to read our scriptures, police officers shouted over us with warnings: "This is the United States Capitol Police. You're engaging in unlawful conduct. If you do not cease and desist at this time, you will be arrested."

After the third warning came, the police began to arrest us. But we continued to read the Bible and to pray even while we were being arrested. And we were literally arrested while reading our Bibles. If you listen to the video of the event carefully, which was watched by more than three million people, you can hear the words of scripture and prayer, and the clicking of handcuffs, as we were forced to put our hands behind our back and were shackled.[18]

After each of us read our scriptures and were about to be arrested, we put our Bibles down on a banner that quoted Isaiah. After we were all taken away, Jim Rice, the editor of *Sojourners* magazine, went to the same police captain and said, "Can we just take all these Bibles away with us?" The captain looked at Jim and said, "No, the Bibles are evidence of a crime being committed." Jim smiled at him and said, "Yes, they are." The captain smiled back and said, "Indeed."

In our current climate, my prayer is that we will gather the lessons many of us have learned over the years about when and how civil disobedience is appropriate and necessary and be ready to act when circumstances call for it. Inevitably there will be moments ahead when nonviolent, prayerful civil disobedience will be part of the way forward. It seems inescapable, given the injustice and dangers we see in America and the rest of the world.

## IS THIS A "BONHOEFFER MOMENT"?

I have been pondering for much of the past two years the question of whether this is a "Bonhoeffer moment," especially in conversation with several church leaders and pastors. Dietrich Bonhoeffer was the brilliant young German pastor and theologian who saw clearly the threat of Hitler's rise to power and the need for the church to strenuously oppose the Nazis. His diligent work eventually cost him his life, being executed in a concentration camp near the end of the war, but his writings have inspired many to bravely confront the world's powers in the name of Jesus. You might have read Bonhoeffer's *Cost of Discipleship*, or *Letters and Papers from Prison*—and if not, you should. Some of us were beginning to ask what a founder of what became called the "Confessing Church" movement has to say to us today. Bonhoeffer taught us to turn back to faith, not just political power, when true crises arise.

I have been giving that question a lot of reflection. Easy or simplistic historical parallels are never helpful. History doesn't repeat, as many have said, but it does sometimes rhyme. Strongman leaders are appearing now in many countries, including here in our United States. These leaders with autocratic tendencies are seldom simply the cause of what they create but are rather a consequence of cultural, political, and moral situations that have been unfolding or unraveling for some time. These allegedly populist but actually authoritarian leaders can lead their people and nations to many different outcomes, each due to their own circumstances, limitations, resistance, and possibilities. *And, critically, one of the most important historical factors to rising autocracy has been the response or lack of response from faith communities to the strongman leaders and their dangerous values.*

I think where Bonhoeffer most comes into our present situation is when he said that the most important question Christians must always ask is "Who is Jesus

Christ for us today?" Hebrews 13:8 says, "Jesus Christ is the same yesterday and today and forever." I believe that with all my head and heart, which gives me great confidence in trying to follow him. But Dietrich Bonhoeffer reminds us that the meaning of Jesus Christ needs always to be applied to our lives and our times today if "following" him is to mean anything. I believe Bonhoeffer's question is the right one always, and for us right now it's an increasingly urgent one. We are no longer in sync with the Savior we name. In Luke 6:46 Jesus says, "Why do you call me 'Lord, Lord,' and do not do what I tell you?" Having been asked this question repeatedly, *I now believe that this is a Bonhoeffer moment*, and I decided after reading Acts early many mornings to try to write a book that would help answer his question "Who is Jesus Christ for us today?" for me and right now.

How we might answer Bonhoeffer's question and Jesus's deepest challenges are what we need to face and better understand. Returning to Jesus requires careful discernment between what belongs to Caesar and what belongs to God in our lives and societies. To restore a close connection to Jesus means Christians need to do a much better job in our current political reality at identifying times when following God's law means challenging and sometimes even disobeying unjust human laws. We need to understand Jesus and his teachings to shape how we need to respond to this historical and moral crisis if those of us who call ourselves "followers of Jesus" want to keep calling ourselves that with any credibility.

This may be a new era in American history, but it is not a new era in human history. From the Roman Empire to Nazi Germany, to the Soviet system, to apartheid South Africa, to dictatorial regimes on every continent, history has demonstrated that the only reality feared by many strongmen as a legitimate threat to their control is the name of the only Rival who can ultimately contend against them. Søren Kierkegaard's warning to nations that would call themselves Christian—that nobody is Christian if everybody is Christian—has come full circle.

Even when Christian culture is compromised by conformity to the values and powers of this world, we can never shed ourselves of Jesus. He has a good record on comebacks.

How do we think the churches and all of us who call ourselves Christian, or religious, or even spiritual are doing with the "Caesar question" now directly before us?

# Chapter 8
# The Peacemaker Question

Blessed are the peacemakers,
for they will be called children of God.

—MATTHEW 5:9

What does it mean to be a peacemaker? Is it the same thing as being a pacifist? Or is pacifism too passive? How do we go about being peacemakers at the interpersonal, family, organizational, community, national, or even global level? Of the various virtues Jesus names in the Beatitudes, why is it the peacemakers specifically who are called "children of God"?

With cultures regularly at war with one another and people around the world waking up to threats against their very existence, we can begin to understand why Jesus reserved special attention and praise for "peacemakers." Wars, rumors of wars, and the politics of personal attack and character destruction fill our media and our conflicted world.

> *Blessed are the peacemakers, for they will be called children of God. . . . You have heard that it was said, "You shall love your neighbor and hate your enemy." But I say to you, Love your enemies and pray for those who persecute you, so that you may be children of your Father in heaven; for he makes his sun rise on the evil and on the good, and sends rain on the righteous and on the unrighteous. For if you love those who love you, what reward do you have? Do not even the tax collectors do the same? And if you greet only your brothers and sisters, what more are you doing than others? Do not even the Gentiles do the same? Be perfect, therefore, as your heavenly Father is perfect. (Matt 5:9, 43–48)*

The first thing to say after reading such a transformational text is perhaps best expressed by poet Wendell Berry: "One cannot be aware both of the history of Christian war and of the contents of the gospels without feeling that something is amiss."[1] One of the answers is again to ask the question, How many times have we heard these texts preached in our churches, especially since 9/11? Let's hear what some of the commentators say.

Evangelical commentator Craig S. Keener says:

> Many first-century Jews had begun to think that revolutionary violence was the only adequate response to the violence of oppression they experienced. Matthew's first audience no doubt could recall the bankruptcy of this approach, which led to crushing defeat in the war of A.D. 66–73. But Jesus promises the kingdom not to those who try to force God's hand in their time but to those who patiently and humbly wait for it—the meek, the poor in spirit, the merciful, the peacemakers. Of course, Jesus' demand does not merely challenge the bloodshed of revolution. *Peacemakers* means not only living at peace but bringing harmony among others; this role requires us to work for reconciliation with spouses, neighbors and all people—insofar as the matter is up to us (Rom 12:18).[2]

Matthew 5:9, in particular, describes the identity of a peacemaker. Listen to what eighteenth-century Methodist preacher and biblical commentator Joseph

Benson said about the biblical meaning of the term "peacemaker." I found it quite a powerful contrast to the wildly contradictory behavior we see and hear every day from the White House, congressional committees, and certainly from campaign ads across the country.

> *The peace-makers*—Those who are themselves of a peaceable temper, and endeavour to promote peace in others: who *study to be quiet*, and, *as much as in them lieth*, to live peaceably with all men: who are so far from sowing the seeds of discord between any of their fellow-creatures, that they both studiously avoid contention themselves, and labour to extinguish it wherever it prevails, laying themselves out to heal the differences of brethren and neighbours, to reconcile contending parties, and to restore peace wherever it is broken, as well as to preserve it where it is. *They shall be called the children of God.*[3]

Of course, what it means to be a peacemaker is most dramatically tested by how we treat our enemies, as Jesus goes on to instruct in Matthew 5:43–44, where he tells us to love even our enemies—which is undoubtedly the hardest teaching of Jesus.

What is clear in the New Testament is that peacemaking is not just a personal characteristic or strategy. Rather, peacemaking is also to be applied in our social and even political situations; how we treat our adversaries, including our hated enemies; and how the peacemaking inspired by Jesus can help us to make social change. Maybe the brashness and bluster of a divisive and dangerous president can be the occasion, the negative example, for our deeper reflection on the meaning of Jesus's words, and his special love for those he calls the peacemakers.

## MORE THAN BEING NICE

During the presidency of Donald Trump, it feels like any commitment to civility in the public square has ended. Even more frightening is how the usual presidential constraints against loose talk, profanity, and even threats of all-out war have also dangerously disappeared. Every day, presidential tweets viciously attack all manner of people (focused on the president's opponents), with the most disrespectful and damning rhetoric ever seen from a White House, while foreign leaders and whole nations come under the American president's violent threats of ultimate destruction.

This political and moral crisis is also why "civility" must mean much more than being "nice" or "polite" in public life. The way we talk to and about one another politically and culturally will either sustain or undermine the health of our civil societies. The violence of language does, in fact, lead to the violence of actions. Character, respect, and decency are qualities that are not merely helpful but also are formational behaviors against the polarization and even violence that human beings are easily drawn to.

Cornell West says we are in a "spiritual blackout, which is the relative eclipse of decency, honesty and integrity."[4] Political leaders who appeal to anxiety, to fear, and even to hatred become themselves instruments of division and danger; and the role of the peacemaker is so instrumental to the ways of respectful dialogue and genuine listening, with an experienced commitment to common sense and practical nonviolence. The lack of civility from political leaders can indeed take us down a road that leads to violence, especially if they actually imply encouragement to civic violence in certain circumstances, as this president actually has done in some of his campaign rallies. And one of the most dangerous consequences of a lack of political civility by political leaders is the reaction to it from their opponents, as some angry critics of the president have also demonstrated. The response to ugly words in politics is usually more of the same, rather than seeking higher ground.

Conflict is inevitable for human beings, and conflict resolution will always be a necessary and urgent task. Most of our human conflicts are resolved every day without violence, and the activity of peacemakers can critically increase those numbers. In my view, peacemaking is not just saying what you are against but also putting your energy and expertise into resolving the conflicts going on—to increase the number of conflicts that can be resolved without violence.

Nearly a decade ago some faith leaders and former members of Congress from both parties collaborated on a Covenant for Civility. That message seems completely forgotten now but has never been more relevant. These were members of Congress speaking also as people of faith who longed for the churches to step into the diminishing political discourse—which has further diminished since these members have all retired. The covenant said in part,

> The church in the United States can offer a message of hope and reconciliation to a nation that is

deeply divided by political and cultural differences. Too often, however, we have reflected the political divisions of our culture rather than the unity we have in the body of Christ. We come together to urge those who claim the name of Christ to "put away from you all bitterness and wrath and anger and wrangling and slander, together with all malice, and be kind to one another, tenderhearted, forgiving one another, as God in Christ has forgiven you" (Ephesians 4:31–32).

We commit that our dialogue with each other will reflect the spirit of the Scriptures, where our posture toward each other is to be "quick to listen, slow to speak and slow to become angry" (James 1:19). . . .

We pledge that when we disagree, we will do so respectfully, without falsely impugning the other's motives, attacking the other's character, or questioning the other's faith, and recognizing in humility that in our limited, human opinions, "we see but a poor reflection as in a mirror" (1 Corinthians 13:12). We will therefore "be completely humble and gentle; be patient, bearing with one another in love" (Ephesians 4:2).

We will ever be mindful of the language we use

in expressing our disagreements, being neither arrogant nor boastful in our beliefs: "Before destruction one's heart is haughty, but humility goes before honor" (Proverbs 18:12). . . .

We believe that it is more difficult to hate others, even our adversaries and our enemies, when we are praying for them. We commit to pray for each other, those with whom we agree and those with whom we may disagree, so that together we may strive to be faithful witnesses to our Lord, who prayed "that they may be one" (John 17:22).[5]

Most people I show this to have never heard of it and find it hard to believe that it was ever said or done. It all seems so impossible now. But those old words need some new meaning. The current dangers and possibilities for peacemakers are illustrated by contemporary stories and examples almost every day. Neither civility nor conflict resolution can be just conceptual ideals to which we aspire. Rather, they must be demonstrated by concrete examples in the world and in our national institutions—which can teach and inspire us. I am particularly encouraged by the growing number of people from a new generation who are being drawn into conflict resolution as a science, art, and vocation.

## IS NONVIOLENCE NAIVE?

I have a very vivid memory of participating in a debate between "pacifism" and "the just war" at Fuller Theological Seminary decades ago. It's the age-old question with the binary categories of war and peace. I was placed in the "pacifist pulpit," and across the way from me on the same stage was another theologian, in the "just war pulpit." And so we began. The arguments were traditional, each being backed by scripture and tradition. There we were high above the congregation, debating back and forth. But the debate seemed frustrating to me, pitting theoretical positions against each other—instead of talking about the real-life conflicts that were then going on and discussing how to best resolve them. I recall looking at my opponent and saying something like, "I think it's time for people like us to get down from these high places and go to the ground. It's time to take up the conflicts that are destroying people's lives and dignity right now, and together apply the best from all our traditions to prevent, stop, and even heal those horrible conflicts. It's time to take our peacemaking from our heads also to our hearts, and from the pulpit to the streets." That moment began to change the conversation for me to one that tries to be more authentic, practical, and real.

I believe the followers of Jesus are now being summoned to a new place in response to international war and violence by new faith-based initiatives that want to move us beyond old binary choices to conflict resolution—just peacemaking and active nonviolence. A hopeful new "nonviolence initiative" is being led by grassroots Christians in the global South—and the Vatican, of all places, is encouraging these Christians, many of whom live or lived in war zones, to help us create some new possibilities.

In a remarkable article provocatively titled "Is Nonviolence Naive?" theologian Andrew Klager wrestles with all the difficult questions raised by Jesus's nonviolent example and teaching. He insightfully distinguishes the difference between "violence" and "conflict" and makes the powerful point that the best way for the followers of Jesus to reduce violence is to take on conflict resolution—to "face conflict head-on."

> Violence is any action that undermines the dignity of another human being, whether direct, structural, or institutional. This can be emotional, psychological, spiritual, or physical abuse; actions that dehumanize the Other; forms of injustice, oppression, or marginalization; and war, genocide, mob violence, and armed insurrection. But violence is not the same as

> conflict. Conflict provides the space to air grievances and expose injustice; nonviolence entails ending conflict by eroding its causes without succumbing to the allure of violence. Nonviolence requires "the willingness to face conflict head on, to resolve it, and to make it a link in the chain of a new process," explained Pope Francis.[6]

Klager goes on to prove that nonviolence is not naive, does not mean a passive withdrawal from conflict, but directly addresses it in better and more effective ways than our old and bad habits of abrasive words and aggressive war—so crudely demonstrated by our current president. Only direct and real involvement in the world's conflicts and violence can provide the practitioners of nonviolence the "front row engagement with injustice, oppression, and exploitation that undercuts any naïveté about the challenges the world faces."[7] This is not just a political option or strategy, or an ideological choice, but is rooted in our commitment as followers of Jesus:

> Jesus, the author of Christian nonviolence, presents us with a choice between the counterintuitive, life-giving behavior of the kingdom of God—humility, compassion, and unity—and the

> "natural," uninspiring logic of empire: violence, exploitation, and competition. . . . Christian nonviolence begins by pledging allegiance to a king who was put on a Roman cross rather than a throne. It's an upside-down kingdom whose constitution is the Sermon on the Mount and whose manifesto is the Beatitudes.[8]

I love the way that Dorothy Day, founder of the Catholic Worker movement, spent all her time each day serving people's needs *and* saw that as a direct and practical alternative to war and violence. She said, "You just need to look at what the gospel asks, and what war does," a great comparison that we should all make. "The gospel asks that we feed the hungry, give drink to the thirsty, clothe the naked, welcome the homeless, visit the prisoner, and perform works of mercy. War does all the opposite. It makes my neighbor hungry, thirsty, homeless, a prisoner, and sick. The gospel asks us to take up our cross. War asks us to lay the cross of suffering on others."[9]

This is all very practical and not just theoretical, as Klager makes clear:

> Think about the Sermon on the Mount: Jesus instructs us to reconcile with those who anger us,

> avoid violently resisting an evildoer, give more than what was stolen, offer the other cheek, go the second mile, love our enemies, and pray for our persecutors. Though counterintuitive, these commandments are often effective ways to disorient the recipients of our behavior. Instead of inviting retaliation, these actions say: "If you can't acknowledge my dignity, I'll take the responsibility to acknowledge yours."[10]

He says, "Jesus refused to confront evil in the world using evil methods." But, he claims, the way of Jesus can practically work in defusing violence and resolving conflict. Unlike the traditional understanding of "pacifism" (a word not found in the Bible), conflict resolution is both an art and a science, not just a naive hope or simply reminding people of what we will and won't do:

> Nonviolent peacebuilders are resolutely pragmatic and science-based, taking and recommending measured responses that consider every conceivable factor, stakeholder, and repercussion. Research by political scientist Erica Chenoweth has shown that, during the 20th century, acts of nonviolent civil resistance were twice as successful in achieving political and socio-economic objectives as acts

> of violent intervention. Nonviolence requires creativity rather than laziness, wisdom rather than impulsiveness, maturity rather than bravado, courage rather than fear.[11]

Historian Theodore Roszak reminds us, "People try nonviolence for a week, and when it 'doesn't work' they go back to violence, which hasn't worked for centuries."[12] "War is impatience," writes theologian Stanley Hauerwas.[13] The way of Jesus takes a longer term and deeper approach than the quick solutions that attack, violence, and war promise.

For followers of Jesus, living as peacemakers and the nonviolent direct action that comes from that is not an emergency reaction to conflict but rather a way of life. Ultimately, the way of Jesus is meant to reverse and replace the cycle of violence with a new practice and cycle of nonviolence in both our personal and public lives.

As all of this implies, peacemaking as a way of life is one of Jesus's most challenging teachings, and one that societies have by and large failed to follow. Warmakers are usually willing to pay a higher cost for war than those of us who are peacemakers are willing to pay for peace. As a teenager who was struggling with the social witness of the church, the first name I ever heard of a Christian who was opposed to the Vietnam

War was "Berrigan," the Jesuit priest who was one of the first religious leaders in the country to come out against the war. As my friend and mentor Daniel Berrigan reminded us,

> We cry peace and cry peace, and there is no peace. There is no peace because there are no peacemakers. There are no makers of peace because the making of peace is at least as costly as the making of war—at least as exigent, at least as disruptive, at least as liable to bring disgrace and prison and death in its wake.[14]

One example of the terrible cost that can come from being a peacemaker and seeker of justice is the life and death of the Reverend Dr. Martin Luther King Jr. After spending the bulk of his ministry fighting for the cause of racial justice and the urgent need to end poverty, Dr. King decided he needed to speak out against the war in Vietnam—given that he came to see racism, poverty, and militarism (the "giant triplets") as inextricably linked. He knew that this was a risky thing for him to do, as it would rupture many of his alliances and relationships with political leaders such as President Johnson, who had slowly come around on civil rights and poverty, and even with other leaders in the civil rights movement who wanted to focus on a singular message. In a famous speech titled "Beyond Vietnam: A Time to Break Silence," delivered at Riverside Church in New York City on April 4, 1967, King spoke powerfully against the war: "I knew that I could never again raise my voice against the violence of the oppressed in the ghettos without having first spoken clearly to the greatest purveyor of violence in the world today—my own government."[15] The black scholar and activist who helped Dr. King write that speech was Dr. Vincent Harding, who later became a primary mentor for me and Sojourners. Harding was also a Mennonite, the church tradition, along with that of the Quakers, that produced the most faith-based opposition to the war in Vietnam. One year to the day after breaking his silence on Vietnam, Dr. King was assassinated on the balcony of the Lorraine Motel in Memphis, Tennessee.

## JUST PEACEMAKING

Staying with the deep meaning of Jesus's words about peacemakers, let me turn to my dear friend and colleague Glen Stassen, the renowned Christian ethicist who passed away in 2014.

It was Glen Stassen who introduced the church that he knew to the powerful vision of *just peacemaking*, both going deeper than—and transcending—the old concepts of pacifism and a just war. Just peacemaking guides us toward the faithful and effective actions that both prevent and end wars, through the creative and critical practices of conflict resolution. More than any other voice on the theological scene, Glen moved us beyond peaceloving to peacemaking. He showed us that what the world needs most from Christians is not theoretical debates about war but the courageous and risky vocation of being peacemakers in the world—the ones whom Jesus called "children of God." Rather than standing above the world's conflicts in our pulpit debates, we must come down to the ground where the conflicts are occurring and find the best ways to reduce and end them. Glen's just peacemaking writings called serious Christians to that task and provided substantial direction for actually doing it. Using the creative and critical practices of conflict resolution, Glen's framework guides us toward effective and faithful actions to both prevent and end wars.

Having diagnosed why we as a society are so easily led to war and the need to offer a clear alternative, Stassen goes deeper and identifies a key shortcoming of pacifism and just war theory as they are often practiced:

> An ethic that focuses on "just say no," as pacifism and just war theory do if they are not assisted by an ethic of constructive peacemaking, is a recipe for losing the debate. . . . A constructive alternative has a much better chance. Jesus didn't just say no to anger and revengeful resistance, but commanded transforming initiatives: Go make peace with your brother or sister; go the second mile with the Roman soldier (Matt. 5:21–25, 38–42).[16]

This evangelical ethicist, also from Fuller Seminary, where I had that big debate, rooted a more active approach in the ethics and actions of Jesus. Stassen lays out what just peacemaking is and what it can look like at its best:

> Just peacemaking theory—the new paradigm for an ethics of peace and war developed by a consensus of 23 Christian ethicists and international relations scholars—shifts the debate to constructive alternatives. It focuses on 10 practices [see below] that have demonstrated their efficacy in toppling dictators and ameliorating causes of war without the killing and chaos of war. For example, the practice of nonviolent direct action toppled Marcos

in the Philippines, and East Germany's Eric Honecker and his Berlin Wall, without a single death.[17]

Before the second war in Iraq, several church leaders in America laid out what we called the Six-Point Plan, which we believed was an alternative to invading Iraq. Glen Stassen lifted up that faith-inspired alternative as a good example of "just peacemaking":

> The genius of [the Six-Point Plan] was that [it] addressed the evil of Saddam's dictatorship directly and proposed a way to depose him without killing Iraq's people and without the destruction and chaos of the war's aftermath. The proposal developed broad support in England, including in the British cabinet, and with a little more time could have developed the momentum to prevent the war.[18]

The British prime minister gave us an hour at 10 Downing Street to lay it out, and I was told it was literally on the table in their cabinet meetings as the alternative to the Iraq war plan, called the American Church Plan. We even were invited to present it to our Secretary of State's council. But the Pentagon and Vice President Cheney prevailed, and Prime Minister Blair went along with President Bush to begin the war that became such a disaster for the country and the world—another war based on lies, like Vietnam.

Stassen concluded his introduction to just peacemaking in the post-9/11 world by emphasizing its inherent practicality—the promise that it is so much more than merely aspirational ideals:

> The ethic we need for a viable future is not only an ethic of restraint in making war, but an ethic of just peacemaking initiatives for preventing war and building a future better than war after war, terrorism after terrorism. The practices of just peacemaking have proven effective in preventing wars in recent history. They are not merely ideals, but empirical practices that make for peace. They point the way to winning the debate—and winning the peace.[19]

*The ten practices of just peacemaking are as follows:* support nonviolent direct action; take independent initiatives to reduce threat; use cooperative conflict resolution; acknowledge responsibility for conflict and injustice and seek repentance and forgiveness; advance democracy, human rights, and religious liberty; foster just and sustainable economic development; work with emerging cooperative forces in the international system; strengthen the United Nations and international efforts for cooperation and human rights; reduce offensive weapons and weapons trade; and encourage grassroots peacemaking groups and voluntary associations.[20]

## WAGING PEACE

What does it look like to wage peace instead of war? How can governments foster creative problem-solving? And how can faith communities challenge them to do so?

Investing early to prevent conflicts from escalating into violent crises is, on average, sixty times more cost-effective than intervening after violence erupts. But the world spends just $1 on conflict prevention for every $1,885 it spends on military budgets.[21] That stems from the habit of war, not from any demonstrated effectiveness—a habit we need to break.

While governments often turn to violence to maintain security and bring perpetrators to justice, it will take much more creative strategies to defeat terrorists. We should consider Paul's strategy of feeding one's enemies to "heap burning coals [of shame] on their heads" (Rom. 12:20). For example, the Muslim world needs assistance from the West in education, especially for its girls and women, the building of technology and infrastructure, and a focus on economic development—not more weapons and money poured into the coffers of corrupt regimes.

The words of Jesus in the Sermon on the Mount are either authoritative for us or they are not. They are not set aside by the threats of terrorism and dictators or by our habits of war. Other alternatives have proven to be effective, such as responding to crises early, promoting preventative actions, using diplomacy, strategically deploying development aid, strengthening civil institutions, and prioritizing international actions, especially in working together to prevent atrocities.

Peacemakers are not utopians. They are the best hope for reducing violence, avoiding the greatest dangers, halting the biggest threats, and moving things (even incrementally) in a better direction. They keep open the necessary and vital option of keeping our greatest conflicts from becoming more bloody. We don't live in a perfect world, but in a broken and fallen world. Therefore, the role of peacemakers is crucial in keeping our inevitable human confrontations from killing more and more of us. War is not merely an activity; it is a system supported by economic and political assumptions and by structures that drive us toward conflict, which is then resolved by chosen methods of violence. The history of those systems and assumptions is deeply embedded in the present conflicts we are now confronting, and it is those assumptions and institutions that we must begin to question.

Any idea of nonviolent conflict resolution must be based on a realistic assessment of our human condition and not predicated on illusive notions of human perfectibility. In other words, human beings will *inevitably* become engaged in conflicts—in their relationships and families, between groups, and certainly among nations. Human conflict will not be ended; to assume that it can be is both politically naive and theologically irresponsible. It is our ways of handling human conflict that must be reexamined.

While human conflict is inevitable, military solutions are not. War is only one system for resolving human conflict. But its costs and consequences are simply too high—for its many victims, for the planet—and especially with the dangerous escalation of violence that the scope and power of today's modern weapons now make possible.

Just as most once believed that it was naive and impractical to think that we could live without slavery, most people today have little imagination of how we could live without military violence. The creation of that imagination is an essential job of nonviolent peacemaking. We must begin to discover that there is a better way.

Here is one potential game changer. What if even some of the 1.2 billion Catholics embraced gospel nonviolence? Read this report from *Sojourners* senior editor Rose Marie Berger:

> Catholic just war criteria assume that a strategically applied use of violence under the right conditions will end violence, creating the possibility of peace. But in an era of weapons of mass destruction and borderless, serial conflicts, the approach no longer works. At least not from the perspective of those on the receiving end of the actions of the remaining superpower. . . .
>
> Across the world, effective alternatives to war and violence are emerging. People are doing serious work to advance these alternatives, to mainstream them, and to scale them up. "Currently 12 international, nongovernmental organizations and many more local groups provide unarmed civilian protection in 17 areas of violent conflict," says Mel Duncan, founding director of Nonviolent Peaceforce. In one year, Nonviolent Peaceforce trained more than 14,000 people in conflict-affected communities in unarmed civilian protection. . . .
>
> The conversation is no longer about justifying cases where armed force may be legitimized, nor is

> it about the pacifism of personal conscience. The focus is on marrying the vast amounts of peacemaking research, civil resistance tactics, and just peace principles with the deep, pervasive peace theology of the church.[22]

I am deeply grateful and hopeful for the new Catholic nonviolence initiative now emerging, especially from the global South, with the warm and strong support of the Vatican under Pope Francis. This international popular process is rising from grassroots nonviolence practitioners who are demanding fresh teaching on issues of war, peace, and gospel nonviolence. In 2019, the nonviolence initiative met for a second time at the Vatican to explore what it would mean for the Catholic Church to fully embrace nonviolence as its forward teaching and practice for engaging conflict. "Nonviolent strategies should be the centerpiece to the church's approach to issues of war and peace and violence," said San Diego Catholic Bishop Robert McElroy.[23] Our friend Marie Dennis, the first Catholic layperson and first woman to be copresident of Pax Christi International, the global Catholic peace movement supporting the nonviolence initiative, said that a papal encyclical on nonviolence would bring the idea "from the periphery of Catholic thought on war and peace to the center, mainstreaming nonviolence as a spirituality, lifestyle, a program of societal action and a universal ethic."[24] I am especially grateful to Dennis, one of Sojourners' founding board members, and our own senior associate editor of *Sojourners*, Rose Marie Berger, a Catholic activist and poet, for their leadership on this vital and hopeful initiative. The group that gathered in Rome unanimously supported an encyclical by Pope Francis on nonviolence. That would be a prayer for peace that would excite me. "May the peace of the Lord be with you . . . and also with you!" Amen!

## IT'S A SIN TO BUILD A NUCLEAR WEAPON

We can't end a chapter on peacemaking without addressing the still-very-real threat of nuclear war in our world posed by the continued existence of so many thousands of the deadliest weapons ever created by human beings. In the current US context, we also need to contend with the frightening reality that our current president—with his temperament, maturity, volatile nature, impulsiveness, vindictiveness, judgment, and unwillingness to listen to others—has his finger on the nuclear button. More broadly, it is terrifying that for decades now we've entrusted the power to destroy civilization as we know it to a single person, whose decision is final and cannot be countermanded. Donald Trump's presidency reveals the extraordinary peril of this system—and that system is always the most immediate danger to the world, no matter who is in power. That system can and must be changed.

The tremendous leadership it took in 2017 to pass the international Nuclear Weapon Ban Treaty came from the global South and from friends like Beatrice Fihn at the International Campaign to Abolish Nuclear Weapons. Pope Francis and the Vatican state were one of the first signatories to the agreement. The United States refused to participate in the proceedings.

I have often claimed, along with many Christian leaders, that our response to the unique peril of nuclear weapons is a matter of faith, not just politics. This is an obligation of those who would follow Jesus, the one who instructs us to be peacemakers, whom he calls children of God. There are many examples we could look to on what a faithful response to the peril of nuclear weapons looks like, but I'll conclude by lifting up a courageous stance taken by one of the twentieth century's most famous US Christian leaders and the world's greatest evangelist on this subject of Christian peacemaking and the danger of nuclear weapons and war.

In 1978, a *Sojourners* subscriber sent me this quote from a European newspaper reporting on Billy Graham's visit to the Nazi concentration camp in Auschwitz, Poland: "The present insanity of the global arms race," Graham said, "if continued, will lead inevitably to a conflagration so great that Auschwitz will seem like a minor rehearsal."[25] The US media had not reported on Graham's statement.

I wrote to Billy Graham and asked if what he said, after visiting Auschwitz for the first time, indicated a change of heart for him on nuclear weapons. Billy wrote back to say it did. He agreed to an interview with *Sojourners* to explain how his thinking had changed about the nuclear arms race, saying that it felt to him like a moral and spiritual question and not just a political issue.

Billy Graham, in that 1979 interview with *Sojourners*, entitled "A Change of Heart," was clear in his view of the threat posed by nuclear weapons:

> Is a nuclear holocaust inevitable if the arms race is not stopped? Frankly, the answer is almost certainly yes. Now I know that some people feel human beings are so terrified of a nuclear war that no one would dare start one. I wish I could accept

> that. But neither history nor the Bible gives much reason for optimism. What guarantee is there that the world will never produce another maniacal dictator like Hitler or Amin? As a Christian I take sin seriously, and the Christian should be the first to know that the human heart is deceitful and desperately wicked, as Jeremiah says. We can be capable of unspeakable horror, no matter how educated or technically sophisticated we are. Auschwitz is a compelling witness to this.[26]

Graham, who died in 2018, had been an important figure in my life and work. Ever since meeting him in the early days of Sojourners' ministry, I found him to be not only gracious and warm, but also a bridge-builder and encourager, and a steady supporter of Sojourners' work for peace and justice, which he called "complementary" to his mission of personal evangelism. He told me that his vocation was to preach the gospel of personal salvation, and he thought mine was to teach the social implications of the gospel. Graham had always been a lifelong learner, passionate about preaching the gospel but always ready to understand more about what that gospel means in the world. It was never surprising to me that this southern-born-and-raised American evangelist decided early on to insist on preaching only to racially integrated coliseums and crusades, while many others just went along with their culture.

But perhaps the most surprising position Graham ever took, which was at odds with many evangelicals of the time, including most of his aides, was his change of heart about nuclear weapons.

As one might expect when talking about Billy Graham, scripture was at the heart of what led to his "conversion" to peacemaking. "I have gone back to the Bible to restudy what it says about the responsibilities we have as peacemakers," Graham said. "I have seen that we must seek the good of the whole human race, and not just the good of any one nation or race." He added, "Is it [God's] will that resources be used for massive armaments that could otherwise be used for alleviating human suffering and hunger? Of course not. Our world has lost sight of true values and substituted false gods and false values."[27]

Billy Graham talked about the unique role that Christians are called to play. "I believe that the Christian especially has a responsibility to work for peace in our world," Graham said. "Christians may well find themselves working and agreeing with nonbelievers on an issue like peace. But our motives will not be identical." And the goal, as he saw it, was the "total destruction of nuclear arms."[28]

Graham told me in our 1979 conversation, "I honestly wish we had never developed nuclear weapons. But of course that is water under the bridge. We have nuclear weapons in horrifying quantities, and the question is, what are we going to do about it?"[29]

That's still the question for Christians today—that is, if we want to reclaim Jesus. There is a distressing and dangerous distance between Jesus's call for us to be peacemakers and the acceptance of weapons and war as the primary way to resolve our inevitable human conflicts. Our disconnection with Jesus's way of loving all our neighbors and even our enemies has had the most devastatingly deadly results. Our human family has been poised, one button away, on the edge of collective suicide for decades, and reclaiming Jesus means we need to seriously and honestly grapple with how we might coax humanity back from this ledge.

Those who help do that shall be called children of God.

# Chapter 9
# The Discipleship Question

Truly I tell you, just as you did it to one of
the least of these who are members of
my family, you did it to me.

—MATTHEW 25:40

We have discussed a number of ways in which too many Christians are disconnected from the life and teachings of Jesus, and what being connected to Jesus looks like in those areas—love of neighbor, seeing all human beings as image-bearers of God, valuing and speaking the truth, being a servant leader, learning how to "be not afraid," distinguishing what belongs to Caesar and what belongs to God, and resolving conflicts as one of the peacemakers. But at the end of the day, is there a basic measure of whether we are behaving as followers of Jesus? If so, what are the implications for personal behavior and public policy?

The twenty-fifth chapter of Matthew's gospel contains Jesus's final discipleship test. *This text was my own conversion passage* coming out of the student movements of the 1960s and into my relationship with Jesus Christ. After battling for civil rights and racial justice and against poverty and war, I believed I had found my life's vocation. But the foundations of it were not yet clear to me, and I found Karl Marx, Ho Chi Minh, and Che Guevara not finally appealing. Having left my childhood faith and home church over the issue of racism as a teenager, I had never quite got shed of Jesus, and I decided to give it all one more chance. I began to reread the gospels on my own after several years of activism. When I got to Matthew 5, 6, and 7, I recalled that I had never heard a sermon in my home church about the Sermon on the Mount—which I could now see was meant to turn the world upside down. I later learned that the Beatitudes and the Sermon on the Mount became foundational, formational, and catechetical teachings for all the new "followers of the way" (what people who decided to believe and follow Jesus were called before they were named "Christians"). But these teachings were never taught in my church growing up, and neither was Jesus's way discussed as a way of life, but rather as a system of beliefs. We were never taught the way of Jesus in my church, or that there even was one.

But it was Matthew 25 that really drew me in and turned me around.

I call it the "it was me" text. I was hungry, Jesus said; I was thirsty, I was naked, I was a stranger, I was sick, I was in prison. It was *me*. You either gave me food to eat or you didn't, you gave me clothes to wear or you didn't, you welcomed me as an immigrant or refugee or you didn't, you looked after me when I was sick or you didn't, you came to visit me when I was incarcerated or you didn't. Whatever you did or didn't do to them, you did to me—that's exactly what Jesus is saying here.

"Lord!" the people cried out (interestingly, all who were there thought they were his followers). "When did we see *you* hungry or thirsty or naked or a stranger or sick or in prison—and helped or didn't help you?" (I often say more lightly, "If we had known we would have at least formed a social action committee!") Jesus's reply just stunned me and invited me back to my faith: "Truly I tell you, just as you did it [or did not do it] to one of the least of these, you did it [or did not do it] to me."

It was a revelation that changed my life. Unusual for Jesus, this was a text of judgment for a teacher who was not normally judgmental. Depending on how they treated the least of these, and therefore how they treated him, he separated his would-be followers like sheep and goats who would either be invited to join him, "Come, you that are blessed by my Father, inherit the kingdom prepared for you from the foundation of the world" or they would "go away into eternal punishment." That clarity was welcome then to me as a young man finding my way; but it sinks in even deeper, now as an older man, as the most challenging test for all of us: to measure our lives by the well-being of those who are always most easily forgotten and invisible—Jesus's final test of discipleship.

That text had never been preached on in my home church either. It begins with, "All the nations shall be gathered before him." They and their people would be separated out by how they treated "the least of these." That is still true today—in all the nations, people separate out by how they treat the poor and vulnerable. For some religious believers it is central to their faith; for others it is nonexistent.

The people who have been my Matthew 25 tutors have usually been poor people themselves or those closely connected to the most vulnerable. My teachers have been people such as Mary Glover, who helped run the weekly grocery bag food line at the Sojourners Neighborhood Center, just twenty blocks from the White House. This powerful Pentecostal woman always said this prayer before hundreds of people came through for the food they truly needed: "Lord, we know you'll be coming though this line today, so help us to treat you well!" Hers was the best commentary on Matthew 25 I had ever heard, and I think I have read most of them. This was Jesus's last teaching before his arrest, death, and Resurrection. And I believe it was his final discipleship test.

In our current political situation, the ones Jesus called the least of these seem to be the ones most targeted. Therefore, in response, we are grateful to now see a "Matthew 25 Movement" that is growing and creating amazing stories, some of which I share here. Joe Scarborough, of *Morning Joe*, now speaks of "Matthew 25 Christians" who might bring us together around a commitment to the poor and vulnerable. A new "Southern California Matthew 25 Movement," their Mateo 25 movement, decided to mobilize around the stunning detention of an undocumented Pentecostal minister, in which ICE had separated him from his wife and children and was threatening to deport him. Young Latino and African-American leaders, many from Fuller Theological Seminary (the largest evangelical seminary in the country), organized across Los Angeles and around the country and eventually prevailed over ICE to set the pastor free and reunite him with his family. It was a great victory. The Matthew 25 movement focuses on three of our most vulnerable populations: undocumented immigrants, young people of color being racially policed, and Muslims under attack. I will tell stories here of people of faith defending people from these three groups and others who are vulnerable and targeted, which are extraordinary examples of applying Jesus to politics today. First, let's look at the text:

> *"When the Son of Man comes in his glory, and all the angels with him, then he will sit on the throne of his glory. All the nations will be gathered before him, and he will separate people one from another as a shepherd separates the sheep from the goats, and he will put the sheep at his right hand and the goats at the left. Then the king will say to those at his right hand, 'Come, you that are blessed by my Father, inherit the kingdom prepared for you*

*from the foundation of the world; for I was hungry and you gave me food, I was thirsty and you gave me something to drink, I was a stranger and you welcomed me, I was naked and you gave me clothing, I was sick and you took care of me, I was in prison and you visited me.' Then the righteous will answer him, 'Lord, when was it that we saw you hungry and gave you food, or thirsty and gave you something to drink? And when was it that we saw you a stranger and welcomed you, or naked and gave you clothing? And when was it that we saw you sick or in prison and visited you?' And the king will answer them, 'Truly I tell you, just as you did it to one of the least of these who are members of my family, you did it to me.' Then he will say to those at his left hand, 'You that are accursed, depart from me into the eternal fire prepared for the devil and his angels; for I was hungry and you gave me no food, I was thirsty and you gave me nothing to drink, I was a stranger and you did not welcome me, naked and you did not give me clothing, sick and in prison and you did not visit me.' Then they also will answer, 'Lord, when was it that we saw you hungry or thirsty or a stranger or naked or sick or in prison, and did not take care of you?' Then he will answer them, 'Truly I tell you, just as you*

> *did not do it to one of the least of these, you did not do it to me.' And these will go away into eternal punishment, but the righteous into eternal life." (Matt. 25:31–46)*

Here are some other commentaries on Matthew 25, in addition to Mary Glover's. Soong-Chan Rah, professor of church growth and evangelism at North Park Theological Seminary, says this about this famous scripture in *The Next Evangelicalism: Freeing the Church from Western Cultural Captivity*:

> Matthew 25 provides a vivid picture of the Judgment Day. In this passage, Jesus comes to judge the earth and divides humanity into the sheep and the goats. The judgment that falls upon the goats is unexpected, as the goats cannot believe that their inaction toward the poor merits God's judgment. The goats are expecting the praise of God for their other accomplishments. They can refer to a long list of material accomplishments for their church. They have built the beautiful buildings, established the successful churches and delighted in material blessings. Why then, are the goats being cast into the lake of fire? Because they have relied upon their economic and material prosper-

ity to measure their successes rather than recognizing that what they've done and not done to the very least of their brothers and sisters is the true measure of success.[1]

Lisa Sharon Harper, author of *The Very Good Gospel,* ties the Matthew 25 and Matthew 5 texts to Black Lives Matter. Solidarity for those regarded as unacceptable challenges society's respectability politics:

> To support #BlackLivesMatter means to support the reality that ALL black life matters, including those who would be seen by white power structures as the least respectable in society. The principle is very much in line with the principle of biblical shalom—the belief that until all of us have peace, then none of us has peace. It is also directly in line with Jesus's Matthew 25 call to do justice for "the least of these." This will challenge evangelicals, especially those who already struggle with the doctrine of grace. If one believes the call of the gospel is to be perfect, then "the least respectable" will disrupt comfortability. But we are called to consider another interpretation of Matthew 5's call to "be perfect as our Father in heaven is perfect"—the call to LOVE perfectly.[2]

The author of *The Politics of Jesus*, Professor Obery M. Hendricks Jr. at New York Theological Seminary, also comments on Matthew 25, and makes it clear that it applies to political leaders as much as it applies to everyone else:

> Indeed, in Matthew 25:31–46, Jesus makes it clear that betrayal of the poor and the vulnerable is among the worst sins possible. Moreover, there Jesus reveals that if nothing else will get one banished to Hell, hurting—even ignoring—those he calls "the least of these" surely will. . . .
>
> Jesus taught—and modeled—that what is most important for those who follow him is to spend their time and treasure in this world, engaging in loving, self-sacrificial actions with the express purpose of manifesting God's love and justice on earth as in heaven.
>
> For me, that is the standard by which all those who seek to lead or govern us must be judged.[3]

I will never forget an unexpected phone call from a well-known former congressman, governor, and even presidential candidate who wanted to talk about whether his policies to fight poverty were good ones because he knew as a Catholic if he didn't get that right the scriptures said he was going to hell! I always wished I got more calls like his.

Lutheran pastor and author the Reverend Nadia Bolz-Webber says Matthew 25 should not be politicized, even by the left side of politics, but is meant to draw us closer to Jesus:

> And as tempting as it seems when we read a Gospel text like this to think, *Look! Even Jesus agrees with us!* We are probably missing something . . . and we can so easily replace the conservative personal morality insurance plan for the hereafter checklist with a liberal social justice, here's what Christianity Really means checklist. Either way we end up not really needing Jesus so much as needing to make sure we successfully complete the right list of tasks. Because in the end every form of Checklist Christianity leaves Jesus essentially idling in his van on the corner while we say "Thanks Jesus . . . but we can take it from here. . . ."
>
> Jesus says I was hungry and you gave me food, I was thirsty and you gave me something to drink, I was a stranger and you welcomed me. Which means . . . Christ comes not in the form of those who feed the hungry but in the hungry being fed. Christ comes not in the form of those who visit the

> imprisoned but in the imprisoned being cared for. And to be clear, Christ does not come to us AS the poor and hungry. Because as anyone for whom the poor are not an abstraction but actual flesh and blood people knows . . . the poor and hungry and imprisoned are not a romantic special class of Christ like people. And those who meet their needs are not a romantic special class of Christ like people. We all are equally as Sinful and Saintly as the other. No, Christ comes to us IN the needs of the poor and hungry, needs that are met by another so that the gleaming redemption of God might be known. And we are all the needy and the ones who meet needs. Placing ourselves or anyone else in only one category or another is to tell ourselves the wrong story entirely.[4]

This really isn't about politics, as Nadia says, or about proving yourself right, and certainly not righteous; it is rather about becoming closer to Jesus. In retrospect, I came to understand how the people who raised me, and spoke of Jesus all the time, had so distanced themselves from the people he called "the least of these" that their isolated location in the world resulted in their becoming distanced from Christ himself—that is the deeper meaning of the text. Ultimately, that came to make me feel more sorry for them, rather than just mad, as I used to be.

That reality has come to me again and again. I remember a chaplain at a Christian college getting in trouble and ultimately losing his job for bringing people like me to speak at his conservative school. It helped make us friends! He ended up working with homeless people in his city instead, and later told me he had never felt closer to Jesus. Another megachurch pastor I know got into the same kind of trouble with his elders for standing up for the poor, for showing solidarity with Muslims being victimized by hate crimes, and for reaching out to LGBTQ people in his city when they were attacked. He too left the church he started and grew so large for the sake of Jesus, to instead help lead the work with the homeless and other people on the edge in his city. He also shared with me how that experience with the most marginalized made him feel closer to Christ than he had ever felt before.

## APPLYING MATTHEW 25

It has always been eye-opening to me how the Matthew 25 text can be applied to many issues—simply by looking at what happens to those on the margins or at the bottom. I have learned that is always the thing to look for when examining a public policy question—how are those who are most vulnerable going to be affected? This text always reminds me why I've learned the most about the world, and my own life and work, by being in the places I wasn't supposed to be and being with people I was never supposed to meet or become friends with. Matthew 25 is a text that continues to convert you over and over again in new ways.

For example, how would the Matthew 25 text apply to an issue such as climate change? That great environmental challenge led me to reexegete Matthew 25 in relation to the growing danger of a rapidly warming planet. The text made me see how virtually all who Jesus named as "the least of these" are already being affected by climate change and will be the ones most devastated by further changes in the future. For the hungry—it means the expectation of massive food shortages and starvation. The thirsty—more terrible droughts, as we are already seeing. The naked—stripping millions of all their resources. The stranger—the clear result of dislocating millions more as migrants. The sick—the spreading of more disease. The prisoner—more destabilization, chaos, poverty, desperation, and therefore crime.

That biblical exegesis of Matthew 25 shows us that climate change isn't just "another issue" among many to elevate on our list of priorities and see how it measures up to our commitment to ending poverty, promoting peace, and so forth. Rather, it impacts all the people we care most about—it's integral to all of those other issues. Pope Francis named it as such in his *Laudato si* encyclical, where he articulates an "integral ecology" that makes clear that our relationships to God, to our neighbors, and to the Earth itself are all interconnected and interdependent.

This text also challenges us as a society and political leaders as to how we treat "the least of these." It is not just a personal examination but also the test of a nation's righteousness and integrity. "Nations" are included in the text, meaning not modern nation-states, which were unknown then, but "the peoples" who made up nations. Indeed, Matthew 25 should be the test of our politics. The least of these should be at the top of our political agendas when, most of the time, those are the very last people whom candidates and politicians generally talk about.

## THE MATTHEW 25 MOVEMENT

As the election results came in on November 8, 2016, and it became clear that a result unanticipated by the vast majority of media outlets and political pundits had taken place, many people found themselves reeling, largely out of fear for the groups of people who would find themselves uniquely vulnerable under the new administration. As people struggled to come to terms with what had happened, "What can I do?" was the question I heard most, and it's what I asked myself. Matthew 25 became an answer to that question.

The direction of national politics was indeed beyond our control—but we could control what we do with our own faith and with our own actions. I began to see the Matthew 25 text talked about in fresh ways across the county from different people in different places—and it was spreading so fast that it began to feel like a movement of the Holy Spirit.

The very familiar gospel text seemed to be saying to us, "Here is what we can do: Stand up and defend those most at risk at this crucial moment in America's political history." Matthew 25 began rising up in the face of a new political regime that was making so many people feel so afraid.

A new Matthew 25 pledge began to emerge throughout the country with local organizers and congregations. Retreats brought together pastors, heads of churches, grassroots activists, and the leaders of national faith-based organizations and networks who prayed and discerned together about the election results and reached a consensus to act in solidarity with those most at risk in the new administration. It was called the Matthew 25 Pledge. It's just one sentence and simply says, *"I pledge to protect and defend vulnerable people in the name of Jesus."*[5]

It was so simple and yet so powerful—at such a dangerous moment when so many were feeling so fearful. Why were people afraid? Because many of those vulnerable people were specifically targeted in the presidential campaign of the candidate who became president. Even before the inauguration on January 20, an alarming number of minority people, as well as their children, had been verbally attacked. "Go back to Mexico!" Hispanic children were told. "Watch out for the police now!" black teenagers were warned by some of their white classmates, with some of them pointing to who won the 2016 election.

Because it was absolutely clear from Matthew 25 that Christians are always called to serve Jesus by sheltering those most in need, the hope came that this could perhaps be a unifying commitment between people of faith on different sides of the political aisle—to protect the most vulnerable together.

Clearly, many people in America were feeling quite vulnerable: racial and religious minorities, women, and LGBTQ people—and especially those who sit at the intersections of marginalized groups. Three groups became a starting point, offered by a broad group of diverse national and local faith leaders and activists.

The pledge had three simple commitments:

1. *Support undocumented immigrants threatened with mass deportation.* Arresting and deporting hardworking and law-abiding people who have lived in America for decades would break up families and potentially put people's lives in danger. Among the most at risk were young "Dreamers," who were brought here as children and who turned in their names and contact information to the administration in response to previous executive orders that allowed them to study and work without fear of deportation.

    Prayerful networks of support were set up in faith communities to offer love, welcome, assistance, and ultimately, resistance to block and obstruct a new wave of deportations. If massive arrests of the people Jesus calls "the stranger" were ordered, immigration police would be forced to arrest many of those immigrants in our churches, seminaries, schools, and homes. Faith communities had the capacity to impose a clear domestic cost on any efforts aimed at massive deportation of those who had become our neighbors and fellow churchgoers. And now we were pledging to do so.

2. *Stand with African Americans and other people of color threatened by racial policing.* Black pastors and parents were especially concerned about how their young people would be treated under an administration that had already fueled racial bigotry and continued to stoke those fears by early cabinet appointments. The new president had already promoted "law and order" and "stop and frisk" in the uncritical code language that racial minorities understand all too well. And if there was little or no accountability from the federal government after January 20 to law enforcement exercising excessive force against our citizens of color, and especially young people, local clergy were promising to hold their police departments accountable.

For Christians, when one part of the body suffers, as it says in 1 Corinthians 12, the whole body should feel that pain and respond. Therefore, racially diverse local clergy from ecumenical and interfaith associations could join together and go to their sheriffs in every community and offer to help support healthy community policing. But they could also promise to watch, monitor, and resist any racial policing by standing against such practices and standing with those they are aimed at, promising to hold law enforcement accountable to racial equity and healing in our communities. That was our pledge.

3. *Defend the lives and religious liberty of Muslims threatened with "banning," monitoring, and even registration.* We also wanted to say that US citizens and immigrants who practice their Islamic faith in this country are our friends and neighbors, and are our brothers and sisters as fellow human beings and children of God. Many Christians, Jews, and others who believe in religious liberty began promising that if Muslims living in America, whether citizens or immigrants, were ever asked to register based on their religious identity, their fellow Christian and Jewish believers would proudly line up before them to declare ourselves to be "Muslims too." That would be a dramatic tactic to make clear that many people of faith would never accept a religious test for entry into the United States. The

new threats from Washington were making many believe that their Christian faith should *compel* them to act—by advocating for and welcoming refugees of all faiths into our country instead of turning them away based on their religion and race. Religious tests and bans, in addition to being morally repugnant, would threaten our nation's democratic principles and the constitutional rights of every American. Our pledge was clearly saying that the violation of the religious freedom of our Muslim brothers and sisters would not be accepted by other people of faith.

This was the beginning of a new Matthew 25 movement. Rather than just watching, grieving, and feeling sorry for what was happening to the most marginalized, we proclaimed the gospel in the twenty-fifth chapter of Matthew, and Christians pledged to join together in circles of support and defense—in the name of Jesus. *A gospel text was the foundation of our actions, not partisan politics or ideology.* We believed that in unjust times, justice often starts in the small places and personal decisions that challenge the big places and structural injustice.

## THE "STRANGER" IN WASHINGTON, DC, AND SOUTHERN CALIFORNIA

Immigrant families are faced with an administration crackdown on undocumented people. Children are afraid to go to school, families are avoiding medical facilities, and some people have expressed their fears of even going to church, where they might be targeted and detained by Immigration and Customs Enforcement (ICE) agents—whose numbers the president has increased as part of a stronger deportation force.

According to a Pew Research survey, about half (47 percent) of Latinos nationwide worry about themselves or someone close to them being deported.[6] Given that the US Latino population is fifty-seven million and growing, that's nearly twenty-nine million people who today are living in fear. Many of the estimated eleven million undocumented immigrants in the United States have loved ones who do have legal status, and these blended families are in greater danger than ever of being separated by our broken and inhumane immigration system.

Here in my own city of Washington, DC, a church shelter was targeted. ICE officials surrounded, questioned, and detained six Latino men who had just left

Rising Hope United Methodist Mission Church's hypothermia shelter in the dead of winter. Their whereabouts were unknown, despite the attempts of area activists, faith leaders, and the church's pastor, the Reverend Keary Kincannon, to obtain information from ICE.

Keary was part of the Sojourners community back when he was a seminarian—and, coincidentally, had just preached at a Sojourners chapel service a few days before. He spoke powerfully of the role we all play in the task of creating God's Kingdom on earth "as it is in heaven," as the Lord's Prayer calls us to do. Keary felt both devastated and outraged that their church shelter for the homeless was targeted by the government to locate and detain undocumented immigrants.

"In the twenty-one years that we've been doing this ministry of sheltering the homeless, I've never seen anything like this before," he told us. "God makes no distinctions between us whether we're undocumented or documented. Our role is to love people the way Jesus loves people regardless of their immigration status, regardless of their faith, regardless of their political affiliation; we are just to love all people."[7] At an early-morning prayer vigil in front of ICE headquarters in Alexandria, Virginia, I heard Pastor Keary

Kincannon lift up the words from Matthew 25: "I was a stranger, and you did not welcome me." Their Rising Hope Mission Church signed the Matthew 25 pledge.

One of the best and ultimately hopeful stories of the Matthew 25 movement came from Southern California, and it also illustrates the capricious cruelty of this administration toward society's most vulnerable.

Pastor Noe Carias was going for a regularly scheduled ICE check-in in Los Angeles. Pastor Noe, married to a US citizen, had never committed a crime beyond his longtime undocumented status from coming into the country at age thirteen with his parents, escaping violence in Guatemala. Now he is the Pentecostal pastor of a thriving Assemblies of God congregation in the Echo Park area of Los Angeles.

But instead of going out with his family for dinner after his typical routine check-in, Pastor Noe was handcuffed, detained, and told he would soon be deported. He was immediately taken to a detention center in Adelanto known for its deplorable conditions.

"We were in shock," said the Reverend Alexia Salvatierra:

> Pastores Melvin and Ada Valiente, co-chairs of Mateo 25, quickly began to organize a united

movement to help Pastor Carias. Pastor Melvin arrived in this country from Guatemala in 1981 when he was a youth during the civil war, and Pastora Ada arrived from Nicaragua as a child in 1972. They both understood the experience of terror and violent chaos; they both knew how a child fleeing Central America would feel and how little that child would know about how to seek asylum. In March, Matthew 25 SoCal went into high gear.[8]

Mateo 25 got letters from church leaders of every Protestant and Catholic denomination in Los Angeles and Orange County. Pastor Noe had been accompanied to an earlier appointment with ICE, where he had received his third stay of deportation, and that group set up a meeting with the deputy director of ICE, whose father, they learned, attended an evangelical congregation. They began to work with the largest networks of Hispanic pastors in Southern California to organize regular prayer meetings and collect signatures on petitions to set the pastor free. They reached out to national allies such as Sojourners, the Christian Community Development Association, and NaLEC (the National Coalition of Latino Evangelicals) to lift his case to a national audience. They began to use social media to get the news out.

The campaign learned that ICE now had "internal mandates to detain and deport people whose only offense was an immigration violation—regardless of the status of their case"—for the first time in more than twenty years. Then, of course, the government began a campaign of falsehoods to discredit and degrade this Pentecostal pastor who had contributed so much to the community.

But Pastor Alexia, who is known as the "godmother" of organizing in Southern California, said this:

> We knew we could not give up. We stood on the word, "We are troubled on every side yet not distressed; we are perplexed but not in despair; Persecuted but not forsaken; cast down but not destroyed; always bearing about in the body the dying of the Lord Jesus, that the life also of Jesus may be manifest in our body." (2 Corinthians 4:8–10)[9]

"Instead of despairing," she said, "we took the campaign to another level."

District superintendents of the Assemblies of God were brought together to petition the general superintendent of the denomination, which has 3.5 million adherents in the United States alone and more than 67 million worldwide.

While there is still some separation between Spanish-speaking and English-speaking members, Dr. George O. Wood, the English-speaking general superintendent, became so "passionate" about the situation that he wrote a letter to the White House, and followed up with a visit—then led national prayers for Pastor Noe at their convention.

The Mateo 25 campaign's strategy was characterized as "national pressure with local persistence." Alexia described what they did next:

> Still determined, we reached out to Matthew 25 leaders around the country in congressional districts with a member of Congress who was on the Homeland Security Committee to see if we could garner support and pressure from above. Vicky Carias was like the persistent widow, speaking to whomever would listen. Pastora Ada Valiente contacted the mayor of Los Angeles and the Guatemalan Consulate to advocate directly for Pastor Carias, and they gladly accepted. Hundreds of emails and calls from Christians all over the country came into the ICE director's office—and we had direct evidence that the director and deputy director were actually reading and listening to them. Local and national media—from CNN to Brave New Films—picked up the story.

> Still, weeks went by without a response as Pastor Carias became sick from the terrible conditions at Adelanto and his wife and children went through psychological torment. . . .
>
> Matthew 25 SoCal was able to hang in there and keep struggling partially because of the unusual Ephesians 2/John 17:21 character of our network: immigrant and second-generation Hispanic evangelicals working together across lines with multicultural and Anglo evangelical and moderate mainline churches. It's a lively stew in which we are committed to prioritizing the perspective of those who are most affected and walk together in intimate solidarity. The miracles of faith required to work together across the lines fuel our capacity to sustain the struggle. We hope that this can become a replicable model across the country.[10]

On Friday, September 22, 2017, after fifty-nine days of detention, Pastor Carias was suddenly and unexpectedly released. The pictures of his children and wife running to him with all of them crying were "achingly beautiful."[11]

In an interview with Sojourners' Jessica Cobian shortly after his release, Pastor Noe spoke movingly of how even in a time of deepest trial for him and his family, he didn't stop being a pastor to other vulnerable people and modeling the way and teachings of Jesus. Even in the detention center,

> God was always with me, and from the first moment that I stepped foot in to the facility. . . . The following day, I began to hold services inside the detention center.
>
> Seventeen people had a reconciliation with Christ while we were there. . . . I had an incredible experience inside the detention center, because even though my family was outside, I understood that God had a purpose for me inside, since I was preaching. The last Wednesday that I was there, I had an incredible experience with God, and he gave me a lot of strength. And miraculously, the next day, he allowed for my release.[12]

Developing replicable models for such solidarity with immigrants; lifting up local examples of standing with young people of color; building trusting relationships between police and the community; holding law enforcement accountable for racial equity; and acting to build relationships among Muslims, Christians, and

Jews with a readiness to defend the religious liberty of everyone are all part of the growing Matthew 25 movement now.

After a long walk on the beach during my summer vacation, a former SWAT team leader and now deputy police captain said to me, "You would be surprised how many people on my side of things are listening to what you and others are saying." Young black pastors are playing crucial roles in linking young people and police chiefs into new conversations toward greater trust, and the young organizers from the streets are making sure that we will never forget the names of Trayvon Martin, Rekia Boyd, Michael Brown, Sandra Bland, Eric Garner, Kendra James, Tamir Rice, Natasha McKenna, Yvette Smith, Philando Castille, Cynthia Fields, Walter Scott, Stephon Clark, and so many more. Local pastors and imams are reaching out to get to know one another, as the moving story from Memphis in chapter 2 describes.

## BRINGING A TEXT TO THE CAPITOL

Can a text such as that in Matthew 25 be brought even to Congress and the White House?

"A budget is a moral document." That was my opening statement at a news conference and prayer vigil of church leaders across from the steps of the US Capitol in 2017. We represented a wide spectrum of the Christian families of America—Protestant, Catholic, Evangelical, African-American, Hispanic, Asian-American, Pentecostal, Orthodox; all part of our Circle of Protection, which was founded in 2011 in service of the biblical mandate to protect poor and vulnerable people. "*A budget is a moral document*," I repeated with energy and passion.

This was originally a statement of principle from the religious community, said to politicians a decade ago. Some politicians now quote it, and even some media pundits point to it, but it was a religious statement from the beginning. I know that because I remember the time when we first offered it to both Democrats and Republicans.

Any budget is a moral statement of priorities, whether it's a budget created by an individual, a family, a school, a city, or a nation. It tells us, mathematically, what areas, issues, things, or *people* are most important to the creators of that budget, and which are least important.

Leaders from Christian families across the theological and political spectrum were speaking together with one voice—saying that the budget cuts envisioned by the White House in 2017 would harm vulnerable people and devastate families living in poverty. It was very significant that the Circle of Protection's first statement after the 2016 election came from such a broad base of Christian leaders, and was focused on protecting those whom God calls us to serve and defend. Despite differences on many other issues, we have consistently come together to form the Circle of Protection around the poor—"the least of these" in the critical budget decisions in Congress—and to ask our legislators across party lines, especially those of faith, to do the same. As Galen Carey, the vice president for government relations at the National Association of Evangelicals, correctly pointed out at our press conference, no federal program is perfect and reforms are often necessary, but "there's a difference between reforming and dismantling" these programs.[13]

Here are parts of the statement we made in response to the proposed White House budget in 2017:

> God instructs us to protect the poor and vulnerable. Jesus tells us to serve and defend "the least of these." The biblical prophets remind us that how we treat the most marginal and vulnerable among us is the test of a nation's moral righteousness—telling kings and rulers that the measure of their governance is the well-being of those most in need. . .

> This budget proposes major cuts to programs for the poor, hungry, weak, sick, and most vulnerable. The lives of low-income African-Americans, Latinos, Native Americans, Asian-Americans, and poor white Americans would be disproportionately impacted. . . .
>
> We do not support sharp increases to defense spending that are made possible by corresponding reductions in non-defense discretionary spending, particularly in programs that help the poor and vulnerable. The biblical prophets teach us that our security depends in part on upholding justice for people in poverty.[14]

As the statement indicates, the Circle of Protection is most powerfully united by the biblical text of Matthew 25. And it's not hard to see why: every category of vulnerable person and situation Jesus names were and are threatened by spending decisions and other policies contemplated by the White House and its allies in Congress.

Jesus said, "I was hungry and you gave me food." Cutting Meals on Wheels, SNAP, and WIC to pay for more tanks is a moral choice. Cutting essential humanitarian foreign aid to a famine- and conflict-riven world to build more weapons is also a moral choice.

Jesus said, "I was sick, and you visited me." Cutting, rationing, and ultimately ending Medicaid as a health guarantee for our poorest and sickest people is a moral choice.

Jesus said, "I was a stranger, and you welcomed me." Demonizing our immigrants and refugees and planning to build a wall against them—that more cuts to the poor would be used to pay for—is a moral choice.

Jesus said, "I was thirsty, and you gave me something to drink." Cutting environmental protections and risking more communities' water getting contaminated like Flint's so shamefully did even under an EPA that actually believed in protecting the environment is a moral choice.

Jesus said, "I was in prison, and you visited me." Mass incarceration systems and policies based on race that disenfranchise men and women of color is a moral choice.

Jesus said, "I was naked, and you clothed me." Cutting programs for the poor while simultaneously making tax cuts for the rich strips the most vulnerable of what little they have and is fundamentally a moral choice.

We have continued to take the gospel text of Matthew 25 to those in power now, as we have done before, and remind this Congress and this White House, as we have done before, that *a budget is a moral document.*

Like budgets, the tax code is also a moral document, a social contract on how we are each going to do our part in sharing our resources with our communities, our neighbors, and those most in need. The fact that the Republican tax bill in 2017 revealed profoundly misplaced moral priorities is why we felt compelled to engage in civil disobedience to contrast the bill's moral priorities with what the Bible says, as discussed in chapter 7.

## "I WAS SICK"

Many of us also came together in opposition to the congressional and White House efforts to cut health care for millions of people—again, for the sake of the most vulnerable, especially those who rely on Medicaid, or it remaining illegal to deny people coverage based on their preexisting health conditions. Countless numbers of individual constituents called, wrote, and met with their members of Congress; activist groups of all kinds took part in major public actions and civil disobedience in Washington; and the protests of disabled people (sometimes in their wheelchairs) and parents of children with complex and life-threatening health conditions helped spark the conscience of the nation. It took the work of everyone to voice their support for the basic principle that all Americans should have the right to quality, affordable, lifelong health care—regardless of their age, location, or income.

During the final consideration of the health care bill, I joined a group of faith leaders in holding a prayer vigil just off the Senate floor, encouraging senators to heed Jesus's words in Matthew 25. Many senators passed right by us on their way in to vote, surprised to see us, and asked why we were there. "Praying for you and your vote," we said, and then asked each one, "Do you want us to pray for you?" Many said yes, please, and came into our circle for prayer as we laid hands on their shoulders.

We stood outside the Senate gallery door, with heads bowed, eyes closed, our hands on the shoulders of a senator or each other. And we prayed. I'm grateful to have had the opportunity to pray with senators from both parties who voted against the bill—as well as a few Republicans who didn't vote "no" but said they felt the need for our prayers.

Without all of these powerful words, contacts, prayers, and actions, the result of the vote could have been very different. We celebrated that victory for defending health care that momentous day but have watched politics chip away at health care for people ever since—showing us that our work is never done. We must remain vigilant and always ready to respond.

## THE DILEMMA OF ABORTION

Matthew 25's focus on the most vulnerable could help us find better paths forward even on the most complicated and divisive issues. For example, abortion, where there are *two* vulnerable lives at stake. A total of 75 percent of women who get abortions are low-income and 86 percent are unmarried.[15] To have an unwanted pregnancy when you are low-income and alone is to be vulnerable. And a potential life growing in the womb is, obviously, also vulnerable.

And, of course, women across our country and the world experience genuine and dangerous vulnerability because of the realities of sexism and the oppressions of gender, which are contrary to the will of God.

In the midst of unwanted pregnancies there are often inequitable male/female power dynamics and sometimes the outright abuse of male dominance. Adding to injustices in male sexual power there are also situations that women often find themselves in—with inequitable pay and benefits; lack of maternal support;

inadequate health care and affordable child care for working mothers, even including lack of basic nutrition; and very different frameworks of economics and career between men and women. So not to admit that women are typically more vulnerable in sexual and family relationships; in the economic, educational, and career structures of society; and, obviously, because it is their body that holds a pregnancy, is to ignore and deny reality.

It also must be admitted, as many "pro-choice" women say, that many of the "pro-life" men who are against abortion do indeed seem to want to control women's bodies, and are consistently unsympathetic to women's rights and equality in both the society and the church.

As every parent in history has learned, the potential and growing life in the womb is the most vulnerable of all—completely dependent on the body of the mother and the care of the parents or parent. Time spent by expecting parents to protect the vulnerability of the life they are waiting for is the overwhelming fact of their lives during their pregnancy.

The vulnerability of the emerging life requires continual medical instructions and monitoring, health care requirements, eating and drinking restrictions, discipline, and exercise, as well as the constant care, caution, and attention of the parents or parent. The way science is moving toward earlier realizations of fetal viability only morally complicates the decision-making.

Yet, not all of those who express moral concerns about the vulnerability of the potential life wish to control women's bodies—especially pro-life feminists and progressives who are equally committed to women's equity and equality.

So how can we find ways to respect and protect the vulnerability of the pregnant mother's body and life, along with the vulnerability of the growing body and life of the emerging child within?

The issues of "life" and "family" have become extremely politically divisive. "Pro-life" and "pro-choice" are now fighting words and turn complicated questions into ideological battles for one over the other—either "for the women" or "for the babies," turning empathy for only one life into single-issue voting on both sides of the political spectrum. How do we go deeper and get better than that? How do we protect vulnerable life in the womb without criminalizing an often tragic and vulnerable choice? Are there any commonsense, commonground solutions to be found that we could agree to or at least compromise on? Solutions will need to show compassion for two vulnerable lives and what science and conscience are teaching us.

Even survey data tells us there's a whole lot more overlap on life issues than the pundits admit. According to the Public Religion Research Institute and a recent Vox poll, 18 percent of Americans and 27 percent of millennials say they are *both* "pro-life" and "pro-choice." Twenty-one percent and 22 percent, respectively, say they are neither.[16] Many Americans want to work together holistically to reduce the number of abortions rather than work against each other fruitlessly.

How could we, *together*, across ideological lines, agree to focus on significantly reducing both unwanted pregnancies and abortions in America, by directly and deeply addressing the circumstances that create such painful choices? All the data shows that providing health care, nutrition, access to free or affordable contraception, and economic progress for low-income women does indeed actually reduce the number of abortions. Can followers of Jesus agree on a consistent "ethic of life" that also includes opposition to the violence of poverty, war, capital punishment, and oppression against all of God's children—including and often especially women, and including both the born and the unborn? Only being pro-birth is simply not the same as being pro-life.

Can we also be honest about the fact that the dignity of human life is more protected by committed covenantal sexuality than it is by casual recreational sexuality? Can we face the reality that recreational sexual behavior outside of committed relationships helps create toxic cultural attitudes and behaviors that lie underneath many of our most difficult and painful social, psychological, and spiritual problems?

Again, it is often a matter of privilege, with affluent people having the freedom and finances to put their sexual pleasure and freedom ahead of the dignity and well-being of others; and they have resources to get away with it—with guilt-free abortion a requirement for such sexual "liberation." But the same ethic of promiscuity becomes so much more destructive for low-income, vulnerable young people and families, causing great dislocation and deeply destructive consequences for the prospects of healthy and successful families. For the rich, settling down after playing around as much as possible has become an ideal lifestyle; but for the poor there are often lifelong consequences for following the cultural ethic of sexual freedom.

I believe it is important to start by saying how much we strongly support marriage—and that we have to begin there. Through this controversial debate, I deeply hope that our country can come together around a new conversation—about how we can all recommit ourselves to marriage and all that comes with it—monogamy, fidelity, and for many of us, parenting. We are losing marriage in this society. While there are many single parents who do a wonderful job taking on the challenges of raising children and holding families together, I believe that if we lose a critical mass of healthy marriages and two-parent families, we are in very serious trouble.

Considerable research in the past few years demonstrates that family itself can be one of the best ways to help protect vulnerable people. As I explained in *The (Un)Common Good*,

> Here are the facts: the poverty rate for married couples in 2008 was 6.4 percent, while for nonmarried, single-headed households, it was 36.5 percent. . . . Isn't it time to get beyond the sound bites and examine the barriers to marriage in low-income communities—for example, our broken criminal justice system and the massive incarceration rates for men of color from poor communities? Or the lack of the kind of jobs that can support a family in vast stretches of poor urban and rural America? Or the number of jobs low-income people need to

> have to pay their bills, and the time that working so many hours takes away from children and family? Yes, let's talk about renewing marriage and family values and overcoming the real obstacles to it.[17]

When it comes to the "abundant life" Jesus promises in John 10:10, it includes the freedom to make choices that help all of our lives flourish. Given Jesus's exemplary treatment of women against the patriarchy of his day, he would clearly include wanting women to flourish as well as men. And Jesus also pulls all of us toward the choices that especially protect the lives of all the most vulnerable. Pro-choice and pro-life labels would likely not well describe the wholeness of Jesus's examples of showing compassion and dignity for all the lives that most need it—especially the most vulnerable ones.

Overcoming the painful and polarizing battles on abortion will never be possible unless we can come together on the principle of the sacredness and sanctity of *all* lives. That means upholding the dignity and image of God in both mother *and* unborn child—and not choosing one or the other's life and dignity to the exclusion of the other.

It is time to move beyond judgment and recrimination. Rather, we need a time of serious reflection; dialogue; understanding; and most of all, for reconsideration of what it means to be deeply committed to abundant life for all concerned—especially vulnerable women, children, and families. In seeking after that truth and striving after consistency in this issue, we will come face-to-face with the need for reconciliation between battling ideological forces.

Many voices need to be heard if we are to determine how to support the dignity and abundance of life and the focus on the most vulnerable in policy on abortion—but especially women's voices. I am the author of this book and a man. And no matter how many women I talk with about these difficult challenges, I will never fully understand the dilemmas, traumas, and tragedies that women go through in such difficult decisions.

## BACK TO MARY GLOVER

The growing momentum behind the Matthew 25 Pledge reminds me of my old friend and mentor Mary Glover, whom I mentioned at the opening of this chapter. She helped me understand the deepest meaning of that gospel text. She was not a theologian or formal biblical commentator, but she showed and taught me the meaning of this scripture many decades ago. Matthew 25 brought me to Christ out of the student movements of my time and led me to help begin Sojourners. We moved into one of the poorest parts of Washington, DC, in the neighborhood where Mrs. Glover lived.

After a while, and in response to growing need, we joined with neighbors to start a simple food line on Saturday mornings, where many people lined up just twenty blocks from the White House to get a big bag of groceries that would get their families through the week. Volunteers, who actually needed their own bags of groceries, helped to collect the food and came to put the grocery bags together each week before we opened the line. Once everything was ready, we prayed. Mary Glover, a powerful Pentecostal woman of faith, would always pray; she prayed like someone who knew whom she was talking to, and it was clear that she and her Lord were in regular communication.

I remember Mary Glover's whole prayer still vividly today. She prayed, "Thank you Lord, for waking me up this morning; that the walls of my room were not the walls of my grave, and my bed was not my cooling board." Then Mary always concluded her prayer with these words: "Lord, we know that you will be coming through this line today, so Lord, help us to treat you well—help us to treat you well. Amen." (I lifted up Mary Glover's prayer so often that it eventually became included in the World Council of Churches' prayer book!)

She was able to see Jesus and to point to him in the hungry people coming through the food line. "I was hungry, and you gave me something to eat. . . . As you have done to the least of these you have done to me."

Mary Glover became an elder to me as a young Christian man, often setting me straight about many things. She did not have much formal education and was a cook in a day-care center who made little money, but she was one of those spiritual leaders who holds neighborhoods together. She showed me where to find Jesus more than any seminary professor or academic theologian I had ever met or read. Mary knew you find Jesus among the most vulnerable members of society: the hungry, the thirsty, the stranger, the naked, the sick, the prisoner—the people Jesus names in Matthew 25 when he says how we treat them is how we treat him.

Mary Glover has passed now. I often miss her but know we would have talked about all of this if she had lived to see the results of the 2016 elections. She would have loved to see a movement around Matthew 25 rising up—and would have been proud to be one of its founders! No matter what the politics said, Mary Glover would have always said, "Lord, we know that you'll be coming through this line today, so Lord, help us to treat you well."

# Chapter 10
# Becoming Salt, Light, and Hope

You are the salt of the earth. . . .
You are the light of the world.

—MATTHEW 5:13–14

What does reconnecting with Jesus mean as we go into the world? How do we see him, recognize him, and follow him? Does reconnecting with Jesus mean reclaiming a way of life or style of life that we can look for?

In his Sermon on the Mount, Jesus lifts up the values of what was literally "a new order" that he came to bring—named the kingdom of God—and then he compares living and walking in this "way" (the early

Christians were first referred to as "followers of the way") to being the "salt" and "light" that the world so desperately needs.

In what are called the Beatitudes, Jesus lays out his vision of the new kingdom of God. It's like a charter or constitution, the clearest and simplest framework for what the new order he came to bring will look like. The Sermon on the Mount and the Beatitudes, in particular, were used by Jesus's disciples to teach others, especially new believers, in the new way of Jesus; this was the church's first catechism. Again, this raises the troubling question of why Jesus's Sermon on the Mount and his Beatitudes get so little attention in American churches today.

One after another Jesus describes those who will be "blessed" and "happy" in this new order of things and how they will turn the world upside down. They will be the poor and poor in spirit, those whose empathy can make them mourn, those who are meek or humble, those who are hungry and thirsty for righteousness and justice (words that in the scriptures often mean the same thing), those who are merciful toward others, those who are pure in heart and therefore have integrity, those who are peacemakers or conflict resolvers, and those who are persecuted for righteousness's sake—for doing the right thing.

These qualities of life, or behaviors, become the signs and signals of the kingdom of God. They are the characteristics of the new order. They comprise how the kingdom begins within each one of us and goes into the world—and is meant to change the world. Living this way, by doing and being these things, is how the kingdom will come.

Those who follow in the way of Christ, in these ways, will not only be blessed and happy in their own lives. They are also essential for both the preservation and the changing of the world, as Jesus describes later in the Sermon on the Mount.

They will be the preserving "salt of the earth" and the shining "light of the world." In the midst of everything else in this world, the flavor and brightness of Jesus's followers will be felt in families and communities; in the economy's workplaces; throughout social services, secular and religious; in the many institutions of civil society; and even in the political order and the many groups trying to change it. Of course, the followers of Jesus are supposed to come together to shape the life of congregations to become Jesus communities. Local, national, and international faith communities are intended to become corporate signs of the kingdom and are meant to impact the neighborhoods, cities, regions, and nations where they live and even impact international issues and crises. And the followers of Jesus, with their communities, will sometimes even create social movements in history (along with morally like-minded people who are not religious) addressed at particular evils when the times call and cry out for that—and all of this personal and collective impact will help keep changing the world.

They will be like *salt*, a *preserving* and stabilizing force, to preserve, protect, and deepen the values and behaviors that human cultures most need to keep and enhance. Jesus said to his followers, "You are the salt of the earth," to literally preserve the important things that sustain and undergird human societies. This is a quality that conservatives often admire—keeping cohesion and positive communal values intact and formative like the glue that often holds things together, values such as honesty, integrity, compassion, fairness, faithfulness, fidelity, and dedication to raising our children in ways that are good and right and for the sake of service to others.

The followers of Jesus will also be like *light*, shining into the darkness *revealing* what is wrong, untrue, and a danger to human life and dignity—and needs to be changed. Jesus said to his disciples, "You are the light of the world," revealing the things we should not let darkness cover up or make us accept—things that should be different. This is what liberals or progressives are often drawn to. Exposing injustice, the light helps point to and promote social, racial, and economic justice where and when it is most needed, because those commitments and goals are integral to the gospel of Jesus Christ. Only when light shines will the darkness go away. The light also serves as a beacon that others can see and be drawn to, modeling loving God and our neighbor in ways that show what true love and justice look like. And remember, as Cornel West has said, "Never forget that justice is what love looks like in public."

Therefore, perhaps being "salt" and "light" transcends political ideology; maybe each undergirds the best of both conservative *and* liberal political philosophies—one preserves what we need and one shines a light on what has to be seen and changed. As I often say, don't go left, don't go right; go deeper. Go deeper into the moral values that a society most needs in the forms of salt and light.

The presence of salt and light in the world is also where our "hope" comes from. As I have often said, *hope is not a feeling, but a decision*; not a mood, but a choice; and one based on faith. When we are both preserving what is good and shining a light on what is bad, we offer hope for both nurture and change. We are not limited by what is, nor do we need to destroy all of what is to change what needs to be changed; rather, we can have the "prophetic imagination," as Walter Brueggemann has taught us, to see how things could and should be different and better. Like salt preserving the food we need to eat, and light ending the darkness and showing us the way forward, we are called to be in the presence of Jesus Christ and his kingdom in the world. When we demonstrate both perseverance and courage in these roles of salt and light we can help both sustain and transform people's lives, root our communities in the most important values, and keep moving our world toward the kingdom of God—which is both here and yet to come, and which was always intended to change the world that God so loves.

To preserve, to shine a light, and to make the decision to hope: these are the substances of our vocation as Jesus followers. Timing is everything, and there is no better time for that spiritual vocation than right now.

## CHARTER FOR A NEW ORDER

Let's look more closely at the first part of the Sermon on the Mount in Matthew 5:

*Now when Jesus saw the crowds, he went up on a mountainside and sat down. His disciples came to him, and he began to teach them.*

*He said:*

*"Blessed are the poor in spirit, for theirs is the kingdom of heaven.*

*Blessed are those who mourn, for they will be comforted.*

*Blessed are the meek, for they will inherit the earth.*

*Blessed are those who hunger and thirst for righteousness, for they will be filled.*

*Blessed are the merciful, for they will be shown mercy.*

*Blessed are the pure in heart, for they will see God.*

*Blessed are the peacemakers, for they will be called children of God.*

*Blessed are those who are persecuted because of righteousness, for theirs is the kingdom of heaven.*

*Blessed are you when people insult you, persecute you and falsely say all kinds of evil against you because of me. Rejoice and be glad, because great is your reward in heaven, for in the same way they persecuted the prophets who were before you.*

> *You are the salt of the earth. But if the salt loses its saltiness, how can it be made salty again? It is no longer good for anything, except to be thrown out and trampled underfoot.*
>
> *You are the light of the world. A town built on a hill cannot be hidden. Neither do people light a lamp and put it under a bowl. Instead they put it on its stand, and it gives light to everyone in the house. In the same way, let your light shine before others, that they may see your good deeds and glorify your Father in heaven." (Matt. 5:1–16,* NIV*)*

I have been struck by how much the Beatitudes from Jesus's Sermon on the Mount have come up on news shows since the 2016 election as such a stark contrast to the language and behavior we see coming from the White House, especially with such seemingly hypocritical silence and support from white evangelical Christians. Bringing such dramatic contrasts to light may be a redemptive consequence of political behaviors that so dramatically violate the fundamental gospel principles that people of faith claim to adhere to.

Even the nonreligious sense that what they see and hear from the current president of the United States, and those Christians who support him, is so different from what they perceive Jesus taught. As author and professor Craig S. Keener explains,

> Inequities of this world will not forever taunt the justice of God: he will ultimately vindicate the oppressed. This promise provides us both hope to work for justice and grace to endure the hard path of love. . . .
>
> Until my conversion in 1975 I professed to be an atheist in part because I looked at the roughly 85 percent of my fellow U.S. citizens who claimed to be Christians and could not see that their faith genuinely affected their lives. I reasoned that if even Christians did not believe in Jesus's teachings, why should I?[1]

Professor Keener, who went on to become a professor of biblical studies, comments on the Beatitudes, "If we truly repent in light of the coming kingdom, we will treat our neighbors rightly. No one who has humbled himself or herself before God can act with wanton self-interest in relationships."[2]

Ethics professor Glen Stassen has a good contrast to the more traditional interpretations of the Sermon on the Mount that he describes as "God's transforming initiatives." More than any other commentator, Glen expresses my own view of that sermon:

> The Sermon on the Mount is not about human striving toward high ideals but about God's transforming initiative to deliver us from the vicious cycles in which we get stuck. It has a realistic view of our world, characterized by murder, anger, divorce, adultery, lust, deceit, enmity, hypocrisy, false prophets, and houses destined for destruction. It announces that in the midst of such bondage, there is also another force operating: God is also beginning to rule with justice and peace, like mustard seeds beginning to grow or leaven beginning to spread, as Jesus said in Matthew 13:31–33. . . . The Sermon on the Mount describes specific ways we can participate in the new initiatives that God is taking. . . .
>
> [T]he sermon does not offer a way of cheap grace, a way of vague passivity. God is taking transforming initiatives, and we are asked to participate in what God is doing, imitating God's initiatives.[3]

And activist Lindsey Paris-Lopez comments on the powerful resonance of the Sermon on the Mount in our current political and moral emergency:

> Jesus's lessons in the Beatitudes and throughout the Sermon on the Mount seem so far removed from our national ethos. We refuse to acknowledge the deep, systemic racism and violence at the core of our cultural consciousness all the while touting our exceptionalism. . . . The Sermon on the Mount is a call to resistance . . . it uproots and overturns a conventional order built on and maintained by violence.[4]

## SIGNS OF SALT AND LIGHT

When I was busy writing this chapter on the meaning of salt and light, I took some time out to go to the funeral of a friend. Andre Pressey was a baseball umpire during all of the twenty-two seasons that I was a Little League baseball coach—and we became friends. Hundreds of people were there. And there was a point in the service that the program called "Family/Friends Tributes (2 minutes)." A long line began to form, and I heard one person after another tell how much Andre loved them—not just saying it but also showing it. Many talked about how much Andre loved his own children and gave everything he had for them. But other young people came up, apologizing for not being experienced in public speaking, but wanting to say how much Andre loved them too, spent so much time talking with them, helping them, protecting them, and guiding them.

Friends told their testimonies of all the personal and practical things Andre did for them day after day. "He changed my oil, fixed my brakes, always took me where I needed to go, cared about what I was going through." His classmates and teammates from Wilson High School talked about what an amazing basketball and baseball player he was—his team's lead-off hitter remembered Andre as the clean-up hitter about whom people would bet to see how long it would take him to hit one out of the park. "He was the one who could have played pro ball." But he looked after his teammates better than anyone else (not something the best players are always known for). The president of Andre's class was there and cried (and there were many tears around the church) when he spoke about how Andre took care of them all, and that is what he will *always* be remembered for. In all the stories, Andre was often the "glue" that kept things together for people wherever he was. I said that Andre was much more than just a great umpire, but also a great coach on the field—teaching kids how to play, training them in good baseball and sportsman-like behavior, and always protecting their safety—all with a smile on his face.

Everyone spoke about how Andre was a mentor to them both on and off the field. I told those gathered for him that Andre the umpire was also the one you could always see loved everybody on the field. Andre was a strong African-American man who was thanked by many for standing up for them when that was needed—always ready to fight for them when something was wrong. But every white kid was also the center of his attention when they walked up to the plate.

The stories about Andre went much longer than two minutes, and when the pastor stood up to finally give the official funeral sermon, he said, "The eulogy has already been spoken." Then Andre's preacher read the text he had prepared and specifically chosen for this day to remember and celebrate Andre's life. It was the text of this chapter, the one I was already working on: "You are the salt of the earth. . . . You are the light of the world." It was the fitting text for someone who had always lived that way.

Look around. Think about Jesus's Beatitudes, which signal the new order he came to bring. Where are the events and who are the people that show us what "salt" and "light" mean today?

The Parkland students come to mind for me, speaking and acting after the horrible loss of their classmates to gun violence in 2018. Like many of you, I was watching and listening very carefully to the students who were speaking out and mobilizing after seventeen of their friends, classmates, teachers, and coaches were killed in another mass shooting with an assault weapon. Now they were turning their grief into action. They no longer felt safe going to school every day and couldn't understand how the older generation and their lawmakers have accepted this situation in which we all now find ourselves: that all Americans are no longer safe at their schools, theaters, concerts, and places of entertainment regardless of where they live.

So the students decided to protect themselves, each other, and their eventual children. Their salt and light began spreading all across the country among a generation that knows how to use social media to mobilize better than any generation before. Their shared values will serve to preserve and protect lives, and to shine a light on what needs to change with our gun laws and regulations.

Likewise, those who bore witness at the Standing Rock Indian Reservation in North Dakota in 2016 have become some of the most important and prophetic leaders protecting God's earth in America today—especially given the threat to our environment that our nation has yet to take on seriously. There is no better example of what the struggle to protect God's creation looks like now, and may look like in the future, than the "water protectors" at Standing Rock, who put their bodies on the line for months to stop the Dakota Access pipeline from being built on sacred tribal lands and endangering the water supply of indigenous people. Native Americans were joined by people of every color and creed, including clergy and military veterans, to prevent the construction from moving forward, despite attacks from private security forces and state law enforcement.

Standing Rock shows that large, multiracial coalitions are still willing and able to come together, first of all in prayer, and then to face enormous adversity, suffering, and even state-sanctioned violence to stand up nonviolently for the rights of disadvantaged groups and the health of the planet. Because of the spiritual witness of the Standing Rock leaders, this spirit of prayerful resistance can infuse and empower us all in years ahead as we carry out our promise to deliver a habitable planet to our descendants and a more equitable world for all of God's children.

The "Dreamers" have also been both salt and light. An issue that has seemed hopeless much of the time, including demoralizing setbacks in 2018, is the debate over our country's broken immigration system. Despite the defeat of legislation that would have protected the Dreamers and offered them a path to citizenship, these brave young people, who are Americans in every sense except their documentation, are continuing the fight to stay in the only country they have known, and to protect their families as well. These eight hundred thousand young people go to school, have jobs, have started businesses, and have served in the military. The way the Dreamers have told their stories and come out of the shadows since the Obama administration's establishment of DACA (Deferred Action for Childhood Arrivals) in 2012 has led to overwhelming public support for them staying in the United States—as many as 80 to 90 percent of the American people.[5] Despite their political defeats, the Dreamers have refused to return to the shadows and also have refused to be used as bargaining chips as this administration seeks to fundamentally restructure legal immigration in this country in ways that will keep families apart and to actually decrease the number of immigrants in America—both undocumented *and* legal. Their courage has, again, changed the narrative, which will ultimately change policies.

Women who marched into the streets after the inauguration in 2017 and many who then headed toward becoming new elected officials after the midterm elections of 2018 have been one of the most powerful and hopeful signs of salt and light in these dangerous times. Women who often provide the love and glue that keeps things together in their families and often serve as "salt" in their communities are also speaking and acting to be "light" as well in our political and moral emergency. The women who have found the courage to stand up to sexual harassment and assault, creating the #MeToo movement, are shining a light on our patriarchal culture, while some of the men who have called out their male peers also give me hope.

Women are also changing the narrative in churches and families. My wife, Joy Carroll, was one of the first women ordained in the Church of England—she is a Brit! And in the United Kingdom she is well known as the real Vicar of Dibley (after the hit television show in which she was a script consultant). One summer we went to the Greenbelt Festival, where we had first met, with our four-year-old son, Luke. Joy was up on the stage celebrating the Eucharist for twenty-five thousand British young people. Our young son, sitting on my lap, was watching his mom lead the service. She would speak and people would respond, as in "The Lord be with you . . . and also with you." She would also ask them to do things, and they would. After watching this for a while, Luke looked up at me and asked, "Dad, can men do that too?" Women in ministry are changing the narrative in the church, the society, and in our families. Doing that offers the salt, and through their visible witness in churches and the world—like when Joy wears her collar—they offer a light that proclaims equality and equity for women denied for so long by both church and society.

This is just one example of why representation is so important in the church and in the culture, in real life and in fiction. When children can look up to real or fictional heroes, and want to be them when they grow up, it expands their sense of what is possible and pushes back against the traditional exclusionary structures when those heroes come from historically marginalized groups. That's why it's so welcome and indeed overdue to see recent developments in pop culture such as Black Panther, Captain Marvel, and Wonder Woman showing that large-scale commercially successful blockbusters with women and/or people of color in the protagonist's role are both possible and welcomed by the vast majority of people. Or, to give another real-life example, that's why the photo of the little boy touching Barack Obama's hair is so iconic and affecting for so many people. The point of much more inclusive depictions of leaders and heroes is not only to demonstrate to girls and children of color that they can be whoever they want to be, but also to show boys and white children that leaders and people we most admire can come from all races, genders, and walks of life, as Joy's priesthood has taught my boys. And for people of faith, this is also a central theological point, that all of us are made in the image and likeness of God—no exceptions.

One of the most powerful signs of change are all the young people of color standing up for what is right and for a better future for *their* children, despite the odds against them, in movements such as Black Lives Matter, and with other young people standing beside them—which is giving many of us a hopeful vision of long-term racial progress, right in the face of the repressive racism of the current regime in Washington, DC. Lots of salt and light going on there. They are providing some of the best organizing of new activist infrastructures in their communities, getting people together and shining a light of accountability on police violence. The black pastors who are willing to speak the truth to power and protect the young people in their church youth groups and those who no longer come to church from increasing racism, by finding themselves in the streets—and not just in their pulpits—are also offering both salt in the streets and light to the society.

Over the past few years, the public revelations of so many tragic killings of young men and women of color, and the rise of a new generation of activists in response, are awakening many people. Because of the power of the witness of black young people in particular, I even hear more white young people ready to speak the truth when they say things like, "If we acted more Christian than white, black parents might have less fear for their children." That discussion is indeed sparking new and deep conversions in and outside of the churches about "whiteness" as an idol, and not just an ideology.

A sign of hope for me is when I see Americans seriously discussing the difficult and deeper questions about the state of race in America—underneath the narrow media and political discussions that still mostly leave "race" out of our public discourse. Beneath the narrow mainstream focus on polls and politics, a deeper conversation is now occurring, which is just what our nation most needs right now. Since the 2016 election, and in some ways because of it, I have seen black, Hispanic, Asian, indigenous, and white voices *together* embracing America's growing diversity and asking how we can build that bridge to a new America. And that's a discussion I almost never hear about in the mainstream media—or in official and "respectable" politics, either conservative or liberal.

I believe that this conversation will take us deeper than politics to a spiritual movement to change politics. As Desmond Tutu often reminded us, we need the "spirituality of transformation." And as Pope Francis told us, building bridges rather than walls is a faith vocation. We have to change the very narrative of race in America, where privilege and punishment are still direct outcomes of skin color, and make it absolutely clear that such a narrative and reality can no longer be accepted or tolerated by the followers of Jesus.

I also believe that many young people, sometimes called the "none of the aboves" because they are reluctant to affiliate with religion and check the "none" box on religious affiliation forms, have still not given up on Jesus. Most still believe in God, if not the religion that has turned them away. But they won't settle for a faith that doesn't make a difference in the world, and that's why they are, for me, signs of salt and light that could even help transform both our churches and our society. Some of the nones even show up at some kinds of churches. My friend pastor Joel Hunter once started one of the biggest megachurches in the country—Northland, A Church Distributed, in Orlando, Florida. But instead of megachurches he now works with "minichurches" in high schools, colleges, and workplaces where often young people sit in circles and talk about how to find and preserve the message of Jesus in changing their lives, their communities, their nations, and their world. And Joel's work with the most vulnerable homeless people in his county has brought him "closer to Christ than I have ever felt." The Reverend Dr. Martin Luther King Jr. famously and painfully said fifty years ago that the most segregated hour in America is 11:00 a.m. on Sunday. But I am in churches now where a new generation is transforming themselves into multicultural communities, and some of these churches have average ages in the twenties—including my family's home church in Washington called The District Church, with pastor Aaron Graham.

Pope Francis has said, "[F]amily is the salt of the earth and the light of the world; it is the leaven of society as a whole."[6] Many of my best and most hopeful experiences are with families who do sports together and end up sharing parts of their lives together, even creating some salt and light. Families can get closer and stronger through their children's sports. We are a baseball family, with our two boys playing on many teams over the years with multiracial teammates, coaches, and leadership in the organizations shaping those programs. The sign outside our front door reads, WE INTERRUPT THIS FAMILY FOR BASEBALL SEASON! I have been a Little League baseball coach for eleven years and twenty-two seasons, and my wife, Joy, has been commissioner at every level. Playing baseball really does bring you closer together. My sons, Luke and Jack, have always said their baseball teammates were their best friends, and at every level of Little League, my players would always testify in our final team meeting of the season how they had become such close friends—and how it felt like a "family." We have often seen how being teammates together really does help overcome racial bias and prejudice, because it is always proximity that finally helps human beings understand one another and learn empathy.

Every black player I ever coached in Little League has had what's called "the talk" with his or her dad or mom—a conversation on how to behave and not behave in the presence of a police officer. It's a talk designed to protect young black men and women from their law enforcement officials where racial bias remains deep and dangerous. This is a talk that *all* black families have, including our young black baseball players, whether their families are low-income or DC elites—with many of both living in Washington, DC.

When I point out that *none* of our white players have ever had that talk, and that few of their parents even know about it, the faces of white parents often look uncomfortable. Does it bother us as white parents that black parents have that talk with their kids when we don't, that our kids' black teammates have all had that talk? When moms and dads, especially moms, talk with each other about their hopes and dreams and *fears* regarding their kids, it becomes a bonding experience—but it doesn't happen much across racial lines. Baseball can help create those relationships and those talks. And when young white players learn about the talk their black teammates and schoolmates have to hear, it makes them angry. It's a great opportunity for white parents to hear from black parents about their mutual hopes and fears for their children's lives. White parents can ask, "How did you feel when you had to tell your son he couldn't trust the law enforcement officials who are supposed to protect him?" White parents can ask themselves, "How would I feel if I had to have that 'talk' with my children?"

The conversation between parents of different backgrounds and between teammates of different backgrounds has a way of powerfully revealing both the values we all have in common—like what we all want for our kids (salt)—while shedding *light* on the deep structural inequities that need to be changed that directly impact the lives of our children. I've even noticed that white members of the House or the Senate, from both parties, who have more open, understanding, and positive attitudes toward the importance of racial justice, are often those who have had long careers in sports on multiracial teams.

When it comes to "light," I also witness a plethora of young videographers and filmmakers, committed journalists and investigative reporters, writers and poets, and musicians and spoken-word artists who are shining the light on so much of our darkness. And a new generation, including my own children and their companions, are offering hope for their dreams and the lives they intend to live—not bound by the limitations and the despair of this moment. There are so many inspiring stories, and many offer the salt and light that the Sermon on the Mount speaks to, some of which we are telling in this book.

## TIME TO GO DEEPER

I often quote Hebrews 11:1, which says, "Faith is the substance of things hoped for, the evidence of things not seen" (KJV). Then I paraphrase the text as, "Hope means believing in spite of the evidence, then watching the evidence change."

Many of the signs of salt and light above are striking precisely because these issues seem so big and hopeless—and are occurring in the context of an administration that has proven explicitly hostile to addressing these systemic problems. Yet we nevertheless see these signs of hope.

These examples remind us that the believers' Resurrection hope we have in Jesus Christ flies in the face of the evidence of this world, and yet we believe in spite of the evidence. Thanks to the courageous actions of many of the people most affected, we may finally see some of that evidence change.

We do have a serious political, religious, and moral crisis in America—and it's likely going to get worse before it gets better, given the polarized politics we now confront. If we are going to survive this crisis; or better yet, respond to it; or *best* yet, put our faith into action to turn dangers into opportunities, we are going to have to go deeper, to be more deeply rooted, in three ways.

First, by going deeper into our faith, whatever that is to us. That means going back to the disciplines and practices that bring that faith to mind and heart—to life each day—must become regular in our lives and schedules. Time, space, and quiet are necessary to deepen faith; we have to stop sometimes in the midst of all the noise and busyness to listen and let go to God.

Second, by going deeper into our relationships to each other. It is especially important to do so across racial lines because of how divided our politics have become. Who our real friends are, who comes for dinner, who our kids have their play dates with, who we share our stories with about our kids and our own lives—will all shape our understanding of the world and of ourselves. What we think and say about a more diverse church and society will be heard; but what we do and whom we do it with will be seen, and ultimately have the most impact on, our congregations, our communities, our country, and us.

Third, by going deeper into our relationships with the poor and vulnerable. What we do and how we treat the most marginal, as we discussed in the previous chapter, will be Jesus's final test of our discipleship. Of course, God loves all people, so that is really a silly point to make. But Jesus always wants to remind us of the people who are most invisible, left out, and left alone in our world—those who are the targets of the politics we have right now. And if we believe chapter 25 from the gospel of Matthew, and act on it, that will bring us in closer proximity to Jesus Christ himself.

Our faith traditions all tell us that there is always hope—but only if people decide to act. And *the decision to show up is what makes change possible*, even in perilous and polarized times. None of us is strong enough to hold up under this relentless onslaught of darkness alone. Not me, and not anyone else. In such a time, justice-minded people have three choices: *burn out*, breaking down and giving up; *shut down and shut out*, retreating into cynicism or private concerns; or *root ourselves firmly*, in our faith in God, our relationships to each other, and our solidarity with the poorest and most vulnerable, who are at greatest risk. We need both sustenance and strategy—not just to keep going, but also to thrive and find the joy we need to live, even in times such as these.

## HOPE IS A DOOR

The more I wrestle with this word "hope," the more I am convinced that we must see hope in a different, and indeed a more biblical, way. You see, hope is not simply a feeling, or a mood, or a rhetorical flourish. It is a choice, a decision, an action based on faith. Hope is the very dynamic of history. Hope is the engine of change. Hope is the energy of transformation. Hope is the door from one reality to another.

Things that seem possible, reasonable, understandable, even logical in hindsight—things that we can deal with, things that don't seem extraordinary to us—often seemed quite impossible, unreasonable, nonsensical, and illogical when we were looking ahead to them. The changes, the possibilities, the opportunities, the surprises that no one or very few would even have imagined just become history after they've occurred. What looked before as though it could never happen is now easy to understand.

The news from the women at the tomb was the greatest hope that the world has ever known. And yet what did the male disciples first call it? "Nonsense." Hope unbelieved is always considered nonsense. But hope believed is history in the process of being changed. The nonsense of the Resurrection became the hope that shook the Roman Empire and established the Jesus Movement. The nonsense of slave songs in Egypt and Mississippi became the hope that let the oppressed go free. The nonsense of a confessing church stood up to the state religion of the Nazi regime. The nonsense of prayer in East Germany helped bring down the Berlin Wall. The nonsense of another confessing church in South Africa helped end apartheid. The nonsense of a bus boycott in Montgomery, Alabama, became the hope that transformed a nation, and the nonsense of saying "Black Lives Matter" defends and continues that transformation today.

This is also how personal transformation takes place. We can't imagine ourselves different than we are today or healed of what binds, afflicts, or addicts us. We can't imagine ourselves forgiven or healed. We can't imagine our own salvation. But when we walk through the door of hope, and we look back at where we have been and where we are now, we see evidence of the grace of God.

For Christians, the Resurrection is that door of hope, and Jesus showed us that the Resurrection comes via a cross. Suffering and hope are always joined in human history. The cost of moving from one reality to another—in our personal lives and in history—is always great. But it is the only way to walk through the door of hope.

Easter is a desperately needed reminder every year that pain, loss, and death don't get the final word. The resurrection of Jesus Christ teaches us that there always is and always will be hope—we do not carry that hope in vain. And *that* resurrection hope is one we can see mirrored in our lives and current events, if we know where to look.

I believe in the Resurrection—the actual historical resurrection of Jesus Christ from the dead. Both my faith and my hope absolutely depend on the resurrection of Jesus. I remember a conversation I had, many years ago, with some of the Jesus Seminar New Testament theologians. One of them asked me, "Do you actually believe in the historical resurrection of Jesus Christ?" I felt the eyes looking at me. "Yes, I do," I replied. "Well, the resurrection is more metaphorical for us," they said. I silently pondered their statement, and whether to start again the endless theological debates about the reality and meaning of the Resurrection in the Christian apologetics. It has all been said before. Instead another question came to mind, so I asked them, "Do you think a merely metaphorical resurrection would have been adequate for Desmond Tutu in South Africa?" The question brought silence to the table and ended the conversation.

Believing in this resurrection helps me more easily see the continuing signs of hope in our world, and our moment. Believing helps me to continue to trust that hope can indeed be *greater* than all the pain.

History depends on those who are willing to walk through the door of hope, those who live and act and even die in hope of a future they know by faith is there—such as the women at the tomb who were given the news of the Resurrection and then opened the door for all the rest of us.

## SPIRITUAL PRACTICES

Let me suggest some practices for the kind of time we are in—for how to embody salt and light in these dark days.

1. *We need to start each day with a "yes" to our faith and to our own personal and public integrity.* There is so much to say "no" to every day now, it is both spiritually and emotionally important to begin every day by saying "yes" to what we believe. We need to say "yes" to engaged citizenship, civil discourse, service to what is right, and courageous resistance to what is wrong. We need to have our "no" begin with a deeper "yes."

2. *Then we need to have the courage to say "no" when that is required and to do whatever is required.* This includes the public arena, the political sphere, in the media and culture, in schools, in workplaces, and especially in the church. It will mean sometimes saying "no" to fellow Christians, and possibly even to members of our own families, when they defend and support ideas and actions that are antithetical to the gospel. It means constantly asking for conversations in churches about our gospel values. It also means not waiting to say "no," or to stand in opposition to what is wrong and dangerous until we see how others will respond. We need followers of Jesus who will not be among the last to

react to breaches of moral and civic behavior, but who will count the cost and show their commitment to justice by being some of the first.

3. *Every day, we need for our "devotions" to hold our Bibles in one hand and the news in the other.* That is the kind of regular devotion and discipline that will serve us in times such as these. Faith must not be allowed to be privatized and kept to only personal matters. Faith must go public, as it was always intended to do. Keep the Constitution close too! Personal faith must make itself felt in public life, especially in a time of public crisis.

4. *We need to answer the biggest challenges ahead by acting on our faith rather than reacting from our emotions.* The habit of responding by acting, and not just complaining and reacting, is central to our spiritual, emotional, and even physical health. Respond to genuine outrages with a deeper commitment instead of cynical anger. And ultimately, learn to respond to hate with a deeper love. That is always the hardest thing, but clearly what the followers of Jesus are called and guided to do.

5. *Spend even more time with our families, not less because we are too busy.* Our children and grandchildren need to know what is going on, and how we and they can respond to it. Try to explain things to them, pray over things that happen in the world with them, and don't try to keep them from seeing or understanding dangerous things. Work to protect them by helping them interpret those things, and by assuring them that we will be together through it all.

6. *Pray, and pray for particular people who will be playing critical roles in the outcomes of political and moral events in our country and the world.* Commit to praying for the courage of the press—including media reporters, broadcasters, columnists, editors, producers, and owners—that they would search earnestly and endlessly for the truth and have the courage to print and otherwise tell it. Also pray for the judiciary to face the hardest questions with a commitment to the rule of law more than the rule of politics. Pray for the leaders in Congress, and all its members, that they would understand themselves as a separate legislative branch of government that holds an absolutely

necessary check on the executive branch, which shows such danger of going out of control. Our scriptures instruct us to pray for all our political leaders, so let us genuinely pray for the president—that he would not see himself as absolute, but rather be humbled to become a public servant.

7. *The opposite of fear is trust, and when fear is the political energy of a nation, we need to rebuild the trust. So let us work and pray to grow in our trust of God, our friends, and our community.* Even if life in this country continues to spiral morally downward, let us be the ones to trust in faith, hope, and love, the three most important things that 1 Corinthians 13 names—and to believe, as the apostle says, that the greatest of these is love. We must ask ourselves each day what it will mean for each of us to be ready to act in faith, in hope, and in love to whatever we are confronting.

These spiritual practices can help us reverse our distance from Jesus and find some paths back to him, which is now the task before us. By responding to this crisis of church and state and culture, those who want to see themselves as followers of Jesus can reestablish a deep and passionate connection with the meaning and message of Jesus Christ.

## THE ROAD AHEAD

As important as protest is, we have to build a movement of what we are *for* and not just what we are *against*. We must go beyond simply reacting to the crazy and dangerous things that happen every day. That can be exhausting, which is, I believe, even part of the plan of the current administration. As important as protest is, each of us has to also be faithful to our own callings in direct response to the crisis we face in America.

I encourage you to read the biblical passage from 1 Corinthians 12:4–31. Verses 4–11 talk about how we are each given unique gifts for unique kinds of service. Verses 14–21 give the body analogy so familiar to many of us—that we are many parts but one body. People have different God-given abilities to use for speaking, serving, caring, helping, protecting, or healing in any time, especially in times such as these. Give this text a good meditation. That means we need to be good teachers and students; artists and activists; nurses, doctors, and other caregivers; lawyers, entrepreneurs, and union organizers; service providers and advocates; pastors, preachers, and laity who lead churches; and workers of every kind in every vocation, all ready to stand in resistance and stand for a better way in what we are facing in this country.

Frodo speaks well to what we are now facing in J. R. R. Tolkien's *Lord of the Rings*, and Gandalf speaks well to a biblical response:

> "I wish it need not have happened in my time," said Frodo.
>
> "So do I," said Gandalf, "and so do all who live to see such times. But that is not for them to decide. All we have to decide is what to do with the time that is given us."[7]

We have only so much control over what happens in the world. As Gandalf reminds us, we don't choose the times we live in, but it's often the case that the times choose us. What that means about how we live out our calling to be salt and light will be different for each of us—different gifts and callings, but all for the common good. Speaking the truth and acting on behalf of what is right will take all of us to the deepest levels.

Preachers should preach ever more prophetically, teachers should teach formation and not just information, writers should write ever more honestly, lawyers should fight courageously for those who need their help, reporters should report the facts ever more diligently and speak the truth to power regardless of what the powers think about that, and artists should make art that nurtures people and makes them think and inspires them to create and act. People who know climate change should fight on climate change, people working for living wages and economic justice should keep organizing, people working for racial justice should continue to build the bridge to a new America, those who work for human rights, voting rights, women's rights, immigrant rights, refugee rights, and LGBTQ rights should keep defending and advocating. We all should serve those around us. We all should always watch for people being left out and alone.

But even in putting our heads down and doing our work ever more diligently, we can't silo ourselves off from each other—we need to stay connected, communicating with one another, and coming together for larger moments and movements of solidarity. Movements are not just events—they are made from many people doing things in their own places and being aware that many others are acting just as they are elsewhere.

In the midst of the painful, shameful, and embarrassing examples of religion selling its soul for power, more and more of us will make clear that we are reclaiming Jesus. Being salt and light in Jesus's name is central to what the world always needs and most needs right now. How do we preserve the values and commitments most necessary for a healthy society, and how do we shine a light on what is wrong and needs to be changed? Both will take courage in times like these. But such courage comes from the hope that is always the best contribution from people of faith. The time we are in is indeed a test for our democracy, but it will also be a test for our faith. May God be with us.

# Epilogue
# The Light of the World

It began with a group of "elders" who met at the beginning of Lent 2018. We were starting to believe that the "political crisis" many were feeling was also revealing a "crisis of faith." We were seeing that this crisis of moral conscience could even be compounded by a constitutional crisis. And we came to believe that a fresh confession of faith in this time of crisis was now required.

Several of us had been talking with one another, and Bishop Michael Curry and I decided to call for a retreat together. As presiding bishop of the Episcopal Church, he hosted us in his New York City official church residence. It was the right time with the right group of diverse leaders from across the spectrum of the churches. The Reverend James Forbes, one of the nation's greatest preachers, said, "We were waiting to be convened and both of you have convened us." We prayed together and experienced a deep sense of lament for our political and moral crisis and the ways we have also been complicit in its unfolding; our first response was communal confession. We confessed our sins on behalf of the churches and our need for repentance, realizing that this word, in Christian, Jewish, and Islamic traditions, means much more than guilt and shame, but a "turning around" and moving in a new direction.

Our concerns were about the future—of our nation's values, heart, soul, and even democracy itself—and they compelled us to respond more theologically than politically, where what we *believe* is the foundation of the things we must vocally *reject*. We agreed that the future of the nation's soul, and the integrity of faith, were indeed now both at stake. Over the season of Lent that followed that Ash Wednesday, we decided to pray, discern, and write a response.

From the beginning of our prayers and discussions, we were adamant that this not be just another "statement" for people to sign or not, but then ignore. We would be the only ones to put our names to this "declaration," not just with our signatures but with our commitment to commend a fresh call to reclaim Jesus in our time and to act on it ourselves as we called others to do the same.

We decided to follow the liturgical arc we were already in beginning with Ash Wednesday and repentance. Throughout Lent, we committed to God our prayer, confession, and collaborative work on finalizing the declaration. We shared the new declaration with some other church leaders and then on Palm Sunday put it up as a full-page ad in one of the nation's premier political publications to make a simple statement to the elected officials and the Washington media, highlighting the clear choice that the dramatic events of Jesus's Palm Sunday pilgrimage into his capital city made clear: Which king are we going to follow? We went on record that "When politics undermines our theology, it is time to examine that politics."

In the Easter season we celebrated our crucified and risen Lord, and recalled with joy how the early church made clear after the Resurrection that "Jesus is Lord," which was clearly perceived as a political statement in a time when Caesar believed that he was. We had decided to call ourselves "followers of Jesus" in the declaration, rather than just Christian leaders, though we all were. But given the low state of many people's perceptions of religion now, we wanted to identify not with Christianity but with Jesus.

We decided that our fresh confession of faith, not politics, would be officially launched in the churches and faith communities on Pentecost, when Christians commemorate that first movement when the Spirit of the ascended Christ descended upon the early believers, who took their faith to the streets.

When the "Reclaiming Jesus" declaration was announced by two dozen church elders across all our church families on Pentecost 2018, an extraordinary event occurred. Scheduled for a Thursday evening, May 24, following Pentecost Sunday, expectations for attendance were modest. One of the biggest churches in downtown Washington, DC, was selected for the launch, with some of the organizing staff for the event just hoping the sanctuary would appear mostly full to those attending and watching via live stream. Yet when the night of the public launch arrived, National City Christian Church overflowed with thirteen hundred people, as did Luther Place across the street—our "overflow" church, which had a projector and a big screen showing a live feed of the service—with seven hundred more. Still hundreds more stood or sat on the beautiful church steps at National City, but no sound was reaching them from the service inside.

People of all ages huddled together watching the service on their phones via Facebook Live—desperately trying to hear. That's when a monastically dressed man in a white robe appeared and asked if he should go fetch his Bluetooth speaker from his car trunk. "Yes!" was the reply. The crowd cheered his solution, but when he set up the speaker on the top of the steps, he confessed he didn't know how to get the wonderful sounds of the church through the speaker to the outside congregation. "Oh, I can do that," said a teenage girl who had overheard the conversation. And she did—through her cell phone, channeling the beautiful music of the Howard University Gospel Choir and powerful words of courage and hope from the elders inside the church to all over Thomas Circle, where people were sitting on benches just listening. A hundred thousand more around the country watched on Facebook Live.

The speaker on the steps from the monk and the teenager was only the first of what felt like many miracles that night. The second was that all the renowned national preachers that night each stuck to their five minutes! During the service, Dr. Barbara Williams-Skinner, one of our African-American elders, whispered in my ear that she could "feel the fear lifting."

During the service launching the Reclaiming Jesus declaration, I made the statement, "Tonight is not about Donald Trump, it's about Jesus Christ!" The crowd's deep response to that simple statement showed how hungry they were to return to the core of their faith in Jesus, as opposed to merely reflecting and submitting to the polarized political divisions of the country.

Following the service, three thousand people (many of them wearing church collars but also including lots of young people) processed in silence to the White House, carrying little battery-powered candles that shone all over Lafayette Park and Pennsylvania Avenue, bringing the light of Christ into our present political and religious darkness. The six core declarations, which had been read out in the elder reflections to spontaneous applause in the church, were now repeated as we moved in a circle together on the sidewalk outside the gates of the White House—offered with the Pentecostal prayers of the gathered Christians from around the country. No one was there to officially receive the declaration, but we all believed it had been delivered, and the fact that the service was reported in 282 media stories that reached 219 million readers confirmed that.

It felt like Pentecost. There was a strong sense from all of us that this was just the beginning of a Reclaiming Jesus *movement*, in this time of political and religious crisis. From a declaration to a movement was the hope and the prayer of the elders from the beginning.

Through these liturgical weeks, Reclaiming Jesus had become not a statement to sign but a call to answer.

A Facebook video simply with the faces and voices of the elders reading from the statement had a million views in the first five days, a million more in the next five, and ended up reaching more than *five million people* (you can watch the video at www.reclaimingjesus.org). It has already been translated into several languages. Clearly, the hunger for listening to Jesus again had an overwhelming response across the country and around the world.

This message of reclaiming Jesus has enabled Christians, and others, in the United States and in many other countries whose leaders have responded to participate in reclaiming Jesus, to courageously clarify what reclaiming Jesus means for times such as these and really for any time. It has also given some new hope even to people who are not Christians or who used to be.

That special night reminded us all how Pentecost, historically, was the beginning of the early Jesus followers taking their faith public after literally hiding together in an upper room. Empowered by the Holy Spirit, they brought their faith to the streets, and that too is what we decided to do again. With our candles passed out at the church, we established candlelight prayer vigils as the signs and symbols of this new Reclaiming Jesus movement in our country. First in the overcrowded church sanctuaries and then on the sidewalk outside the White House gates, we declared that "Jesus is our light" and that the "light of Christ" is our way of pushing back the darkness.

The heart of the declaration, which is really more of a pastoral letter to the churches, is the six declarations that embody a "we believe" therefore "we reject" confessional framework we had agreed to on the Ash Wednesday retreat. Taking in and taking stock of these six declarations is an important way to understand the unique danger of this political and spiritual moment, the distance that presently exists between Christians and a Jesus that too many Christians desperately try to avoid, and some fundamental cores of Jesus's ministry and meaning that can help us find our way back to him, even and especially amid this fearful time.

As we look toward what the future will hold, what reclaiming Jesus will look like in the months and years ahead, and why reclaiming an authentic witness to what it means to follow Jesus is so urgently necessary, I keep thinking about light and darkness, and my mind is drawn again and again to the gospel of John, which begins with an image of Christ as light. "The light shines in the darkness, and the darkness has not overcome it" (1:5 NIV).

I just loved the question that came from some of the people planning to come to the Pentecost launch of the

Reclaiming Jesus declaration in 2018. They asked, "Do we need to bring our own candles?"

It was a practical question, but it drew me to thinking about what we were doing that night in stark, almost elemental terms: the vigil, and our declaration calling us to reclaim Jesus in this moment, were both figuratively and literally about light and darkness. A candlelight vigil has clear theological significance for us: the good news of Jesus Christ—his life, death, Resurrection, and teachings—must be our light that we shine amid the current darkness in this time of political and religious crisis.

In the news that we see every single day, there is a darkness that has infected the heart of our faith and our democracy. And the truth is that it's almost certainly going to get worse before it gets better. Yet merely focusing on all the growing darkness and even just keeping up with all of the daily scandals and outrages can be a morally and spiritually exhausting task. Naming the darkness is crucial, but we must not become overwhelmed by it or, worse yet, even get caught up in it.

*Here's where the light comes in.* The call to reclaim Jesus: that Jesus needs to be reclaimed and is worth reclaiming is being responded to by millions of people in America and around the world—representing both individual and collective light in the darkness. It shows that there are Christians everywhere who are determined not to be complicit or silent as their faith is hijacked for political ends, nor as their democracy and rule of law are hijacked for the personal gain of corrupt leaders and their families, friends, and wealthy allies.

The thousands who overfilled and then spilled out of those Washington churches in May 2018 were just the vanguard of a much larger spirit that is bringing the light of Jesus to this dangerous moment in our nation's history and in the history of Christianity. This isn't about politicizing our faith. Rather, it's about bringing the wisdom, the insights, the truth, and yes, the light, of our faith to bear on our politics and our politicians. This isn't bringing politics into faith but rather bringing faith into politics, to confront it, transform it, and—as Jesus did in the temple just before his death in another capital city—to upend the corrupt tables of religion and politics.

This is neither the first nor the last time in history that the symbolism of a *candlelight vigil*—of a host of lights together shining in the darkness—has been used in dark political or religious times and made a difference. Candlelight vigils were widespread in South Africa during the struggle against apartheid and were among the tools that helped end it.[1] In the mid-1980s in the Philippines, peaceful demonstrations including candlelight vigils culminated in a nonviolent intervention in 1986 led by Cardinal Jaime Sin that toppled the dictatorship of Ferdinand Marcos.[2] In South Korea, in 2016 and 2017, the president was impeached and forced to leave office in large part because the revelations of her corruption led to what has been called the "candlelight revolution," with hundreds of thousands of people taking to the streets each weekend for twenty weekends in a row, the number growing from week to week, peacefully shining hundreds of thousands of lights to show that South Koreans were demanding that their elected leader be subject to the rule of law.[3]

One of the most powerful examples of the power of a candlelight vigil to capture national and even global imagination and spur changes many thought impossible is what happened in Leipzig, East Germany, in October 1989. After seven years of weekly "Prayers for Peace" at St. Nicholas Church, where a sign outside proclaimed the prayers as "Open to All," a series of "Monday demonstrations" gained steam.[4] Two days after the East German government violently put down demonstrations on the fortieth anniversary of East Germany's founding on October 7, about eight thousand people attended the October 9 prayers at St. Nicholas. After the service, they joined a crowd of seventy thousand people holding candles and marched through the streets of Leipzig; the images were broadcast around the world. The rest, as they say, is history, as 120,000 people took to the streets the following week and 300,000 the week after that. On November 9, exactly a month after the October 9 candlelight vigil, the Berlin Wall came down. That's the power of light in the darkness.

And that brings us back to John 1:5: "The light shines in the darkness, and the darkness has not overcome it (1:5 NIV)." I like this translation of this verse best. Another common translation (the NRSV) reads "the darkness did not overcome it," but I like "has" better. It implies that the struggle between the light and the darkness is eternal and continues today. Even while our faith tells us the light will prevail, it is an issue of faith, because we can't know for certain that the light will prevail. In our current situation, it tells us two things: First, we must always let our light shine and always remain vigilant for threats to that light, because the darkness will always seek to overcome it. Second, we can take heart and take hope that the light of Christ is indeed the light of the world, and it is our best and ultimately only reliable tool to keep the darkness at bay. As the Reclaiming Jesus declaration says, "Jesus is our light." As many have done before, it is time again to trust the light of Christ, join the light of Christ, and take the light of Jesus into the world—believing that the darkness, in the end, cannot overcome that light.

But it is vitally important to realize that our hope isn't finally in politics, but always in the renewal of our faith and a revival of moral conscience in our personal and public lives. This crisis is not just about politics but also shows how a political crisis could and should provoke a resurgence of faith, and as far as we Christians and others are concerned, a moment and movement to reclaim Jesus. In the end, everything comes down to hope, which is the most important contribution that faith communities make to their societies—to the common good. And my ultimate conviction because of my faith is this: *Hope means believing in spite of the evidence, then watching the evidence change.*

With that confidence, we can take our light into the darkness—and just maybe change history. Yes, brothers and sisters, this is a dark time. But I have good news: as I told the people coming to Washington from a church in Pennsylvania, "There will be enough candles for everybody!"

The moral, political, and faith crisis continues to deepen as I finish this book. So I would like to finish this book with the declaration of *Reclaiming Jesus*, not as a way to end, but as a call to begin again.

# The "Reclaiming Jesus" Declaration

To close this book, here is the full text of the "Reclaiming Jesus" declaration. I commend it to your careful reading, reflection, prayer, and action.

**We are living** through perilous and polarizing times as a nation, with a dangerous crisis of moral and political leadership at the highest levels of our government and in our churches. **We believe the soul of the nation and the integrity of faith are now at stake.**

It is time to be followers of Jesus before anything else—nationality, political party, race, ethnicity, gender, geography—our identity in Christ precedes every other identity. We pray that our nation will see Jesus's words in us. "By this everyone will know that you are my disciples, if you have love for one another" (John 13:35).

When politics undermines our theology, we must examine that politics. The church's role is to change the world through the life and love of Jesus Christ. The government's role is to serve the common good by protecting justice and peace, rewarding good behavior while restraining bad behavior (Romans 13). When that role is undermined by political leadership, faith leaders must stand up and speak out. Rev. Dr. Martin Luther King Jr. said, "The church must be reminded that it is not the master or the servant of the state, but rather the conscience of the state."

It is often the duty of Christian leaders, especially elders, to speak the truth in love to our churches and to name and warn against temptations, racial and cultural captivities, false doctrines, and political idolatries—and even our complicity in them. We do so here with humility, prayer, and a deep dependency on the grace and Holy Spirit of God.

This letter comes from a retreat on Ash Wednesday, 2018. In this season of Lent, we feel deep lamentations for the state of our nation, and our own hearts are filled with confession for the sins we feel called to address. The true meaning of the word repentance is to turn around. It is time to lament, confess, repent, and turn.

In times of crisis, the church has historically learned to return to Jesus Christ.

Jesus is Lord. That is our foundational confession. It was central for the early church and needs to again become central to us. If Jesus is Lord, then Caesar was not—nor any other political ruler since. If Jesus is Lord, no other authority is absolute. Jesus Christ, and the kingdom of God he announced, is the Christian's first loyalty, above all others. We pray, "Thy kingdom come, thy will be done, in earth, as it is in heaven" (Matthew 6:10). Our faith is personal but never private, meant not only for heaven but for this earth.

The question we face is this: Who is Jesus Christ for us today? What does our loyalty to Christ, as disciples, require at this moment in our history? We believe it is time to renew our theology of public discipleship and witness. Applying what "Jesus is Lord" means today is the message we commend as elders to our churches.

What we believe leads us to what we must reject. Our "Yes" is the foundation for our "No." What we confess as our faith leads to what we confront. Therefore, we offer the following six affirmations of what we believe, and the resulting rejections of practices and policies by political leaders which dangerously corrode the soul of the nation and deeply threaten the public integrity of our faith. We pray that we, as followers of

Jesus, will find the depth of faith to match the danger of our political crisis.

**I. WE BELIEVE** each human being is made in God's image and likeness (Genesis 1:26). That image and likeness confers a divinely decreed dignity, worth, and God-given equality to all of us as children of the one God who is the Creator of all things. Racial bigotry is a brutal denial of the image of God (the imago dei) in some of the children of God. Our participation in the global community of Christ absolutely prevents any toleration of racial bigotry. Racial justice and healing are biblical and theological issues for us, and are central to the mission of the body of Christ in the world. We give thanks for the prophetic role of the historic black churches in America when they have called for a more faithful gospel.

**THEREFORE, WE REJECT** the resurgence of white nationalism and racism in our nation on many fronts, including the highest levels of political leadership. We, as followers of Jesus, must clearly reject the use of racial bigotry for political gain that we have seen. In the face of such bigotry, silence is complicity. In particular, we reject white supremacy and commit ourselves to help dismantle the systems and structures that perpetuate white preference and advantage. Further, any doctrines or political strategies that use racist resentments, fears, or language must be named as public sin—one that goes back to the foundation of our nation and lingers on. Racial bigotry must be antithetical for those belonging to the body of Christ, because it denies the truth of the gospel we profess.

**II. WE BELIEVE** we are one body. In Christ, there is to be no oppression based on race, gender, identity, or class (Galatians 3:28). The body of Christ, where those great human divisions are to be overcome, is meant to be an example for the rest of society. When we fail to overcome these oppressive obstacles, and even perpetuate them, we have failed in our vocation to the world—to proclaim and live the reconciling gospel of Christ.

**THEREFORE, WE REJECT** misogyny, the mistreatment, violent abuse, sexual harassment, and assault of women that has been further revealed in our culture and politics, including our churches, and the oppression of any other child of God. We lament when such practices seem publicly ignored, and thus privately condoned, by those in high positions of leadership. We stand for the respect, protection, and affirmation of women in our families, communities, workplaces, politics, and churches. We support the courageous truth-telling voices of women, who have helped the nation recognize these abuses. We confess sexism as a sin, requiring our repentance and resistance.

**III. WE BELIEVE** how we treat the hungry, the thirsty, the naked, the stranger, the sick, and the prisoner is how we treat Christ himself. (Matthew 25:31–46) "Truly I tell you, just as you did it to one of the least of these who are members of my family, you did it to me." God calls us to protect and seek justice for those who are poor and vulnerable, and our treatment of people who are "oppressed," "strangers," "outsiders," or otherwise considered "marginal" is a test of our relationship to God, who made us all equal in divine dignity and love. Our proclamation of the lordship of Jesus Christ is at stake in our solidarity with the most vulnerable. If our gospel is not "good news to the poor," it is not the gospel of Jesus Christ (Luke 4:18).

**THEREFORE, WE REJECT** the language and policies of political leaders who would debase and abandon the most vulnerable children of God. We strongly deplore the growing attacks on immigrants and refugees, who are being made into cultural and political targets, and we need to remind our churches that God makes the treatment of the "strangers" among us a test of faith (Leviticus 19:33–34). We won't accept the neglect of the well-being of low-income families and children, and we will resist repeated attempts to deny health care to those who most need it. We confess our growing national sin of putting the rich over the poor. We reject the immoral logic of cutting services and programs for the poor while cutting taxes for the rich. Budgets are moral documents. We commit ourselves to opposing and reversing those policies and finding solutions that reflect the wisdom of people from different political parties and philosophies to seek the common good. Protecting the poor is a central commitment of Christian discipleship, to which 2,000 verses in the Bible attest.

**IV. WE BELIEVE** that truth is morally central to our personal and public lives. Truth-telling is central to the prophetic biblical tradition, whose vocation includes speaking the Word of God into their societies and speaking the truth to power. A commitment to speaking truth, the ninth commandment of the Decalogue, "You shall not bear false witness" (Exodus 20:16), is foundational to shared trust in society. Falsehood can enslave us, but Jesus promises, "You will know the truth, and the truth will set you free." (John 8:32). The search and respect for truth is crucial to anyone who follows Christ.

**THEREFORE, WE REJECT** the practice and pattern of lying that is invading our political and civil life. Politicians, like the rest of us, are human, fallible, sinful, and mortal. But when public lying becomes so persistent that it deliberately tries to change facts for ideological, political, or personal gain, the public accountability to truth is undermined. The regular purveying of falsehoods and consistent lying by the nation's highest leaders can change the moral expectations within a culture, the accountability for a civil society, and even the behavior of families and children. The normalization of lying presents a profound moral danger to the fabric of society. In the face of lies that bring darkness, Jesus is our truth and our light.

**V. WE BELIEVE** that Christ's way of leadership is servanthood, not domination. Jesus said, "You know that the rulers of the Gentiles (the world) lord it over them, and their great ones are tyrants over them. It will not be so among you; but whoever wishes to be great among you must be your servant" (Matthew 20:25–26). We believe our elected officials are called to public service, not public tyranny, so we must protect the limits, checks, and balances of democracy and encourage humility and civility on the part of elected officials. We support democracy, not because we believe in human perfection, but because we do not. The authority of government is instituted by God to order an unredeemed society for the sake of justice and peace, but ultimate authority belongs only to God.

**THEREFORE, WE REJECT** any moves toward autocratic political leadership and authoritarian rule. We believe authoritarian political leadership is a theological danger that threatens democracy and the common good—and we will resist it. Disrespect for the rule of law, not recognizing the equal importance of our three branches of government, and replacing civility with dehumanizing hostility toward opponents are of great concern to us. Neglecting the ethic of public service and accountability, in favor of personal recognition and gain often characterized by offensive arrogance, are not just political issues for us. They raise deeper concerns about political idolatry, accompanied by false and unconstitutional notions of authority.

**VI. WE BELIEVE** Jesus when he tells us to go into all nations making disciples (Matthew 28:18). Our churches and our nations are part of an international community whose interests always surpass national boundaries. The most well-known verse in the New Testament starts with "For God so loved the world" (John 3:16). We, in turn, should love and serve the world and all its inhabitants, rather than seek first narrow, nationalistic prerogatives.

**THEREFORE, WE REJECT** "America first" as a theological heresy for followers of Christ. While we share a patriotic love for our country, we reject xenophobic or ethnic nationalism that places one nation over others as a political goal. We reject domination rather than stewardship of the earth's resources, toward genuine global development that brings human flourishing for all of God's children. Serving our own communities is essential, but the global connections between us are undeniable. Global poverty, environmental damage, violent conflict, weapons of mass destruction, and deadly diseases in some places ultimately affect all places, and we need wise political leadership to deal with each of these.

**WE ARE DEEPLY CONCERNED** for the soul of our nation, but also for our churches and the integrity of our faith. The present crisis calls us to go deeper—deeper into our relationship to God; deeper into our relationships with each other, especially across racial, ethnic, and national lines; deeper into our relationships with the most vulnerable, who are at greatest risk.

The church is always subject to temptations to power, to cultural conformity, and to racial, class, and gender divides, as Galatians 3:28 teaches us. But our answer is to be "in Christ," and to "not be conformed to this world, but be transformed by the renewing of your minds, so that you may discern what is the will of God—what is good and acceptable, and perfect." (Romans 12:1–2)

The best response to our political, material, cultural, racial, or national idolatries is the First Commandment: "You shall have no other gods before me" (Exodus 20:3). Jesus summarizes the Greatest Commandment: "You shall love the Lord your God with all your heart, your soul, and your mind. This is the first commandment. And the second is like unto it. You shall love your neighbor as yourself. On these commandments hang all the law and the prophets" (Matthew 22:38). As to loving our neighbors, we would add "no exceptions."

We commend this letter to pastors, local churches, and young people who are watching and waiting to see what the churches will say and do at such a time as this.

Our urgent need, in a time of moral and political crisis, is to recover the power of confessing our faith. Lament, repent, and then repair. If Jesus is Lord, there is always space for grace. We believe it is time to speak and to act in faith and conscience, not because of politics, but because we are disciples of Jesus Christ—to whom be all authority, honor, and glory. It is time for a fresh confession of faith. Jesus is Lord. He is the light in our darkness. "I am the light of the world. Whoever follows me will not walk in darkness, but will have the light of life" (John 8:12).

**Bishop Carroll A. Baltimore,** *President and CEO, Global Alliance Interfaith Network*
**Rev. Dr. Peter Borgdorff,** *Executive Director Emeritus, Christian Reformed Church in North America*
**Dr. Amos Brown,** *Chair, Social Justice Commission, National Baptist Convention USA, Inc.*
**Rev. Dr. Walter Brueggemann,** *Professor Emeritus, Columbia Theological Seminary*
**Dr. Tony Campolo,** *Co-Founder, Red Letter Christians*
**Dr. Iva Carruthers,** *General Secretary, Samuel DeWitt Proctor Conference*
**The Most Rev. Michael B. Curry,** *Presiding Bishop and Primate, The Episcopal Church*
**Rev. Dr. James Forbes,** *President and Founder, Healing of the Nations Foundation and Preaching Professor at Union Theological Seminary*

**Rev. Wesley Granberg-Michaelson**, *General Secretary Emeritus, Reformed Church in America*

**Rev. Dr. Cynthia Hale**, *Senior Pastor, Ray of Hope Christian Church, Decatur, GA*

**Rev. Dr. Richard Hamm**, *former General Minister and President of the Christian Church (Disciples of Christ)*

**Rev. Dr. Joel C. Hunter**, *Faith Community Organizer and Chairman, Community Resource Network*

**Rev. Dr. Jo Anne Lyon**, *General Superintendent Emerita, The Wesleyan Church*

**Bishop Vashti McKenzie**, *117th Elected and Consecrated Bishop, AME Church*

**Rev. Dr. Otis Moss, Jr.**, *Co-Convener National, African American Clergy Network*

**Dr. John Perkins**, *Chair Emeritus and Founding Member, Christian Community Development Association and President Emeritus, John & Vera Mae Perkins Foundation*

**Senior Bishop Lawrence Reddick**, *Christian Methodist Episcopal Church*

**Fr. Richard Rohr**, *Founder, Center for Action and Contemplation*

**Dr. Ron Sider**, *President Emeritus, Evangelicals for Social Action*

**Rev. Jim Wallis**, *President and Founder, Sojourners*

**Rev. Dr. Sharon Watkins**, *Director, NCC Truth and Racial Justice Initiative*

**Dr. Barbara Williams-Skinner**, *Co-Convener, National African American Clergy Network; President, Skinner Leadership Institute*

**Bishop Will Willimon**, *Bishop, The United Methodist Church, retired, Professor of the Practice of Ministry, Duke Divinity School*

# Acknowledgments

I am grateful to many people for this book. Thanks to all the pastors and leaders from many sectors who called me to talk about what to do after the 2016 election. Those questions woke me early in the mornings and led to this book. Thanks, in particular, to Michael Curry, Presiding Bishop of the Episcopal Church, who came to Washington for a long, late conversation that led to the "Reclaiming Jesus" declaration and eventually to this commentary on the questions of Jesus—and who wrote the foreword to the book.

Thanks to my Sojourners team, who help make my work possible, and especially J.K. Granberg-Michaelson, who did the research on this book and became my companion in its completion. Thanks to Jim Simpson, who every day helps advise and direct my strategy and time and has been the point person for this book project, and to Patrick Hubbard, who faithfully and miraculously keeps me on schedule and on task.

I am always grateful for my close lifelong friend Wes Granberg-Michaelson, also board chair of Sojourners, for continual conversations that help shape my thinking and message—including on this book. Thanks to Adam Taylor, our new executive director, for his leadership at Sojourners, and for helping to keep me accountable to the next generation of leaders. Thanks to Rob Wilson-Black, the CEO of Sojourners, who makes sure the organization runs smoothly so that we (and I!) can get our message of faith in action for social justice out into the world. And thanks to leaders like Peggy Flanagan, who is part of my family, and dear friends like Yvonne Delk and Barbara Williams-Skinner, who all help keep me on the ground for the people most affected by our nation's original sins.

I am tremendously grateful to my literary agent, Kathy Helmers, who believed in this book and message from the beginning and played an important role in its early framing. And I feel so fortunate and grateful to be working once again with Mickey Maudlin and his team at HarperOne, who saw the transformational potential of this message for these times from our very first conversation about it.

Mary Ann Richardson and Rick Little offered needed hospitality for the creating and writing of this book for which I am very thankful. And many thanks go to my wife, Joy Carroll, a "village priest"—she ministers to the people around her everywhere she is—for sustaining a household that makes our family's life and work and studies and baseball (!) possible, and for our two sons, Luke and Jack—young men now—who often ask me questions that make me think and write and act.

Finally, thanks to all who read this book and are, I hope, inspired and encouraged to help save the soul of this nation and the integrity of faith for "a time such as this."

# Notes

## Chapter 2: The Neighbor Question

1. Martin Luther King, Jr., "I've Been to the Mountaintop (speech, Mason Temple, Memphis, April 3, 1968), https://www.americanrhetoric.com/speeches/mlkivebeentothemountaintop.htm.
2. N.T. Wright, "The Road to New Creation," NTWrightPage.com, September 23, 2006, http://ntwrightpage.com/2016/03/30/the-road-to-new-creation/.
3. Gustavo Gutiérrez, in *Seeds of the Spirit: Wisdom of the Twentieth Century,* ed. Richard H. Bell and Barbara Battin (Louisville: Westminster John Knox, 1995), 78.
4. Darrell L. Bock, *Luke* (The IVP New Testament Commentary Series) (Downers Grove, IL: InterVarsity, 2010), accessed September 13, 2018, at BibleGateway.com, https://www.biblegateway.com/resources/ivp-nt/Parable-Good-Samaritan.

5. Sharon Ringe, *Luke* (Louisville: Westminster John Knox, 1995), 160.
6. See, e.g., Tim Dixon et al., "Attitudes towards National Identity, Immigration, and Refugees in Italy," More in Common, August 2018, 8–9, https://www.moreincommon.com/italy-report1.
7. Wes Granberg-Michaelson, "More Than Demographics," Sojo.net, May 11, 2015, https://sojo.net/articles/more-demographics.
8. Miriam Jordan, "Family Separation May Have Hit Thousands More Migrant Children Than Reported," *New York Times*, January 17, 2019, https://www.nytimes.com/2019/01/17/us/family-separation-trump-administration-migrants.html.
9. "'Suffer the Little Children': A Call to Reclaim Jesus," ReclaimingJesus.org, accessed September 13, 2018, http://reclaimingjesus.org/sites/default/files/downloads/reclaimingjesus.family.pdf.
10. Mark Galli, "Loving Our Neighbors Knows No Borders—Even Political Ones," *Christianity Today*, June 20, 2018, https://www.christianitytoday.com/ct/2018/june-web-only/loving-our-neighbors-knows-no-borders-even-political-ones.html.
11. For more on the resistance across society and the church to the administration's cruel child separation policy, see chapter 7.
12. Martin Niemöller, "First They Came for the Social-

ists . . . ," quoted in *Holocaust Encyclopedia*, US Holocaust Memorial Museum, accessed September 13, 2018, https://encyclopedia.ushmm.org/content/en/article/martin-niemoeller-first-they-came-for-the-socialists.

13. Michelle Goldberg, "First They Came for the Migrants," *New York Times*, June 11, 2018, https://www.nytimes.com/2018/06/11/opinion/trump-border-migrants-separation.html.
14. Steve Stone, "Why We Opened Our Church to Muslims," Sojo.net, January 31, 2011, https://sojo.net/articles/why-we-opened-our-church-muslims.
15. Peter Wehner, "What Wouldn't Jesus Do?" *The Washington Post*, March 1, 2016, https://www.nytimes.com/2016/03/01/opinion/campaign-stops/what-wouldnt-jesus-do.html.
16. Michael Gerson, "A Case Study in the Proper Role of Christians in Politics," *The Washington Post,* June 21, 2018, https://www.washingtonpost.com/opinions/a-case-study-in-the-proper-role-of-christians-in-politics/2018/06/21/39acd0bc-7578–11e8-b4b7–308400242c2e_story.html?utm_term=.770904bc0de0.
17. Pope Francis, "Message of His Holiness Pope Francis for Lent 2015," the Vatican, October 4, 2014, https://w2.vatican.va/content/francesco/en/messages/lent/documents/papa-francesco_20141004_messaggio-quaresima2015.html.
18. Pope Francis, "*Evangelii Gaudium*," the Vatican, November 24, 2013, http://w2.vatican.va/content/francesco/en

/apost_exhortations/documents/papa-francesco_esortazione-ap_20131124_evangelii-gaudium.html, paragraph 54.

19. Pope Francis, "*Evangelii Gaudium*," para. 2.

## Chapter 3: The Image Question

1. Sabrina Tavernise, "In Trump's Remarks, Black Churches See a Nation Backsliding," *New York Times*, January 14, 2018, https://www.nytimes.com/2018/01/14/us/black-churches-trump.html.
2. Jynnah Radford, "Key Findings About U.S. Immigrants," Pew Research Center, June 3, 2019, https://www.pewresearch.org/fact-tank/2019/06/03/key-findings-about-u-s-immigrants.
3. Anna Flagg, "Is There a Connection Between Undocumented Immigrants and Crime?" *New York Times*, May 13, 2019, https://www.nytimes.com/2019/05/13/upshot/illegal-immigration-crime-rates-research.html.
4. Jim Wallis, *America's Original Sin: Racism, White Privilege, and the Bridge to a New America* (Grand Rapids, MI: Brazos, 2016), 126.
5. Martin Luther King Jr., "Where Do We Go from Here?" address delivered at the Eleventh Annual SCLC Convention, August 16, 1967, https://kinginstitute.stanford.edu/king-papers/documents/where-do-we-go-here-address-delivered-eleventh-annual-sclc-convention.
6. Sandra L. Colby and Jennifer M. Ortman, "Projections of the Size and Composition of the US Population: 2014 to

2060," US Census Bureau, March 2015, https://www.census.gov/content/dam/Census/library/publications/2015/demo/p25-1143.pdf.

7. "Reclaiming Jesus—DC Vigil Event," *Sojourners* Facebook page, May 24, 2018, https://www.facebook.com/SojournersMagazine/videos/10155616183912794/.
8. Nora Samaran, "The Opposite of Rape Culture Is Nurturance Culture," NoraSamaran.com, February 11, 2016, https://norasamaran.com/2016/02/11/the-opposite-of-rape-culture-is-nurturance-culture-2/.
9. Jenna Barnett, "How Churches Can Stand for Survivors, Not the Accused," Sojo.net, April 27, 2018, https://sojo.net/articles/how-churches-can-stand-survivors-not-accused.
10. Jenna Barnett and Jim Wallis, "'I Believe You': Church Leaders Respond to Survivors," sojo.net, September 27, 2018, https://sojo.net/articles/i-believe-you-church-leaders-respond-survivors.
11. For one thoroughly researched examination of these issues in a way that respects the views of people in different places on the theological questions, see James V. Brownson, *Bible, Gender, Sexuality* (Grand Rapids, MI: Eerdmans, 2013).
12. See, e.g., Fr. James Martin, SJ, *Building a Bridge: How the Catholic Church and the LGBT Community Can Enter into a Relationship of Respect, Compassion, and Sensitivity* (New York: HarperOne, 2017).
13. "Our Issue," True Colors Fund, https://truecolorsfund.org/our-issue. Accessed September 13, 2018.
14. Jonathan Greenblatt, "Right-Wing Extremist Violence

Is Our Biggest Threat. The Numbers Don't Lie," Anti-Defamation League, ADL.org, January 24, 2019, https://www.adl.org/news/op-ed/right-wing-extremist-violence-is-our-biggest-threat-the-numbers-dont-lie.

15. Greenblatt, "Right-Wing Extremist Violence."
16. Eric Rosand, "When Fighting Domestic Terrorism, You Get What You Pay For," Brookings.edu, November 2, 2018, https://www.brookings.edu/blog/order-from-chaos/2018/11/02/when-fighting-domestic-terrorism-you-get-what-you-pay-for.
17. Ron Nixon and Eileen Sullivan, "Revocation of Grants to Help Fight Hate Under New Scrutiny After Charlottesville," *New York Times*, August 15, 2017, https://www.nytimes.com/2017/08/15/us/politics/right-wing-extremism-charlottesville.html.
18. Erin Banco and Sam Stein, "House Judiciary Committee Planning Hearing on the Rise of White Nationalism," *Daily Beast*, March 18, 2019, https://www.thedailybeast.com/house-judiciary-committee-planning-hearing-on-the-rise-of-white-nationalism.
19. John Cohen, quoted in Banco and Stein, "House Judiciary Committee Planning Hearing."
20. Adam Serwer, "White Nationalism's Deep American Roots," *The Atlantic*, April 2019, https://www.theatlantic.com/magazine/archive/2019/04/adam-serwer-madison-grant-white-nationalism/583258.
21. Colby Itkowitz and John Wagner, "Trump Says White Nationalism Is Not a Rising Threat After New Zealand At-

tacks: 'It's a Small Group of People,'" *Washington Post*, March 15, 2019, https://www.washingtonpost.com/politics/trump-offers-us-assistance-after-horrible-massacre-in-new-zealand/2019/03/15/931833d2-4712-11e9-aaf8-4512a6fe3439_story.html?utm_term=.9f190cc54e46.

22. Felica Sonmez, "George W. Bush: 'May We Never Forget That Immigration Is a Blessing and a Strength," *Washington Post*, March 18, 2019, https://www.washingtonpost.com/politics/george-w-bush-may-we-never-forget-that-immigration-is-a-blessing-and-a-strength/2019/03/18/9b5aaf6a-49b1-11e9-93d0-64dbcf38ba41_story.html?utm_term=.9472eab34b37.
23. "'Islam Is Peace' Says President," George W. Bush White House Archives, September 17, 2001, https://georgewbush-whitehouse.archives.gov/news/releases/2001/09/20010917-11.html.
24. Daniel Cox, Rachel Lienesch, and Robert P. Jones, "Beyond Economics: Fears of Cultural Displacement Pushed the White Working Class to Trump," Public Religion Research Institute, May 9, 2017, https://www.prri.org/research/white-working-class-attitudes-economy-trade-immigration-election-donald-trump/.

## Chapter 4: The Truth Question

1. Andreas J. Köstenberger, "'What Is Truth?': Pilate's Question in Its Johannine and Larger Biblical Context," *Journal of the Evangelical Theological Society* 48, no. 1 (March 2005): 34–35.

2. Köstenberger, "'What Is Truth?,'" 45.
3. Köstenberger, "'What Is Truth?,'" 51.
4. Miroslav Volf, *Exclusion and Embrace: A Theological Exploration of Identity, Otherness, and Reconciliation* (Nashville: Abingdon, 1996), 266.
5. Köstenberger, "'What Is Truth?,'" 60.
6. Köstenberger, "'What Is Truth?,'" 62.
7. "Simone de Beauvoir," Wikiquote, accessed September 13, 2018, https://en.wikiquote.org/wiki/Simone_de_Beauvoir.
8. Several reporters and outlets are attempting to do so, but differing methodologies as to what constitutes a lie or false claim result in different totals. That said, Daniel Dale's project with the *Toronto Star* is among the best for staying up to date on the current president's falsehoods and can be found here: http://projects.thestar.com/donald-trump-fact-check/.
9. Matthew Henry, *Concise Commentary on the Whole Bible*, Matthew 7, accessed March 6, 2019, https://biblehub.com/commentaries/mhc/matthew/7.htm.
10. Richard Rohr, "The Plank in Your Eye," CAC.org, July 14, 2016, https://cac.org/the-plank-in-your-eye-2016-07-14/.
11. Martin Luther King Jr., "Splinters and Planks," July 24, 1949, accessed at the Martin Luther King Jr. Research and Education Institute, Stanford University, https://kinginstitute.stanford.edu/king-papers/documents/splinters-and-planks.
12. Brian McLaren, "A Call for Evangelical Rhetorical Ac-

countability," Sojo.net, June 26, 2008, https://sojo.net/articles/call-evangelical-rhetorical-accountability.

13. David Leonhardt, "All the President's Lies," *New York Times*, March 20, 2017, https://www.nytimes.com/2017/03/20/opinion/all-the-presidents-lies.html.
14. Leonhardt, "All the President's Lies."
15. Jerry Brewer, "The NFL Beat Trump. Soundly," *The Washington Post*, September 24, 2017, https://www.washingtonpost.com/sports/the-nfl-responds-to-trump-by-embracing-its-diversity/2017/09/24/07d57814-a15c-11e7-ade1–76d061d56efa_story.html?noredirect=on&utm_term=.c6b28350740e.
16. Adam Ericksen, "Truth, Lies, and the NFL," Sojo.net, September 26, 2017, https://sojo.net/articles/truth-lies-and-nfl.
17. Michael Gerson, "Under Trump, Christians May Have It Easier. They'll Also Be in Grave Spiritual Danger," *The Washington Post*, January 23, 2017, https://www.washingtonpost.com/opinions/under-trump-christians-may-have-it-easier-theyll-also-be-in-grave-spiritual-danger/2017/01/23/16cdb6ac-e19e-11e6-a453–19ec4b3d09ba_story.html?utm_term=.ec22c20542be.
18. Courtney Hall Lee, "When Did Christians Become Comfortable with the Loss of Truth?," Sojo.net, February 15, 2017, https://sojo.net/articles/when-did-christians-become-comfortable-loss-truth.
19. Stanley M. Hauerwas, "Bonhoeffer on Truth and Politics," Conference on Lived Theology and Civil Courage,

June 14, 2003, http://www.livedtheology.org/wp-content/uploads/2015/05/20030614PPR.04-Stanley-M.-Hauerwas-Bonhoeffer-on-Truth-and-Politics.pdf.

## Chapter 5: The Power Question

1. Steven J. Cole, "Lesson 100: Who's the Greatest? (Luke 22:24–30)," Bible.org, accessed September 13, 2018, https://bible.org/seriespage/lesson-100-who-s-greatest-luke-2224–30.
2. John Calvin, *The Institutes of the Christian Religion,* ed. John McNeill, trans. Ford Lewis Battles (Louisville: Westminster John Knox, 1960), 2:1–2.
3. Alexander MacLaren, *Expositions of Holy Scripture,* Luke 22:24–Luke 22:37, Biblehub.com, accessed September 13, 2018, https://biblehub.com/commentaries/luke/22–24.htm.
4. St. Thomas Aquinas, *Commentary on the Gospel of St. John,* trans. Fabian R. Larcher, OP (Albany, NY: Magi Books, 1998), para. 1781, https://dhspriory.org/thomas/John13.htm.
5. Rodney A. Whitacre, *John* (The IVP New Testament Commentary Series) (Downers Grove, IL: InterVarsity, 2010), accessed September 13, 2018, at BibleGateway.com, https://www.biblegateway.com/resources/ivp-nt/Jesus-Washes-Disciples-Feet.
6. Kristine Phillips, "'Make Lindsborg White Again': Racist

Messages Target College President with Biracial Children," *The Washington Post*, September 22, 2016, https://www.washingtonpost.com/news/grade-point/wp/2016/09/22/make-lindsborg-white-again-racist-messages-target-college-president-with-biracial-children/?utm_term=.c18b8a0e7f9c.

7. Phillips, "'Make Lindsborg White Again.'"
8. "Bethany College President Demonstrates Hospitality Message," Bethany College, August 31, 2018, https://www.bethanylb.edu/2018/08/bethany-college-president-demonstrates-hospitality-message/.
9. Rachel Donaldo, "On Gay Priests, Pope Francis Asks, 'Who Am I to Judge?,'" *New York Times*, July 29, 2013, https://www.nytimes.com/2013/07/30/world/europe/pope-francis-gay-priests.html.
10. Pope Francis, "*Evangelii Gaudium*," para. 45.
11. C. S. Lewis, "Equality," *Spectator* 171 (August 27, 1943): 192, accessed September 14, 2018 at http://www.tlchrist.info/cs_lewis.htm.
12. Reinhold Niebuhr, *The Children of Light and the Children of Darkness: A Vindication of Democracy and a Critique of Its Traditional Defense* (Chicago: Univ. of Chicago Press, 2011), xxxii.
13. Vincent Harding, quoted on the Practicing Democracy Project, Spiritualityandpractice.com, accessed September 14, 2018, https://www.spiritualityandpractice./com projects/practicing-democracy-project/quotes.

14. Nancy Gibbs, "The Danger of Governing on Social Media," *TIME*, May 11, 2017, http://time.com/4775429/donald-trump-james-comey-twitter/.

15. Donald Trump on *Good Morning America*, published to YouTube on April 2, 2011, accessed September 14, 2018, https://www.youtube.com/watch?v=6o5GxmMIbok.

16. Donald Trump, "Full Text: Donald Trump Announces a Presidential Bid," *The Washington Post*, June 16, 2015, https://www.washingtonpost.com/news/post-politics/wp/2015/06/16/full-text-donald-trump-announces-a-presidential-bid/?utm_term=.209ed6989fe1.

17. Jesse Byrnes, "Trump: 'You Have to Be Wealthy in Order to Be Great,'" *The Hill*, May 26, 2016, http://thehill.com/blogs/blog-briefing-room/news/281433-trump-you-have-to-be-wealthy-in-order-to-be-great.

18. Danielle Kurtzleben, "Poll: White Evangelicals Have Warmed to Politicians Who Commit 'Immoral' Acts," NPR.org, October 23, 2016, https://www.npr.org/2016/10/23/498890836/poll-white-evangelicals-have-warmed-to-politicians-who-commit-immoral-acts.

19. The full declaration can be found in the back matter of this book and at www.reclaimingjesus.org.

## Chapter 6: The Fear Question

1. Rodney A. Whitacre, *John* (The IVP New Testament Commentary Series) (Downers Grove, IL: InterVarsity, 2010), accessed March 7, 2019, at BibleGateway.com,

https://www.biblegateway.com/resources/ivp-nt/Jesus-Rescues-His-Disciples-on-Sea.

2. Charles John Ellicott, *Commentary on the Whole Bible*, 2 Timothy 1:7, Biblehub.com, accessed March 6, 2019, https://biblehub.com/commentaries/2_timothy/1–7.htm.

3. Ellicott, *Commentary on the Whole Bible*.

4. Gordon D. Fee, *Philippians* (The IVP New Testament Commentary Series) (Downers Grove, IL: InterVarsity, 2010), accessed March 6, 2019, at BibleGateway.com, https://www.biblegateway.com/resources/ivp-nt/Rejoice-Give-Thanks-Pray.

5. "2015 National Drug Assessment Summary," US Department of Justice Drug Enforcement Administration, DEA.gov, accessed March 6, 2019, https://www.dea.gov/sites/default/files/2018–07/2015%20NDTA%20Report.pdf.

6. Ashley Parker, Phillip Rucker, and Josh Dawsey, "Trump and Republicans Settle on Fear—and Falsehoods—as a Midterm Strategy," *The Washington Post*, October 22, 2018, https://www.washingtonpost.com/politics/trump-and-republicans-settle-on-fear—and-falsehoods—as-a-midterm-strategy/2018/10/22/1ebbf222-d614–11e8-a10f-b51546b10756_story.html?noredirect=on&utm_term=.c12ee4350f93.

7. Tanya and Tracy Connor, "Fox News Commentator Says Migrants Are Carrying Smallpox, a Disease Eradicated in 1980," *Daily Beast*, October 29, 2018, https://www.thedailybeast.com/fox-news-commentator-says-migrants-are-carrying-smallpox-a-disease-eradicated-in-1980.

8. Oriana Pawlyk, "Number of Troops at Border Has 'Peaked,' Defense Official Says," Military.com, November 15, 2018, https://www.military.com/daily-news/2018/11/15/number-troops-border-has-peaked-defense-official-says.html.
9. Gordon Adams, Lawrence B. Wilkerson, and Isaiah Wilson III, "Trump's Border Stunt Is a Profound Betrayal of Our Military," *New York Times*, November 19, 2018, https://www.nytimes.com/2018/11/19/opinion/president-trump-border-military-troops.html.

## Chapter 7: The Caesar Question

1. Wes Granberg-Michaelson, "Asking 'Which Jesus?' in 2018," Sojo.net, March 26, 2018, https://sojo.net/articles/asking-which-jesus-2018.
2. Whitacre, *John*, https://www.biblegateway.com/resources/ivp-nt/Glory-Is-Revealed-Jerusalem.
3. Min-Ah Cho, "What Is Empire?," Sojo.net, accessed September 14, 2018, https://sojo.net/preaching-the-word/what-empire.
4. Ched Myers, "By What Authority?," *Sojourners*, May 1983, https://sojo.net/magazine/may-1983/what-authority.
5. Willard Swartley, "Answering the Pharisees," *Sojourners*, February 1979, https://sojo.net/magazine/february-1979/answering-pharisees.
6. Swartley, "Answering the Pharisees."

7. Swartley, "Answering the Pharisees."
8. " 'Suffer the Little Children': A Call to Reclaim Jesus," ReclaimingJesus.org, accessed September 13, 2018, http://reclaimingjesus.org/sites/default/files/downloads/reclaimingjesus.family.pdf.
9. " 'Suffer the Little Children.' "
10. Amy Pollard, "Flight Attendants Want No Part in Separating Immigrant Children from Parents," Slate.com, June 20, 2018, https://slate.com/news-and-politics/2018/06/flight-attendants-oppose-trump-administrations-family-separation-policy.html.
11. Ed Mazza, "Montana Man Quits Government Job Rather Than Help ICE 'Hunt Down and Deport' Undocumented Immigrants," HuffPost.com, February 9, 2018, https://www.huffingtonpost.com/entry/montana-man-quits-over-ice_us_5a7d2b14e4b08dfc9302751c.
12. Camila Domonoske and Richard Gonzales, "What We Know: Family Separation and 'Zero Tolerance' at the Border," NPR.org, June 19, 2018, https://www.npr.org/2018/06/19/621065383/what-we-know-family-separation-and-zero-tolerance-at-the-border.
13. Adam Taylor, "At What Cost to Our Soul?," Sojo.net, June 26, 2018, https://sojo.net/articles/what-cost-our-soul.
14. Trip Gabriel, "An ICE Raid Leaves an Iowa Town Divided Along Faith Lines," *New York Times*, July 3, 2018, https://www.nytimes.com/2018/07/03/us/ice-raid-iowa-churches.html.

15. Gabriel, "An ICE Raid."
16. Oscar Cullmann, quoted in Swartley, "Answering the Pharisees."
17. Swartley, "Answering the Pharisees."
18. "Christians Arrested Reading Scripture in Senate Office Building," Sojo.net, November 30, 2017, https://sojo.net/media/christians-arrested-reading-scripture-senate-office-building.

## Chapter 8: The Peacemaker Question

1. Wendell Berry, *Blessed Are the Peacemakers: Christ's Teachings about Love, Compassion, and Forgiveness* (Washington: Shoemaker & Hoard, 2005), 4.
2. Craig S. Keener, *Matthew* (The IVP New Testament Commentary Series) (Downers Grove, IL: InterVarsity, 2011), accessed September 14, 2018, at BibleGateway.com, https://www.biblegateway.com/resources/ivp-nt/Kingdom-Rewards-Repentant.
3. Joseph Benson, *Commentary on the Old and New Testaments*, Matthew 5:9, Biblehub.com, accessed September 14, 2018, https://biblehub.com/commentaries/matthew/5–9.htm.
4. Cornell West, "Cornel West on Why James Baldwin Matters More Than Ever," interview by Christopher Lydon, *Radio Open Source,* transcribed on Lithub.com, March 2, 2017, https://lithub.com/cornel-west-on-why-james-baldwin-matters-more-than-ever/.

5. "A Covenant for Civility: Come Let Us Reason Together," quoted in Jim Wallis, *The (Un)Common Good: How the Gospel Brings Hope to a World Divided* (Grand Rapids, MI: Brazos, 2014), 176–178.
6. Andrew Klager, "Is Non-Violence Naive?" *Sojourners,* July 2018, https://sojo.net/magazine/july-2018/nonviolence-naive.
7. Klager, "Is Non-Violence Naive?"
8. Klager, "Is Non-Violence Naive?"
9. Dorothy Day, quoted in Klager, "Is Non-Violence Naive?"
10. Klager, "Is Non-Violence Naive?"
11. Klager, "Is Non-Violence Naive?"
12. Theodore Roszak, quoted in *The Search for a Nonviolent Future: A Promise of Peace for Ourselves, Our Families, and Our World* (Novato, CA: New World Library, 2010), 87.
13. Francis Phillips, "Is the Concept of Just War Still Valid?," review of Stanley Hauerwas, *Hannah's Child: A Theologian's Memoir, Catholic Herald,* August 17, 2010, http://www.catholicherald.co.uk/commentandblogs/2010/08/17/is-the-concept-of-just-war-still-valid/.
14. Daniel Berrigan, *No Bars to Manhood,* quoted in Jim Wallis, "The Unchained Life of Daniel Berrigan," *Sojourners,* August 2016, https://sojo.net/magazine/august-2016/unchained-life-daniel-berrigan.
15. Martin Luther King Jr., "Beyond Vietnam: A Time to Break Silence," speech at Riverside Church, New York City, April 4, 1967, https://www.americanrhetoric.com/speeches/mlkatimetobreaksilence.htm.

16. Glen H. Stassen, "Winning the Peace," *Sojourners*, January 2005, https://sojo.net/magazine/january-2005/winning-peace.
17. Stassen, "Winning the Peace."
18. Stassen, "Winning the Peace."
19. Stassen, "Winning the Peace."
20. Glen H. Stassen, "Ten Practices of Just Peacemaking," *Sojourners*, January 2005, https://sojo.net/magazine/january-2005/ten-practices-just-peacemaking.
21. Bob Baskin, "2017 Federal Budget: Support Intl. Peacebuilding Funding—Sign Congressional Petition Today," Peace Alliance, March 24, 2016, https://peacealliance.org/2017-federal-budget-support-intl-peacebuilding-funding-sign-congressional-petition-today/.
22. Rose Marie Berger, "Game Changer?," *Sojourners*, December 2016, https://sojo.net/magazine/december-2016/game-changer.
23. Robert McElroy, quoted in Joshua J. McElwee, "Vatican's Second Conference on Nonviolence Renews Hope for Encyclical," *National Catholic Reporter*, April 23, 2019, https://www.ncronline.org/news/justice/vaticans-second-conference-nonviolence-renews-hope-encyclical.
24. Marie Dennis, quoted in McElwee, "Vatican's Second Conference on Nonviolence Renews Hope for Encyclical."
25. Billy Graham, "A Change of Heart," interview with Jim Wallis and Wes Michaelson, *Sojourners,* August 1979, https://sojo.net/magazine/august-1979/change-heart.
26. Graham, "A Change of Heart."

27. Graham, "A Change of Heart."
28. Graham, "A Change of Heart."
29. Graham, "A Change of Heart."

## Chapter 9: The Discipleship Question

1. Soong-Chan Rah, *The Next Evangelicalism: Freeing the Church from Western Cultural Captivity* (Downers Grove, IL: InterVarsity, 2009), 61.
2. Lisa Sharon Harper, "Four Things Evangelicals Should Know About Black Lives Matter," Sojo.net, January 15, 2016, https://sojo.net/articles/faith-action/four-things-evangelicals-should-know-about-black-lives-matter.
3. Obery Hendricks, "The Truth About Obama's Faith," Sojo.net, January 28, 2008, https://sojo.net/articles/truth-about-obamas-faith-0.
4. Nadia Bolz-Weber, "Matthew 25: How I Met My Husband," Sojo.net, December 7, 2011, https://sojo.net/articles/matthew-25-how-i-met-my-husband.
5. You can take the Matthew 25 Pledge at https://sojo.net/matthew-25-pledge.
6. "Latinos and the New Trump Administration," Pew Research Center, February 23, 2017, http://www.pewhispanic.org/2017/02/23/latinos-and-the-new-trump-administration/.
7. Keary Kincannon, quoted in "People of Faith Are Pledging to Protect People Under Threat by Trump's New Policies," Sojo.net, February 22, 2017, https://sojo.net/articles

/people-faith-are-pledging-protect-people-under-threat-trump-s-new-policies.

8. Alexia Salvatierra, "How to Protect Communities from Deportation," Sojo.net, September 28, 2017, https://sojo.net/articles/how-protect-communities-deportation.
9. Salvatierra, "How to Protect."
10. Salvatierra, "How to Protect."
11. Salvatierra, "How to Protect."
12. Noe Carias Mayorga, "59 Days in an ICE Detention Center," interview with Jessica Cobian, Sojo.net, October 4, 2017, https://sojo.net/articles/59-days-ice-detention-center.
13. Galen Carey, quoted in Jim Wallis, "Truth That Bears Repeating: A Budget Is a Moral Document," Sojo.net, March 30, 2017, https://sojo.net/articles/truth-bears-repeating-budget-moral-document.
14. "Christian Leaders Speak Out Against Cuts to Poverty-Focused Programs," Circle of Protection, June 21, 2017, http://circleofprotection.us/wp-content/uploads/2017/06/circle-of-protection-june-21-2017-budget-statement.pdf.
15. Jenna Jerman, Rachel K. Jones, and Tsuyoshi Onda, "Characteristics of U.S. Abortion Patients in 2014 and Changes Since 2008," Guttmacher Institute, May 2016, https://www.guttmacher.org/report/characteristics-us-abortion-patients-2014.
16. Jim Wallis and Sandi Villareal, "How We Talk About Life—and Death," Sojo.net, July 23, 2015, https://sojo.net/articles/how-we-talk-about-life-and-death.
17. Wallis, *The (Un)Common Good*, 167–168.

## Chapter 10: Becoming Salt, Light, and Hope

1. Keener, *Matthew*, https://www.biblegateway.com/resources/ivp-nt/Ethics-Gods-Kingdom.
2. Keener, *Matthew*.
3. Glen H. Stassen, "God's Transforming Initiative," *Sojourners*, April 1992, https://sojo.net/magazine/april-1992/gods-transforming-initiative.
4. Lindsey Paris-Lopez, "The Sermon on the Mount: A Theology of Resistance," Sojo.net, February 10, 2017, https://sojo.net/articles/sermon-mount-theology-resistance.
5. Jennifer De Pinto et al., "Most Americans Support DACA, but Oppose Border Wall—CBS News Poll," CBSNews.com, January 20, 2018, https://www.cbsnews.com/news/most-americans-support-daca-but-oppose-border-wall-cbs-news-poll/.
6. Pope Francis, "Homily of Pope Francis," Holy Mass for the Family Day on the Occasion of the Year of Faith, the Vatican, October 27, 2013, http://w2.vatican.va/content/francesco/en/homilies/2013/documents/papa-francesco_20131027_omelia-pellegrinaggio-famiglia.html.
7. J. R. R. Tolkien, *The Lord of the Rings* (Boston: Houghton Mifflin, 1987), I, 60.

## Epilogue: The Light of the World

1. Cecelie Counts, "Divestment Was Just One Weapon in Battle Against Apartheid," *New York Times*, Janu-

ary 27, 2013, https://www.nytimes.com/roomfordebate/2013/01/27/is-divestment-an-effective-means-of-protest/divestment-was-just-one-weapon-in-battle-against-apartheid.

2. Julio Alicea, "Filipinos Campaign to Overthrow Dictator (People Power), 1983–1986," *Global Nonviolent Action Database*, October 5, 2011, https://nvdatabase.swarthmore.edu/content/filipinos-campaign-overthrow-dictator-people-power-1983-1986.
3. Ha-Joon Chang, "South Koreans Worked a Democratic Miracle. Can They Do It Again?," *New York Times*, September 14, 2017, https://www.nytimes.com/2017/09/14/opinion/south-korea-social-mobility.html.
4. Peter Crutchley, "Did a Prayer Meeting Really Bring Down the Berlin Wall and End the Cold War?," *British Broadcasting Corporation*, October 9, 2015, http://www.bbc.co.uk/religion/0/24661333.